Praise for
THE GEOGRAPHY OF MEMORY

"Alzheimer's and the death of a parent is a journey that others have told us about but few with such penetration and humane wisdom as Jeanne Walker. Her story is a map of memory with mythical overtones, by which I mean that while its shape is recognizable, its details are utterly unique. I read it, mesmerized, wondering my way through this deeply moving portrait of a mother, a daughter, a family. Against expectation we are invited to join their hilarious, daunting dance: a boogie of decline whose haunting music persists."

—Luci Shaw, poet, author of
*The Crime of Living Cautiously* and *What the Light Was Like*,
writer in residence at Regent College

"With THE GEOGRAPHY OF MEMORY, Jeanne Murray Walker, a master wordsmith, takes us on a journey—dare I say sacred pilgrimage—into the inner world of Alzheimer's. While Walker does not flinch from the calamities and sorrows of this journey, she also provides us with fresh glimpses into hidden joys and startling surprises along the way. I commend THE GEOGRAPHY OF MEMORY to you."

—Richard J. Foster, author of
*Celebration of Discipline* and *Sanctuary of the Soul*

"In a kind of family alchemy, a mother's failing memory somehow excites the synapses of her daughter's. The result is a child-adult memoir of grace, poignancy, and rich compassion."

—Philip Yancey, bestselling author

"As the lively, witty, energetic character who was her mother begins to become hopelessly lost in Alzheimer's, poet Jeanne Walker readily shoulders her share of caregiving, a commitment of love requiring three-hour plane rides: disrupting the rhythms of her own life as a wife, mother, and professor, disquieting her with grief, and taxing her relationship with her beloved sister almost to the breaking point. Yet the narrative as a whole says much more. At some point, knowing so well the story of her mother's life, Walker begins to find her crazy communications intelligible—realizing that her mother is talking in metaphors and understanding them. The farther away her mother wanders, the closer their relationship. The love between them strengthens. Trying to follow the details of her mother's life as she recalls them, now, in fragments, Walker finds to her surprise that she is not only recovering her own childhood memories but also understanding them in a new way—a set of insights ranking among the most precious of her life. In plainsong prose evoking her heartland roots, Jeanne Walker locates the gifts to be found in the darkest days of a loved one's decline and death, a story of redemption that will inform and encourage anyone caring or expecting to care for ill and aging parents—or anyone at all."

—Peggy Anderson, author of *New York Times* bestsellers *Nurse* and *Children's Hospital*

"Alzheimer's is a word that strikes terror in most of us, particularly as we and our parents age. Poet Jeanne Murray Walker's memoir of her pilgrimage through her mother's illness and death doesn't gloss over the difficulties, but it removes the terror. What remains is a sturdy witness to unexpected meanings and beauties and even humor that surface in lives of faith and suffering. A friend once told me 'Anything can be endured if you make a story of it.' This magnificently written story is the latest evidence."

—Eugene H. Peterson, professor emeritus of Spiritual Theology, Regent College, Vancouver, B.C.

"Jeanne Murray Walker's story of a mother with Alzheimer's, like reports from other recent conflicts, is disorienting. How could it be otherwise? There are no 'front lines,' no clear distinctions between friends and enemies. How did this war even get started? How will it end—and what would 'victory' look like? Maybe, she suggests, we need to see this disease with fresh eyes. 'As I spent thousands of hours with her,' Walker says of her mother, 'I began to recover my own past.' There's nothing syrupy about this book, but it's full of joy as well as sorrow. What a gift she has given us."
—John Wilson, editor, *Books & Culture*

"Jeanne Murray Walker has written one of the most elegant, tender, and intelligent memoirs of Alzheimer's I have read. At once heart-wrenching and richly rewarding, intimate and objective, coldly cutting, and full of clear-eyed promise, THE GEOGRAPHY OF MEMORY is a beautiful gathering of moments: an artful mosaic of shards that builds to a portrait of faith and hope and love."
—Bret Lott, author of *Letters and Life: On Being a Writer, On Being a Christian* and *Jewel*

"In describing her mother's long passage into dementia and its reverberations through a family, Jeanne Murray Walker has given us a powerful tale of loss but also renewal, pain but also love. In simple yet beautiful language, she shows how the light of hope and grace can illuminate even the darkest journey. For many, many readers THE GEOGRAPHY OF MEMORY will be a treasure."
—Alan Jacobs, author of *The Narnian*

"Those of us who've accompanied a beloved parent through the valley of the shadow will instantly recognize the terrain in this lyrical and profoundly wise account of aging unto death. Jeanne Murray Walker's THE GEOGRAPHY OF MEMORY is, hands down, one of the most beautiful books I've ever read."
—Paula Huston, author of *Simplifying the Soul* and *A Season of Mystery*

"This book is not about 'silver linings,' though the author believes 'the news about Alzheimer's is more hopeful than what we hear on the street.' Fully acknowledging the anxieties, frustrations, bewilderment, and tensions that arise in caring for a parent with dementia, Jeanne Murray Walker manages to lead us through those rocky passages to a place not only of acceptance but of fascination and gratitude for the way that such caregiving brings her to new terms with her own memories, with the legacy of stories that are now hers to tell, and with shifting roles that offer rigorous lessons in humility and compassion. The way her own stories mingle with her mother's mirrors a striking truth about how what we call our own life stories are composites, our materials recycled, and everything we call 'ours,' a gift from those who continue to shape us even as they take their leave."
—Marilyn McEntyre, author of
*Caring for Words in a Culture of Lies*

"If you believe there is only darkness and loss in caring for a parent with Alzheimer's, you clearly haven't read Jeanne Murray Walker's book, which sets us straight. This page-turning memoir, fastidious in detail, delivers surprise and wit on nearly every page, teaching us about the immutability and transcendence of human personality, worth, and love. I needed this book."
—Leslie Leyland Fields, author of *Surviving the Island of Grace: A Life on the Wild Edge of America*

"This deeply humane memoir is at once a memorial to a mother whose memory failed before her body gave way, a poignant reflection on the sister who lived close by while the author flew in repeatedly from afar, and an insightful exposition on memory itself. With a poet's eye for the apt image, THE GEOGRAPHY OF MEMORY is also a case book of spiritual disciplines taught by what Jeanne Murray Walker calls "the ugly twins, aging and death."
—Mark Noll, Francis A. McAnaney Professor of History, University of Notre Dame, author of *American Evangelical Christianity: An Introduction*

"A beautifully written memoir of a daughter's journey with her mother over the changeful, perilous landscape of Alzheimer's. The author's compassion, humanity, and humor shine through a chaotic, if not amazing, kaleidoscope of family plans, places, and emotions. What powerfully winds through the narrative is a poet's wonderful reflections on her own history and the nature of memory, identity, and self. A dazzling, engaging story of the grace of holding on and letting go."     —Dr. Myrna Grant, faculty emerita, Wheaton College, Illinois

"There is so much more to this book than the subtitle indicates. Yes, it is a pilgrimage through the Alzheimer's that befell Walker's mother, told with unflinching yet compassionate honesty, and invaluable for any reader wrestling with a loved one's parallel journey. But the telling of the story involves the connections between mother and daughter, and both with family. It evokes reflections on memory, the nature of the human person, and love itself, that should endlessly engage your soul. It is one of the best memoirs you will ever read, period. A masterpiece."     —Warren Farha, owner of Eighth Day Books, Wichita, KS

"Jeanne Murray Walker's loving account of caring for her Alzheimer's-stricken mother is also the occasion for the author to reflect on her own memories of growing up as a fundamentalist. She engagingly relates her own journey in leaving that heritage even while remaining a Christian and also intensely loyal to her memorable fundamentalist mother."     —George Marsden, author of *Fundamentalism and American Culture*

"Jeanne Murray Walker elegantly affirms the value of memory while mourning its loss in her mother's life. She untangles complex threads of family, illness, and faith in a way that sheds light on the aging and dying process—much needed in our death-phobic culture."     —Hannah Faith Notess, editor of *Jesus Girls: True Tales of Growing up Female and Evangelical*

"Walker offers an irresistibly candid account of her mother's slide into dementia and the challenges of helping her in her final days. As her fragmented memory becomes a mosaic of the family's history, her children are forced to confront issues from the past as well as crises in the present. Walker, a poet, creates a rich texture of remembered physical detail that not only lends beauty to the narrative but anchors events and emotions in the reader's memory even as they were anchored in her own."

—Stephanie Kraft, journalist and author of
*No Castles on Main Street*

"THE GEOGRAPHY OF MEMORY is as brave and poignant a tale of a mother's passage into Alzheimer's as you are likely to find. But what truly sets it apart is the way it triumphantly disproves our worst fear about this disease: that it robs its victims of their humanity. Like one of Shakespeare's late tragicomedies, this book moves through loss and discord to discover, by the end, wellsprings of unexpected grace and reconciliation."

—Gregory Wolfe, editor of *Image* magazine

# THE GEOGRAPHY OF MEMORY

A Pilgrimage
Through Alzheimer's

JEANNE
MURRAY
WALKER

**CENTER
STREET**

New York    Boston    Nashville

*The Geography of Memory* is represented by D.C. Jacobson & Associates
LLC, an Author Management Company.

Center Street
Hachette Book Group
237 Park Avenue
New York, NY 10017

www.CenterStreet.com

Printed in the United States of America

RRD-C

First edition: September 2013
10 9 8 7 6 5 4 3 2 1

Center Street is a division of Hachette Book Group, Inc.

The Center Street name and logo are trademarks of
Hachette Book Group, Inc.

The Hachette Speakers Bureau provides a wide range of authors for
speaking events. To find out more, go to
www.HachetteSpeakersBureau.com or call (866) 376-6591.

The publisher is not responsible for websites (or their content) that are not
owned by the publisher.

Library of Congress Control Number: 2013939103

ISBN: 978-1-4555-4498-1

*For Julie and Rich*

# CONTENTS

We possess nothing certainly except the past.
—EVELYN WAUGH, *BRIDESHEAD REVISITED*

We shall not cease from exploration
And the end of all our exploring
Will be to arrive where we started
And to know the place for the first time.
—T. S. ELIOT, "LITTLE GIDDING"

# PREFACE

I wrote this book because I believe the news about Alzheimer's is more hopeful than what we hear on the street. And it needs to be told. Alzheimer's scares Americans quite literally to death. The Alzheimer's Association claims that between 2000 and 2008 deaths from Alzheimer's increased by 66 percent while every other major cause of death decreased. It's risen to the sixth leading cause of death in the United States. By 2050 the incidence of Alzheimer's is expected to quadruple worldwide. As a recent op-ed in the *New York Times* has argued, fear of the disease causes children to abandon their parents, and parents to consider suicide, rather than living through dementia. What a parent has to gain from being cared for by her children may be obvious, but it's less clear what the child has to gain. Nevertheless, I learned that to stay and struggle through Alzheimer's is to reap gifts that may not come any other way.

One of the surprising gifts of those years was that I began to understand even the most wacky of my mother's comments; I gained a new appreciation for dementia victims. In fact, often my mother's conversation seemed fresh and surprising. Some of her comments were funny, though I felt guilty about laughing. Slowly it dawned on me that what she said wasn't random, though it sometimes sounded that way. In fact, all her life she had sprinkled so much metaphor around her speech that my father often teased her about it. Toward the end she often drew her metaphors from her early life. A lot of what she said was hard to decode. But because I knew her story, I could often guess what she meant.

Mother, like all of us, carried her former selves inside her, almost as if they were characters in a play. During her final decade, her earlier selves would emerge. Not that I could predict which Mother would speak next. She might be eight years old, talking to her grandmother (me), or a school nurse, at forty, speaking to her high school principal (me), or at twenty, explaining (to me) the odd thing one of her gentleman callers had done that day. As she verged into dementia, her earlier selves came and went at will. I sometimes thought, now I have several mothers.

As I spent thousands of hours with her, I began to recover my own past. I had never reflected at length on my early life: I had forged a path straight through graduate school to a teaching job, which I combined with raising children, keeping house, and writing. I was always casting myself into the future, reinventing courses, writing in new genres, applying for grants, scanning the horizon. The past got crowded out. Maybe that's what I wanted. Why should I hang myself on the hook of my past, especially such a traumatic past as I'd had? For me the last decades of the twentieth century were such razzle-dazzle, jaunty, surge-forward years.

And then I had to slow down to take care of Mother. Ironically, as she lost her memory, I gained mine. During the hours and hours I spent with her, scenes from earlier years that I had entirely forgotten leapt back so forcefully that they almost seemed to be happening in the present. I began to comprehend my own history in a fresh way. I saw how I had defined myself against Mother, how hard I had to fight to get away from her, and what it had cost us both. This unexpected recovery of my own memories that came during Mother's Alzheimer's calamity became one of the most spectacular gifts of my life.

I also developed a deep bond with my sister. As the two of us cared for our mother, the connection between us blossomed into a remarkable friendship. This friendship is not without conflict. In fact, our last decade with Mother might be called a difficult spiritual journey. But looking back, I see that it *was* a journey, an unpredictable one with abrupt declines, giddy periods of recovery, and, of course, plateaus. In emergency phone calls, through violent differences of opinion, from very different points of view and different regions of the country, my sister and I honored one another as co-partners. We came to know one another better and appreciate one another more.

And even after Mother was almost incapable of talking, she was teaching me about life and death. What she had to teach was not always what I wanted to learn. In our society, where cosmetics companies make billions helping us eradicate wrinkles and other signs of aging, news about the ugly twins, aging and death, is not welcome. Our Disneyfied culture barely acknowledges that they exist. But in the end, it's better to know about them. What we suppress pops up to govern our behavior. If we can't bear to look at death, it rules us. It begins to manifest itself in ongoing anxiety, to spring up in nightmares. To face it squarely can be freeing. To think about death can change the way a person decides to live. Taking care of Mother gobbled up vast quantities of my life; watching her change was agonizing. But it left me different, wiser, better.

I received one final gift. Utterly lost on a dark Dallas expressway at two a.m. one terrifying Thursday morning, I saw that I was not just slogging through what seemed like endless repetitive years of horror. I was on a kind of pilgrimage. That long pilgrimage with my mother and my sister taught me—perhaps it taught all three of us—spiritual disciplines. Among them I count prayer, hospitality, patience, forgiveness, humor, imagination, meditation, silence, empathy, and letting go. For much of that long slog I wasn't thinking in religious language. But these spiritual disciplines and gifts appeared and reappeared, braiding their way through our daily experience, lingering like a faraway melody on some of the darkest mornings. These graces came very slowly and at the beginning they had no names. It is only now that I am beginning to identify them.

Alzheimer's is bleak. It is. But it's not all horror. My mother's last years reveal that for all the heartache, there can still be joy and laughter, insight and love. In this book I have tried to focus on more than just the catastrophes the disease brings. I have tried to bear witness to and name the gifts that came to us. This naming, I trust, will offer hope to Alzheimer's patients, to their spouses and children, to all the disease has terrorized.

# ACKNOWLEDGMENTS

Thanks to the editors who, long before I thought of writing this book, published some of these chapters as essays in their journals (which I read regularly and love): Greg Wolfe and Mary Kenagy Mitchell at *Image* and Rod Smith at *Shenandoah*. Their enthusiasm for this story, in its early stages, fueled me with fire to write more. Thanks also to the editors at Word Farm Press, Sally Sampson Craft and Marci Johnson, who read the manuscript in its earliest stages and backed it.

I am grateful to my friends in the Chrysostom Society for their ongoing repartee about our mutual projects, for how carefully they listened to some of these chapters, and for their comments. I'm thinking particularly of Rudy and Shirley Nelson, Bob Siegel, Jack Leax, and Luci Shaw. I am grateful, especially, to my Chrysostom buddy, Virginia Owens, for her book, *Caring for Mother: A Daughter's Long Goodbye*, which confirmed my sense that understanding metaphor was crucial to understanding Alzheimer's victims.

Thanks to my friends who slogged through the manuscript during the years I was drafting and revising it, particularly to Nancy Hoffman, with whom I walk on the Haverford College nature trail, and to my friends, Deborah Burnham (who read many versions) and Elaine Terranova, both of them remarkable poets.

Thanks to students in the Seattle Pacific University low residency MFA program, who listened as I read some of these essays and who registered their pleasure or displeasure—equally helpful. Thanks and special love to my fellow faculty members in the MFA program, who often feel like kin as we share writing and teaching experiences—Jeanine Hathaway, Leslie Leyland Fields, Gina Ochsner, Bret Lott, Robert Clark, Lauren Winner, and Paula Huston. Thanks also to the smart and endlessly generous staff: Tyler McCabe, Dyana Herron, and Beth Bevis.

Thanks to Sydelle Kramer, who read the manuscript at an early stage and gave me shrewd advice.

Thanks to many long-time writers and readers, fellow travelers on the journey, among them Julie Moore, Marjorie Maddox Hafer, Peggy Anderson, Ejner Jensen, Jill Baumgaertner, Cordelia Biddle, Anne Colwell, Ron Reed, Tom Montgomery-Fate, Dan Hoffman, Barbara Crooker, Denise Brown, Greg Djanickian, Allison Funk, Rod Jellema, Skip Renker, and Dabney Stuart.

Thanks to David Jacobsen, my kind and brilliant agent.

Thanks to Joey Paul, senior editor at Center Street, who believed in these words and shepherded them through the publishing process. Thanks to Laura Laffoon for her vigilance and optimism.

Thanks to my wonderful sister, Julie, and her fantastic husband, Rich. I am grateful to them for the many years they hosted me when I flew to Dallas to care for mother, even when it might not have been convenient for them.

Thanks to Jack and Molly, and Matt and Bobbie, who helped us take care of their grandmother.

Thanks to my mother's friends at Lake Ridge Bible Church—who loved her and never deserted her. And thanks to the aides, particularly in the Christian Care Alzheimer's unit, who showered her with fond attention.

Thanks to my husband, Daniel. He read this book at every stage, faithfully commented, and managed never to seem tired of it.

I am grateful to the Dean of Arts and Sciences at the University of Delaware for a travel grant to do research, as well as to the University for several GUR grants to write parts of the manuscript.

And a final thank you to the readers of this book.

*Chapter 1*

# THE PHONE CALL

Far away, as if through a mist, I hear my husband calling. Swimming up from a dream, I roll over, open my eyes. He's leaning on one elbow in bed, facing me, softly repeating my name. In the milky gloom, I can barely make out his figure.

"What?" I ask. We're in Paris in a hotel room. That much I remember. I push farther down into the warm sheets. I don't get back to sleep easily.

"I think something's happened to your mother," he says.

Sitting bolt upright in the dark, I watch as my husband swabs the floor for his phone. There's a cold breeze leaking in the closed windows. I pull the duvet around my shoulders and press the stem of my watch, which lights up the dial. It's two thirty a.m.

My husband is mistaken, I think. How can he know that something is wrong with my mother? She's in Dallas.

He's jumpy. We're both jumpy after the recent news: that my mother's been in a car accident; that the Christian Care Center is moving her to the Alzheimer's unit; that she needs hospice care; that she has broken her hip.

He sits in bed pushing buttons on his cell phone, pressing

the phone against his ear. The curtains ripple. A monotonous, vengeful January wind whips the trees outside.

"Hi, Rich," my husband says. Rich is my brother-in-law in Dallas.

Silence. My husband looks troubled.

He takes the phone from his ear. "Your mother has died," he says.

I try to believe this, but I don't understand it. I might as well be a stone, unable to feel water pouring over its back. How did he know she was dying? Did she visit him? I wonder. Did he feel her leaving?

He holds out his phone.

I take it.

"We were with her," Rich tells me. "She was asleep. She didn't seem to be in pain. She just never woke up."

With dementia, finally the brain and lungs shut down. But the progress of the disease varies so much with each victim that no one can predict in what month or even what year the end will come. I thought, as her doctors did, that we had many months to go.

Outside, the gnarled treetops boom and crack as they thrash in the wind. When the trees go, I think wildly, everything is in danger. Whipping branches cast shadows against the filmy curtains. My mind keeps slipping its groove, slipping its groove like a vinyl record. Rich goes on talking, this man who has lived through so many emergencies, offering me valuable facts in his calm voice.

"Her favorite aide was with her. And her hospice nurse."

"I'm glad."

I'm *not* glad. I don't feel a thing. But one has to say something.

"You want to talk to Julie?" Rich offers.

"Yes."

"Don't feel like you have to come home," Julie says immediately.

"I want to."

"Don't you have another week to teach?"

I fumble for the answer.

The program. Oh, yes, she must mean the University program I'm teaching this month in London. How much longer does it run? I can't remember.

My husband is pulling on his clothes. When he flicks on the light, the massive ornate furniture rears up around us: a walnut dresser, the maroon duvet with a giant green and burgundy and white paisley pattern. He stands at the window, lifting the curtain at one corner to look out. I feel as if I'm watching a movie of someone else's life.

"How many students do you have?" Julie asks.

"Twenty."

"You can't leave them in the middle of the program, can you?"

"I don't know. I *want* to come home," I say, hoping I really do.

"I can take care of things here," Julie says.

By *things*, she must mean the body. The body that held me before I came into the world, the body that held her. She means my mother's body has to be buried, the final thing we can do for her. My mother looked like a little hollowed-out canoe a month ago, when I last saw her. She weighed barely a hundred pounds.

For almost a decade my sister and I together have taken care of our mother's clothes, her medicine, her friends, her housing. We've gone fifty-fifty, each with different tasks. Julie, who lives close to her in Dallas, makes quick trips to check in with her weekly. She and Rich entertain her at lunch on Sunday. They take care of her finances. I fly to Dallas four or five times a year and stay with her for a week, or part of a week, to wash her clothes, buy her shoes with rubber soles, take her to lunch in a restaurant, encourage her friends to keep visiting her, bring candy to her nurses, stock her apartment with flowers, whatever needs to be done. For years Julie and I have been phoning and e-mailing one another about what might keep Mother safe and occupied and challenged. As we cluck and fuss over her, we are getting to know one another better, coming to rely on one another.

I understand that this, too, has come to an end. I understand it better than I understand that my mother is dead.

"Promise me something," I say to Julie.

"What?"

"That we'll still see one another."

"Sure," Julie replies.

She means it, I can tell; I just don't believe her. Both our lives are monopolized by children and houses and demanding jobs.

"Mother would want us to," I tell her. "You promise?"

"Okay."

"Really?"

"Yeah." But without a crisis, I wonder what will bring us together.

The wind rattles the glass in the windows. It sounds cold and hysterical. My husband is going through the receipts in his billfold, glancing over at me from time to time.

"Can I let you know our plans tomorrow?" I ask Julie.

"Sure."

"We'll call the kids and tell them what's happened."

"Okay. And if you can't come home, we really are okay here," Julie says.

I look at my watch. My mother died on January 27, 2008.

It's a long night. Time slows down, lengthens out. We sleep fitfully, or rather, we don't sleep, lying in a semiwakeful stupor of demonic, distorted thoughts and images. The prayer I have been teaching our three-year-old granddaughter comes to me in the bell-like clarity of Sophia's voice. *O Lord, support us all the day long, until the shadows lengthen, and the evening comes, and the busy world is hushed, and the fever of life is over, and our work is done. Then in your mercy, grant us a safe lodging and a holy rest, and peace at the last. O Lord, support us all the day long, until the shadows lengthen, and the evening comes.*

The evening, I think. The evening means Death.

*Chapter 2*

# THE CHOICE

The next day, charcoal clouds hang low over Paris and the air outside the window of our hotel is heavy and gray. We drink coffee and eat croissants in a neighborhood hole-in-the-wall, while locating an Internet café on our brightly colored tourist map. Then we pull on our hats and coats and gloves and step out into the bitter January wind to search for it. It's Sunday. We called the children first thing. Now we need to e-mail my office to let them know that I have to leave the program. Or maybe that I'll stay.

I need to settle this.

The trouble is, I can't remember the names of streets. A few minutes after I see a name on the side of a building, it's gone. A windshield wiper keeps everything clean and blank in my head. I am supposed to be the navigator, but we wander like home-less people through the damp fog. Finally we notice that we've circled past the same shops several times. We stop in a computer store so my husband can ask for directions in his elementary French, which is better than mine. Then we start out again, in the opposite direction, where the salesperson has told him, in French, to go. Following this route for a mile or so, we turn left and then right, and then left again, but we find no Internet café. So my husband steps into a stationers' to ask again.

My feet are so brittle and icy that I can no longer use my toes for balance. I feel as if any moment I may topple over. I open and shut my hands inside my gloves to get the blood going. With dismay I begin to recognize buildings. We're looping back toward the restaurant where we had breakfast. It's getting dark and we have wandered for almost the whole day, it seems to me, though when I look at my watch, I discover that it's only eleven. We again hone our attention like zombies to find some Internet café. I must confer with my university administrators. We must decide whether to fly home.

By noon we are exhausted and frozen. Finding ourselves close to Notre Dame Cathedral in surreal darkness, we allow ourselves to be carried along by a stream of worshippers. We drift by the immense flying buttresses, beside the tall stone angels and saints, through the massive doors rimmed with multiple levels of sitting and standing granite figures. Who gets to sit, I wonder, and who has had to stand up in this cathedral entryway for seven hundred years?

In the gloom of the interior, my eyes take time to adjust. Overcast daylight shines through the splinters of stained glass in the great rose window, illuminating points of turquoise and sapphire and cobalt blue. I hang on to these pricks of light with my eyes as we sit down on wooden chairs in the cavernous nave. Notre Dame is a tourist destination, but it looks like we are surrounded by French people, mainly. Each is stylish, with a clever hat here or a distinctive tie pin there or an orange scarf. The man sitting beside me is bundled in a bold black-and-white houndstooth checked coat.

Above us soars the vaulted ceiling, its ribs and barreling

webbed in shadows. Stone gargoyles with distorted lips and bulging eyes leer down from columns and pedestals. They are faces of idiots and fools the stone carvers remembered from the back alleys of their villages. I feel like them, stupid, dumb. But it's not nice to stare. I avert my eyes, then move my gaze to the gigantic altar. I blink dizzily at the golden chalices and ornate boxes.

It comes to me that a great cloud of witnesses really does surround us in this cathedral, spirits of generations. By kneeling here, I can see where they wore down the stone floor. The tall altar candles flicker. Fire endures while the candle gets used up. The spirit is more enduring than the body; that's what the candle says. Oh, images and their poignancy! We sail together, the living and the dead, as if nestled together in a massive ship.

As this congregation of strangers stands and steers through the French liturgy, I think about my mother lying alone in a funeral parlor. Or rather, not my mother, but my mother's *body*, her arthritic, knobby hands, her mouth, her forehead. They've laid out her body in the room where my stepfather was displayed years ago beside Chippendale chairs with striped mulberry and mustard upholstery. The sideboard. The wallpaper. Those funeral directors wanted their parlor to look as much like a living room as possible.

In my daze, I'm jarred by the sound of French droning through the Dallas funeral parlor. Then I recall that we're in a church in Paris. Translating the French, I catch snatches of meaning. *We lift our hearts up to God. It is meet and right for us so to do.*

My mother's spirit left her body fewer than twelve hours earlier. I think with some panic that I'd better consider what that means, while the rupture is still fresh. It feels like being at the scene of a car accident, needing to write down the details. I wonder whether

her spirit is floating between earth and heaven. Such airy existence is new to her. I wonder whether she feels out of place. I wonder whether she is trying to make herself understood to other spirits, trying to make friends on this first day after her death.

And I wonder how my husband knew when my mother's spirit departed her body. What made him wake up soon after she died? He loved her, of course—or rather, not *of course*, because most sons-in-law and mothers-in-law do not love one another. Did she wake him? I wonder again.

But how?

The priest stirs, begins moving his hands, raising the chalice. He's far away, in heavy robes, looking like a magician. At some primitive level, I feel that my mother cannot be dead, because, very simply, she gave me life. My life poured into her and then my body tumbled out into the world. How can I still exist, when the person who caused my existence has died? I hold one hand out and stare at it. I see its familiar jade ring.

My fingers tremble slightly. I fear that I am not doing well, that we have decisions to make, that I cannot afford to fall apart, that I need to do whatever people mean when they say they are pulling themselves together.

When the mass of people rise to their feet and sing "Holy God, We Praise Thy Name," I try to recall the English words: *Holy God, we praise Thy Name; Lord of all, we bow before Thee! All on earth Thy scepter claim, All in Heaven above adore Thee.* As the priest begins his homily, the cathedral brightens the way the sky opens when a cloud passes from the sun.

In that moment I sense my mother. I feel a little frightened and improbably buoyant. I don't know why her spirit has come back, or how. I just know that I am in a French Catholic church the day after mother died, and her presence, like light, falls across me through one of the cathedral windows. It strikes me as odd that she's here, funny, really, because she was such an anti-Papist. And as the child of German immigrants, she held no truck with the French. But even in the later stages of Alzheimer's she had a sense of humor.

—

The following day, when I speak with the administrator at my university, she offers me the condolences of the whole staff. They'll be thinking about me, she says. She tells me I should do whatever I need to do. But no, unfortunately, each Study Abroad Program is unique, and there's no one to take over my program. If I leave Europe, my students' program may be over.

"Will they get credit?" I ask her.

"We'll have to figure that out," she tells me.

"They've worked hard all month."

She doesn't reply.

—

Two days later the students and I climb to our classroom on the fourth floor of our Russell Square walkup, where I meet the Study Abroad students for classes, our feet shuffling on the carpeted steps. The room smells stuffy. I sit on the desk at the front. The students peel off their coats and drop into the chairs. A radiator crackles. In the eaves just outside the windows, birds chirp frugally.

My students' faces glow with the adventure of their recent travels to Rome and Edinburgh and Dublin, where they have gone during the five day break that my husband and I spent in Paris. They laugh and call to one another. They pass around pictures on their cell phones and laptops. They tell jokes and exchange souvenirs. As a group, we've gotten close. Right now we would do anything for each other.

I watch them numbly. I have no idea what I will tell them. In thirty years of teaching, I've never felt so dimwitted in a classroom.

Eventually the students notice me. Quiet descends on them gradually, and they settle down slowly the way a bedsheet, after being snapped, flutters to the floor. Several of them turn their faces toward me, a bunch of sunflowers swiveling toward light. In that moment I cannot conceive of how to explain that their London Study Abroad program is over, that they waited tables for two summers to earn money for the trip that now may go down the drain, that they will have to fly home immediately, and they may not get credit.

I know perfectly well that I have the right to leave. It's my *mother*, after all. But if I do, I can't imagine what would happen to these children who have been put in my charge. And besides, I think my mother would want—no, that my mother *does*, actually, *right now*—want me to stay. Didn't she always tell us to finish what we start? If I could ask her and she could answer, she would tell me she doesn't need me in Dallas. She's gone to a better place. She's with my father. Those are the exact words she would use.

So I don't leave my students. The students never learn that my mother has died. On Wednesday morning, my mother is quietly buried in Dallas while I am teaching a class in London.

*Chapter 3*

# THE ROILING HEAVENS

It's spring 1998, about ten years before the phone call that informed us of Mother's death. I'm sitting on her couch, paging through a photo album of her flower arrangements. She is a national flower show judge and with every year her arrangements, which were initially cluttered, have grown simpler. Now they appear almost Asian in their stark beauty. Even I can see how startling and original some of them are.

"These are great, Mom," I call.

"You think so?"

"Yeah, I do." Over Mozart's greatest hits, which are playing on her stereo, I hear her banging pots and clanging bowls happily in the kitchen. "You want some coffee?" she yells.

"Nope," I shout back. I'm like her tennis partner. We volley words, keeping the connection going between us.

For almost two decades, until his death, she was married to my father, a Swede, whose mother taught her to keep the coffeepot on day and night. If nobody wants to drink the stuff, that's okay. Mother swirls its dreggy blackness down the sink before she goes to bed. Meanwhile, we live and move and have our being in a heavenly aroma of coffee.

In her middle age, a decade after my father died, my mother

married Jim, a cigar-smoking, sweet-tempered Southern civil engineer who told her she could do anything she wanted, as long as she permitted him to support her. She joyfully resigned her job as a school nurse and launched herself into the flower-arranging world. She began oil painting, too. Then she set up a Bible study group and began to teach Sunday school. She spent time reading to kindergartners at the local school, and lunched with friends, and persuaded Jim to attend the Dallas Symphony with her.

I close the photo album and squint at the oil painting my mother has brought out from her closet and set up for me to admire. It's her childhood Minnesota farm in winter. She's worked on the painting for months. Across the top of the canvas, navy blue clouds roll in. The heavy sky bears down on a tiny farmhouse that's already smothered in snow.

I kick off my shoes and swing my feet onto her sofa, keeping my eyes on the painting. The roiling heavens look alive and vindictive. My hands tingle and I feel as if I've just jumped out of a plane. The bottom is dropping out of my stomach. The longer I stare at the painting, the more distraught I feel. My mother's specialty is bright pictures of fruit and halcyon landscapes.

"How about a walk?" she yells from the kitchen.

I pause. All day we've been gadding about in her silver Saturn—to shopping malls, to lunch, to the Dallas Museum of Art. But I volley back, "Okay."

She emerges from the kitchen, bringing the smell of basil with her. She looks like a million dollars in a lively patterned, hot-pink suit. "You don't want to?" she asks, disappointed.

"I said *yes*." This is one of the things that drives me crazy about my mother.

"I don't want to force you, darling."

"I'd love a walk."

"I have to walk every day," she explains.

"I know."

"For my back."

"I know, Mom. Do you want me to change before we go out?"

She assesses my jeans and T-shirt. I am dressed in what Texans think of as eastern liberal jeans and hiking boots. Her neighbors and friends wear vividly colored knits duded up with pins or beads and cute black pumps. As do their visiting middle-aged children. My dressed-down clothes probably lower my mother's status among her friends. But I love her enough to visit her often. I hope that makes up for it.

"You look fine," she tells me. "We'll just take a couple of turns around Bentley."

She ducks into her bathroom to check her appearance in the mirror. Her Tweed perfume wafts by me, her signature fragrance. "Oh, darling, I remember what I was going to tell you," she calls.

I mosey over and lean against the door jamb, listening.

"Remember how your grandmother raised a hundred laying hens every spring?"

"Yeah?"

"Well, she sold the eggs and kept the money in her checking account. And did she ever guard that money. Oh boy! Well, one day a raccoon got into Mom's hen yard. She stomped her foot and screamed, *Whhhhist!* Like that. *Get out!*" Mother fans the air, making a shooing motion. "But the coon grabbed the rooster and scuttled up a pine tree. So Mom got Dad's rifle. I'd never seen her hold a gun. I was terrified. She aimed. She pulled the trigger."

"And what happened?"

"The raccoon curled up and fell to the ground. And the rooster flew down." My mother is giggling. I can see the kerfuffle of clucks and flying feathers in the hen yard, the rooster strutting proudly among his recovered harem.

"Were you scared?"

"I hid my eyes in her skirt."

"That woman was something, wasn't she?" Mother likes me to say this.

"That's where you come from, sweetheart." This is my mother's groove.

"Um hum," I murmur.

"You can do anything you put your mind to." I've heard all my life how my grandmother baked bread every day, fed twenty at her table, sewed clothes for five children, served as a sounding board and adviser for her impulsive husband, midwifed babies into the world, tooled around Murray County in her car. After my grandfather died, Mother flew to Pipestone, Minnesota, every fall to bring her mother to Dallas, where they spent the winter together.

I watch my mother tame her mop of black curls. She snatches a tube of scarlet lipstick and freshens her lips, flawlessly outlining their peaks and valleys while she talks, without looking in the mirror. I never got the hang of that. I suspect the optimum age for learning such a lipstick trick is thirteen. I was not allowed to wear lipstick when I was a teenager. Of course, my mother couldn't have been fooling around with Revlon at thirteen on the farm, either.

"Here," she says. "Try it." She holds the tube out to me.

I take this as a hint that I need to put on lipstick before we go out. So I reach for my overnight bag on the bathroom counter.

"Don't you love the color?" my mother asks. She screws the tongue of her lipstick out farther so I can fully appreciate its blazing scarlet.

"That's really *red*," I say, trying to sound excited.

"Come on."

"No thanks."

"Don't you like the color?"

"I'd look like a kid playing grown-up." I learned a long time ago that I can't wear violent reds.

"Just test it."

"I will, when we're not going out."

"O-kaaay," she sings. She means *You're passing up a good deal. Too bad for you.*

She places the lipstick just so in a bin in her orderly makeup drawer. Then she moves toward her front door.

I follow.

"Wait, wait, wait," she chants under her breath, detouring to the kitchen. She picks up a pad, grabs a Magic Marker, and writes in large black cursive: PUT IN ROAST. My mother, who is eighty-three, has scrawled notes to herself ever since I can remember. She had me doing it as soon as I could write. Get up. Brush teeth. Get dressed. Learn to drive. Find a man.

"The roast has to go in at five," she explains. "Or we won't be able to eat by seven. Is seven a good time for you to eat?"

"Seven is great."

"I mean, on the East Coast, you're an hour ahead of us."

"Daniel and I eat late."

"What time?"

"Around seven thirty."

"So you'd rather eat later than seven."

"Seven is just fine."

"I want to do things the way you like."

"Really, seven is good. Then we can watch *Wall Street Week*."

"You like that program, too?"

"Yep."

"Isn't that amazing," she chirps happily. Jim, her second husband, who has been dead for a decade, got her into the habit of watching *Wall Street Week*. She possesses a twenty-year unbroken string of good advice from stockbrokers and financial advisors, all of which has left her essentially untouched by any skill at investment. She still believes a dollar is a dollar and the stock market is a casino. But she is devoted to her rituals, and whenever I visit, we watch *Wall Street Week* together. In the corner of her living room her gray-faced TV waits for its moment.

*Chapter 4*

# FOREBODING

All right, here we go," my mother announces, moving smartly toward the front door.

The phone bleats.

I hope my mother will not answer it. I'm sick of waiting around for this walk we're supposed to be taking. But she gives me a consequential look, which means someone might need her. Then she picks up.

"Erna Kelley," she vocalizes musically.

Pause. "Oh, yes, Bertha."

Bertha is famous in our family as one of the people Mother counsels.

This is bound to take time, I know, so I decide to get a drink of water. Stepping into the kitchen, I open the freezer door for ice cubes. It's so packed with food that a couple of solid things clunk onto the floor. When I pick them up, I notice they're packages of ham. I try to fit them back in the freezer, but they tumble out again. To make room, I ease out six or seven other packets, hoping if I rearrange the freezer I can fit everything back in. I lay the packages on the counter beside the refrigerator. They include six or seven different kinds of ham.

My mother doesn't eat ham.

What's going on? I wonder. Is she involved in some kind of ham testing project? Maybe she's planning to make a large dinner for a church group. But really, this many packages of ham?

I can hear Mother murmuring to Bertha in the living room. "Oh, I know, honey. I know. Isn't that the truth. Yes. Have you prayed about it, Bertha?"

I haul more packages out of the freezer. There are several roasts, one as big as a shoebox, one bigger. There is a whole frozen goose. Gray ice crystals web the packages together and cling to the sides of the freezer compartment. I am the sort of housekeeper who lets my freezer get out of control, but my mother is not. This seems like a freezer owned by a mother on another planet.

I begin to repack the frozen food. As pieces keep slipping out, I catch them and fit them back. My hands buzz with cold and then they turn numb.

I hear Mother say, "Well, my daughter's here, and we're going out. That's right. But I'll call you back. Yes, honey. Tonight. I won't forget. No trouble at all."

She clicks the receiver into its cradle.

I cram everything back into the freezer and slam the door. Then I amble over to the sink and draw a glass of water.

My mother finds me in the kitchen. "I'm sorry that took so long. That was Bertha. Bertha is so needy."

"What's the latest?"

"Her husband lost his job. Did I tell you that?"

"Yeah, on the phone a couple of weeks ago." I take a sip of water.

"Oh, that's right. Well, and Bertha is impractical. Just utterly helpless. The woman has every symptom in the book. And she can't afford any therapist but me."

"She's lucky to have you."

"I'm cheap." My mother sighs ruefully.

"That's true." I laugh. "The price is right."

"I can't imagine what some of these people would do without me."

"Neither can I," I say. In truth, without my mother I think that some of her friends might get up, tie their shoes, and change their behavior. I haven't told her this, but she probably knows it crosses my mind. On the other hand, it is remotely possible that some of her friends might commit suicide without her.

My mother tends to feel they would.

I move toward the front door, hoping to get on with our walk.

"Just a second." My mother grabs a paper towel from the kitchen counter and wipes out the sink. She wants her house clean in case anyone stops by.

"Take your time," I say. I have vowed a hundred times that when I am with her, I will really *be* there. I tense the muscles in my arms. I clench and unclench my hands.

"Are you okay?" she asks.

"Fine."

"What's wrong?"

"My hands are cold. I was getting ice."

"I run a regular counseling business from this place," she tells me.

"How many patients do you have?"

"Oh, about six."

"Doesn't that take a lot of time?"

She's wiping the counter now. "I call it Kelley's Krazy Klinic. All *K*'s," she says. "Did I tell you my joke?" She is realigning the salt and pepper shakers on the stove.

"No."

"Welcome to my psychiatric hotline. If you're obsessive-compulsive, please press 1 repeatedly. If you're codependent, please ask someone to press 2. If you've got multiple personalities, please press 3, 4, and 5."

She is squaring the paper napkins. I am laughing.

"I thought you would like that." She puts the napkin holder down and rummages around in her memory to find the rest of the joke. "If you're paranoid, we know who you are . . . and we know what you want. Just stay on the line so we can trace the call.

"And then . . . wait. I forget. Oh! If you're depressed, it doesn't matter which number you press. No one will answer."

"I love it!" I say.

"That's all I can remember. I'm terrible at jokes."

"Where'd you get it?"

"I made it up."

"No, really."

"You think your mother can't make up a joke?"

"I think you're very clever."

"If I remembered where I got my jokes, I wouldn't have any space in my head for what's really important."

"Wherever you got that one, you should go back for more."

"Come on, let's get out of here," she shouts. She grabs my arm and pulls me out to the mesquite-lined sidewalk at the Christian Care Center. Around us floats the smell of roses and far away a lawn mower drones. Even at five thirty, the Texas light is rosy. Mother's little brick bungalow casts a shadow across the coarse green lawn that's so solid I feel I could lean my shoulder against it and move it.

When houses in the neighborhood where Mother and Jim lived began losing value and crime was ramping up, Mother had nightmares that a thief might break her garden-room window and climb in. After six months of worried discussion, I flew to Dallas and the two of us toured housing options. Christian Care won hands down. It was well constructed, wonderfully kept, and staffed with satisfied workers. The campus boasted an independent living high rise, a grassy neighborhood of two bedroom bungalows, and an assisted living facility with light, spacious apartments. They were planning to build an Alzheimer's unit, not that we paid attention to that at the time. It just showed how forward-thinking they were. The buildings were laid out on well-kept lawns next to a city golf course, behind a fence with a gate and a guard. Mother moved there when she was full of lip and zest, in her mid-seventies.

Now strolling downhill, I raise my face full into the balmy late Texas afternoon air, lagging behind Mother. The glossy leaves on the towering magnolia sparkle.

"Come on, darling. A slow walk doesn't do anything for you." Mother pulls me along briskly.

Her neighbor, a woman with leathery, cinnamon-colored skin, is kneeling in her small garden patch, digging with a trowel. Though it's only early March, her irises are up, trembling in a slight breeze.

When she sees us, she rocks back on her heels. "Haaaaaah there, Eeeeer-na," she drawls, shading her eyes against the molten sun.

My mother turns to me. "You remember Ellie."

I smile. "Hi, Ellie," I respond, slipping into the role of my mother's friendly daughter.

"Have I met this one?" Ellie points her trowel at me. "No. I met the other one, with dark hair." She stands up with difficulty, getting a start by leaning on her trowel, a tall, broad-shouldered woman in a rodeo blouse. Her big turquoise jewelry dramatically sets off her tan. She inspects me.

"This is our little professor from the East Coast," my mother explains proudly.

"Oh, my Gawd, don't listen to my English!" Ellie shrieks, covering her mouth with her trowel hand.

"She writes stories," my mother says.

"Do you!"

"That get published."

"Well, I'll be!" Ellie bleats.

Ellie's irises and pansies and geraniums and volunteer snapdragons are the first I've seen this season. We have snow back in Philadelphia.

"What a gorgeous garden!" I gush.

"Honey, your mother's the flower show judge. I just trudge along in the dirt." Ellie shifts her weight to her other foot. At the end of her long, tan, shapely legs, she's wearing sweet, ferocious yellow alligator heels.

"There's nobody at Christian Care like Ellie," my mother crows. She's one of a kind."

"Here in Texas your mother's learned to talk bull," Ellie barks.

My mother ducks her head with embarrassment. "You can't get up earlier in the morning than Ellie!"

We move away from the Trowel Lady, calling out cordial good-byes.

My mother spots a group of her friends in the distance by the fountain. She aims us in that direction.

"Darling, don't be upset by Ellie's crude talk. She's from the country," my mother confides.

"So are you," I remind her.

"I left the farm when I was seventeen."

"You just told me a story about the farm."

"I never belonged on that farm. I took piano lessons. I sang in the Minneapolis nurses' choir. Ellie got trapped in the country all her life." My mother wants me to see the difference between her and Ellie.

I say, "I bet Ellie loved the Hill Country."

"And it shows."

"I like Ellie," I argue.

"So do I."

We walk by children jumping rope and I stop to watch. *Miss Mary Mack, Mack, Mack, All dressed in black, black, black, With silver buttons, buttons, buttons, All down her back, back, back, She asked her mother, mother, mother, For fifty cents, cents, cents, To see the elephant, elephant, elephant, Jump the fence, fence fence.* No children live at Christian Care, only people aged sixty-five and up. The kids must be visiting grandparents.

My mother hauls me forward.

I stop to admire a bed of yellow flowers with brown centers. "I love those."

"They're just rudbeckia. Nothing special. Come on."

The sidewalks winding through the manicured Christian Care campus are narrow. As we walk together, Mother drifts farther toward my side until she's run me off the path into the grass. She's never been able to walk straight. It's some kind of inner ear thing. You either have to bump her back into her own lane or lag, do a two-step behind her, and then fall in with her on the other side. I decide to come around on the other side. Ten yards later, I reverse the process. She doesn't even notice. Dancing this dance together, we finish out the Dallas afternoon.

—

Around eight that night, after we watch *Wall Street Week*, I tell Mother it's time for me to turn in. She asks me whether I need anything: a snack, help with the pull-out couch, maybe some Benadryl so I can get to sleep. No, no, and no. "Okay, darling," she says, "help yourself to anything you need." And she tilts her face up so I can kiss her good night.

I step into her study, a small second bedroom where I keep my suitcase when I visit, where I try to sleep on her spongy sofa.

I close the door.

Then I remember that I need something to write on. I'm working on a new play. Earlier in the day I thought of a solution to a plot problem. I want to make a note of it before I forget it.

I could open the door and ask my mother for paper, but I don't want to start things up again. I look around, but no paper. She told me to help myself to what I needed. I think she was talking about the refrigerator. But I decide to extend her invitation to her desk.

I pull out the center drawer, where I see scissors, tape, Magic Markers, pencils, and paper clips. There is also a round plastic object I can't identify. I pick it up. Feeling a surge of guilt for snooping, I carefully edge it back and shut the drawer.

The drawer on the top right contains stationery and stamps.

In the large middle drawer, I expect to see neat stacks of envelopes wound with rubber bands. But it is a hodgepodge of papers. I reach in, scoop up some, and slide them onto the desk: old Christmas letters and picture postcards, including several from me, and bills and coupons from grocery stores, and birth announcements, and birthday cards, and photos, and catalogs, and shopping lists. My mother has always been obsessively clean and orderly. I have seen her line her paper clips in rows.

I pick up an envelope, pull a folded paper from it, and read it. It's from one of my mother's cousins, a pleasant, unremarkable letter. Still, I have no right. I should not be prying. I examine the expiration date on a coupon for dog food. It's a year and a half old. My mother has not had a dog since we were kids. There's a paper in her handwriting that lists birds and butterscotch and an iron hook. I hold it beneath the light. The paper trembles in my hand. Could it be a shopping list? Birds might mean bird seed, but I can't imagine what the iron hook stands for. *Iron hook* sounds menacing.

I keep unfolding papers, opening letters, faster and faster. I'm jumpy, waiting for her knock at the door. Or maybe she'll just barge in and catch me going through her desk. But I am hungry to find out what's going on. My hand trembles so that I can hardly read the bill I'm holding. I put it down and shovel the mishmash of paper back into the drawer. I can't remember what the drawer looked like when I opened it. I wonder whether she will be able to tell that I've been spying on her.

I sit on the couch. Oh Mama! Butterflies of panic flutter in my chest. I have crossed a boundary I should not have crossed. My mother would rather die than appear undignified. I have seen her muddled drawer and she has no idea.

Or does she?

Did she leave it there so I would find it?

The flight home is uneventful. But I believe something is wrong with my mother.

# FIELD NOTE I

## ADAGES

*The irony of my mother's losing her memory is that for so long she functioned as a system for retrieving information from the past.*

  *I thought about this in the shop where I get my hair cut. Minnie, my favorite shampoo guru, was explaining to me why she goes to the gym every morning.*

"Because my mother used to tell me, You can die of being lazy."

*I can smell almond, which must be the shampoo.* "Sounds like my mother. She always said, Haste makes waste."

Many hands make light work, *Minnie shoots back.*

*The two of us take turns like Quick Draw McGraws.*

Good things come when you least expect them. *I fire.*

Great oaks from little acorns grow.

Stick to your guns.

Stick to your knitting.

Beauty is in the eye of the beholder.

All good things come to those who wait.

Enough is as good as a feast, *I sing out.*

*But that's a cheat, the name of a play I read in graduate school. I'm running out of sayings.*

Birds of a feather flock together, *Minnie cries. Then to add insult to injury,* By their fruit you will know them. *Minnie could probably go on indefinitely.*

*She gets quiet, then says,* "Those old adages, you know, they gave us standards. They gave us something to live by."

*Not only did Mother tell stories, but she could also reel off a twenty-minute-long prayer, a pastiche of phrases and clauses that explained her story to God.*

*And into her everyday speech she dropped dozens of maxims:* Prayer changes things. Too soon old and too late smart. Give thanks in all things. Don't rush me and I'll work cheaper. Out of the mouths of babes.

*Before Alzheimer's, my mother functioned for all of us as a regular memory retrieval system.*

## Chapter 5

# MY PHANTOM MOTHER

After that visit, my mother, who for twenty-five years had lived a controlled existence in my mind, began to walk right in without knocking. Regularly. I thought about her all the time. I'd be in the jam aisle at the grocery store and imagine I saw her around the corner by the ice cream cones. I'd hear a snatch of Vivaldi and catch her voice asking, "What's the name of that piece again?" I'd lecture my children: "If you expect it to happen, you've got to practice," and imagine a cartoon of myself with her words floating out of my mouth.

One day when I spotted the maple in our front yard and turned into our driveway, I thought: Mother is like that tree; you see her and you know where to turn.

*Ugh, how sappy*, I thought. Getting the emotional pitch right between me and this phantom mother was a challenge.

We invited my actual mother to visit us at Christmas. I wanted to honor her in some way. I decided to throw a party for her. The two of us brainstormed for weeks on the phone about the menu: poached salmon with sauce and little sandwiches with cut-off crusts. Olives and pickles, smoked trout, cured herring, goat cheese, and Stilton. Butterscotch bars and brownies and bells and snowmen and wreathes decorated with green sprinkles and Red Hots.

And I cleaned. I entered into personal combat with the mold in our shower. I battled white rings on our end tables. I dusted the intricate crevices of the radiators. I walked around the kitchen on my knees bearing a rag and probing into the recesses between cabinets. I wiped down our spooky, spiral basement stairs (on which I'm certain I will someday fall and break my neck), trying to ignore the hanging ice skates with sharp blades that provoke nightmares. I wanted Mother to believe I had learned to keep house.

One afternoon I called her and ask for advice about how to perk up our house plants for the party.

"What do you mean, *perk up*?" she asked suspiciously.

"They look tired."

"Plants don't get tired. What have you done to them?" she demanded in her flower show judge voice.

"We had to bring them in from the porch the first week of October."

"They're not getting enough light."

"Maybe," I admitted. Our house stands close to other brick townhouses on our city block and it shares a wall with the neighbors', which means no windows on one side.

"Just pitch them."

"What do you mean, *pitch?*"

"Pitch! Throw out. Toss. Leave them for the garbage man."

"I can't do that. We've had them for a long time."

"Oh, for pity sakes! Don't be such a novice."

"What do you mean, *novice?*"

"Am I a dictionary? You're the one who studied English."

"What do you mean, novice?

"No one but a novice would get so sentimental about plants."

And now here we are, finally, on the evening of the party, Daniel, my mother, and our teenage son, Jack, as well as my own novice, sentimental self, pulling up chairs at our dining room table for a quick snack an hour before the guests arrive. The old, frowsy, yellowing houseplants stand watch like grateful sentinels around us.

I've taken a shower and changed to a long black skirt and a white blouse, serviceable enough for my role as the maid at my own party. Mother is still wearing the beat-up old black slacks she wore to dust the furniture and on her feet are her flats with the broken heel. This is not like her. She sports classy clothes and prides herself on never appearing in public without makeup. She loves parties and meets new people as eagerly as a cocker spaniel.

"What are you wearing tonight?" I ask her.

"You're looking at it."

"You're wearing that to the party?"

"I'm watching videos upstairs with Jack."

"This is your party!"

"I don't have anything to wear."

"You bought a new dress this spring."

"I did not."

"You buy a new dress every spring."

"Not this spring."

She begins attending scrupulously to her grilled cheese sandwich.

"Mom, this party's for you. Our friends are coming to meet you!"

"You can get together with your friends without me."

"I promised them you'd be here."

"I didn't ask you to give me a party, darling."

The two of us have been planning it for weeks. Half an hour and someone will be ringing our doorbell. It takes Mother an hour to get into her full regalia.

Her face is set in an unfamiliar, stony expression.

"Come on." I scrape my chair back and stand up. "We'll find you something."

She allows herself to be led up the long flight of stairs to our bedroom, where she chooses an olive skirt and a mustard blouse from my closet, not her customary blazing sequin and rhinestone outfit, but still, with her fluffy black curls and slender figure, she looks lovely.

—

After the doorbell stops ringing, after we hang up our friends' heavy wool coats, after we pour wine, Mother descends into the hullabaloo of voices. I chime a kitchen knife on a glass and introduce her. Our friends beam and clap. She ensconces herself on the blue couch in the second parlor, where Michele, my exercise partner, a canny businesswoman, sits beside her on the floor, chattering happily as other friends come and go.

Mother is a teetotaler. She refuses wine all evening. But when I come around with a bottle of Merlot and bend over her, she allows me to pour about two fingers into stemware. I hand it to her.

"I'm just a social drinker," she announces to the gathered crowd.

They chuckle.

She swirls the wine in the glass, sniffs deeply, takes a sip, grimaces, and takes another sip as they laugh.

As the evening wears on toward ten thirty, I hear laughing and clapping coming from the second parlor. I follow the sound and find that my mother has hopped down to the floor where she lies flat on her back, pulls her knees to her chin, grasps her hands demurely under her skirt and pivots back and forth like a rocking horse. She is demonstrating her back exercises for Michele. A middle-aged crowd is gathering. "You should all do these exercises," she's instructing them. "They'll keep you limber till you're ninety."

"Oh, my god," our friends say as they leave, "your mother is totally a pistol."

"How did you get so lucky?" they ask.

## Chapter 6

# FALLING

Several days later Mother, as usual, is wearing her large pink plastic trifocals that turn dark and sinister when she steps into the sun. We are about to take Jack to chess. She is walking downstairs when she trips and falls down the last rack of steps to our first floor.

I race down the steps to pick her up. "Are you okay?"

She yanks her arm away from my clutches and hauls herself to her feet. "These steps are impossible!" she shouts. She turns around and kicks a step.

I kick the step, too. "There," I say. "Take that."

She laughs.

"You've never had trouble with steps before." But I can guess what happened. She lost her balance because the heel of her shoe is crumbling.

She pulls off her trifocals. "You try steps with these." She twirls them over her head as if she were performing a musical number at Radio City Music Hall.

"Not me. I can't even manage bifocals."

"Well, I'm perfectly fine with trifocals." She pulls herself up haughtily.

"Then what's wrong?"

"I can't see a thing through these."

"When did you last visit your eye doctor?"

"Three years ago," she says, "and I'm not going back."

"But you need to get the right prescription."

"These cost three hundred and seventy dollars and I'm not paying that again."

"Are you telling me you're not going back to your eye doctor?"

"That's the down payment on a house!"

"Wait. You have to take care of your eyes, Mom."

"That's more than my parents paid for the farm!"

"A hundred years ago."

"I'm getting my next glasses at a dollar store."

"No. You need the right prescription."

"These doctors have us jumping through hoops." She narrows her eyes shrewdly. "Are you working for them?"

I lower my voice. "Is it the money?" I ask.

"The doctors own the toll roads. They're highway robbers."

"Are you okay for money, Mom?"

She changes the subject. "What are we doing today?"

Mother's dignity has always depended on keeping her private life locked up. She believes in something she calls Family Secrets. As we were growing up, she commanded us to stash what we heard at home into the vault of Family Secrets and throw away the key. Life, my mother taught us, is a game in which other people try to gather information about you. You can never tell what they'll use it for. They're probably up to no good. And in spite of my mother's real and passionate love for her children, "other people" might include us. Therefore, Family Secrets can mean keeping secrets from your family. This habit of Mother's, keeping secrets, now thrusts me into a predicament. I have no idea whether she has enough money to live on. Maybe she's unwilling to buy new trifocals because she can't afford them. Maybe that's why she didn't buy a new dress this spring and why she hasn't gotten the heel of her shoe fixed.

*Chapter 7*

# SAFE

When I consider Mother's need for privacy and her passion to keep what she cared about locked up, I think of our family's safe. Mother kept it on the floor of the clothes closet in her bedroom, covered by a jolly-looking red-and-white-checked picnic tablecloth, which she hoped would throw burglars off track. In fact, our whole extended family was into safes. My father's father, who owned and ran the general store in Parkers Prairie, Minnesota, kept one in his office. My mother's father also kept a clandestine safe in his cold, dank basement vegetable room under the shelves of canned tomatoes and peaches. When I was about nine he motioned me to follow him down there, and I stood shivering in the musty-smelling, freezing damp air, where little chips of the basement wall were peeling off, while he opened the safe and flashed what he said were sixty thousand dollars in bills. He warned me to never breathe a word about it.

I assumed that every family in America kept a vault. I confess, this perplexed me. If everyone kept a safe, how could any of them be secret? A burglar (who probably possessed a safe, too) would surely guess we had one.

Our own family's safe was a heavy cube, a foot and a half long and wide and tall, made of brushed steel with a door on one side. On top of the door was a round, black combination lock. This was probably the safe my father kept at his store in Parkers Prairie, Minnesota, the one my parents moved with us when we piled everything into an American Van Lines truck and took off for Nebraska.

On slow Sunday afternoons Mother would call us kids together to witness the opening of the safe. Once we had gathered, she would close the bedroom door and whisper that she needed to check the deed to the house. Or find an insurance policy. Or show us our collection of silver dollars.

Papers she kept in the safe might as well have been holy writ, they were so enshrined and mysterious. She would hike up her skirt so we could all see the knee she had smashed when she was a child running from the bull on the farm (from which she barely escaped and then almost bled to death, though God spared her at the last minute when her parents found a surgeon to sew her up). On that knee and her other good one, she would kneel before the safe, her left hand grasping an envelope where my father had scrawled the combination before he died. She held her hand up for silence, then twirled the dial, cocking her head to listen for the clicks.

By the time my brother, Michael, was sixteen, he refused to join the rest of us, reverently kneeling around the safe. One Sunday Mother bribed him with the promise of hamburgers for dinner. He fidgeted impatiently as she penetrated the gloom of the closet and lifted off the picnic cloth. After prolonged twirling, she murmured, "I almost got it that time," and started spinning the dial all over again.

Michael snorted, "I've got other things to do."

"You need to know how to find these papers in case something happens to me," she whispered, modeling good Family Secret behavior.

"Nothing's going to happen to you," Michael grumped.

"That's what we thought about your father," Mother hissed fiercely.

"What's the point of having a safe anyway?" Michael's adolescent voice slid to a squeak.

"Shhh! Do you want everyone in the neighborhood to hear?"

"No one's listening," he scoffed. "Anyone who isn't an I-dot is watching baseball right now."

Mother stopped twirling the dial and twisted around to confront him. "What do you know about the world?"

"There's nothing in there anyone would want!" Michael said.

"Oh, come on, Michael," I beseeched. I figured that if the two of them had a skirmish it would slow down Mother's safe ritual and we might be sitting there all afternoon.

Mother's brown eyes were snapping with anger.

"This safe isn't even *safe*," Michael reasoned, as if logic were the main goal. He got up from the floor where he had been sitting cross-legged and stepped over to the safe and hoisted it up and strode out of the room with it.

"Where are you taking that?" Mother yelped.

"I'm showing you," he called back, "the safe isn't safe! If someone really wants it, he can just pick the whole thing up and walk off with it."

"You bring that back here!" Mother shouted, scrambling to her feet.

Michael brought the safe back and dropped it with a clunk on the hardwood floor beyond our raging mother. Then he walked out of the room.

He didn't get hamburgers that night. He stayed in his room sulking while the rest of us reheated spaghetti and red sauce from earlier that week. That was the last time Michael ever participated in the ritual of the safe. I set the table because I didn't like Michael to defy Mother. I was mad at him because he sentenced Julie and me to spaghetti, when we could have enjoyed hamburgers. Defiance that seemed perfectly reasonable to Michael would never have occurred to me. I worried about him and I worried about how he baited our Mother. Next he might climb out on the roof and shout our family secrets to the people who drove by on Fifty-fourth Street.

In hindsight, I recognize Mother herself was like a safe. For all her chatty, off-the-cuff friendliness, she herself was profoundly enigmatic.

After my father died, people asked one another, "How does she do it?" The apparent serenity with which she navigated my father's and brother's deaths endowed her with authority and charisma. Maybe she had learned her inscrutability from living in a town so small that you could pick up your phone and hear people gossiping about you on the party line. All I know for sure is that during Mother's last decade she might as well have been a safe whose secrets I couldn't unlock.

*Chapter 8*

# IT'S IGOR STRAVINSKY

After Christmas Mother flew back to Dallas and I launched into the complete Elizabeth Bishop and other poets with my students, a pleasure I probably relish more than they do. But beneath the bliss of reading poetry every day, my attention kept getting snagged on the rough bedrock of worry. I could not figure out how to break through mother's privacy shield. I should have checked into her finances long ago.

For months I tried to work myself up to pry from Mother information about her finances. What would happen to her if she couldn't see well enough to drive? If she couldn't afford shoes that would help her keep her balance as she walked around Dallas? If she couldn't buy new clothes or afford to take her old clothes to the cleaner? What if she was running out of money?

Oh, come on, I told myself. This is stupid. Empathy is one thing; obsession is another. So I took a walk on the Haverford Nature Trail and took an inventory of what I knew. I knew that when Mother married Jim, my stepfather, he had a little money. After all, he taught my sister and me how to invest conservatively; that is, to invest in supermarkets and toothpaste companies, which produced or sold products that people would still have to buy if there were a depression. He was invested in those companies himself and had enough money so that after she married him, Mother was initiated into middle-class luxuries. She started buying fresh bread instead of day-old, picking out a new dress for each season, driving a car that wasn't a rattletrap.

Seventeen years later, when Jim died, Mother resumed the routine of bill paying. At that point Jim's investments must have needed tending. I doubted that she was managing her own money. She knew nothing about it. She always claimed that investing in the stock market is no better than betting on a horse race. Jim's broker, I assumed, was doing pretty much whatever he wanted with her stock.

I wondered who was keeping tabs on the broker.

Not her children. At least I wasn't.

—

I vow during my next call to Mother to lead her into a frank discussion about money. The week comes and goes and none of our phone conversations present the opportunity. I make excuses to myself and renew my oath to do it the following week. But no. Every week that spring I swear to myself that I'll speak to her about money before Friday. But I never do. In February I decide the reason I can't launch the topic is that we need to talk face-to-face.

So I book a flight to Dallas in March and we gad around and when I leave, we still haven't had our candid discussion about her finances. By April the agony of worry becomes more intense than the pain of confronting the issue head on. I take an oath before God during silent prayer in church that after spring break, I will force the discussion.

So one night as I fry chicken and cook rice, my husband dials Mother. When she answers, Daniel flips on the speaker phone, hoping that I can glean information about her mood before the Big Talk.

"This is Igorrrr Stravinsky," Daniel growls.

"Oh, hello," my mother responds enthusiastically.

"I know you luffff museeek."

"I do. I love music."

"I vant to half you to my house for dinner."

"I'm sorry. *Who* is this?"

"I yam Igor Stravinsky. I yam inviting you for dinner."

"What are you having?"

"Cheeeekin und rrrrrice."

"Who are you? I don't think I know you," she says apologetically.

"I yam a vamous composer!"

"Oh, Daniel!" my mother giggles.

When Daniel hands the phone to me, I clamp it between my shoulder and chin while I snip parsley.

"How are you, darling?" she wants to know.

"We're doing our taxes," I tell her, launching into my pretext before the money showdown. With my mother, if you want to go to the left, first you have to tack right.

"It's the tax time of year," she says agreeably.

"Daniel's got papers spread all over the table."

"That's the ticket. Give him the job!"

"Have you done your taxes?"

"I sent the stuff off a long time ago."

"Are you getting money back?"

"I suppose a little," she says absentmindedly. I can tell from her voice that she's wearying of this topic, that I'd better go for it.

"What's your tax bracket?"

"Why are you suddenly so interested in taxes?"

"I wonder if you'd like help with your money."

"I have an accountant."

"For taxes."

"That's all I need her for. I've taken care of my own check-book since I went to nurses' training."

"At Christmas—remember—" I begin. "I thought you told me...." I can't bear to humiliate Mother, but I made a vow before God, so I bravely forge ahead. "You said you couldn't afford a new dress."

"Oh, good grief," she bursts out, sounding as if she pities me for being gullible. "You can't believe everything you hear."

Outside, wind shears through the rhododendron hedge. The porch light swings, sending eerie shadows back and forth across the darkened veranda. I remember her painting of her child-hood farm. I remember her glasses, her broken flats.

"Mother, look. If I knew something about your finances, at least I could remind you that you don't have to worry."

"Honey, if I get worried, you just remind me to trust God," she says.

"Okay. Let's say *I'm* the one who worries."

"Oh piffle! You don't worry."

"I worry about *you*."

"Where's your faith, darling?"

"In the little finger of my left hand! Mother, I don't give a flying—"

"Don't talk like that!"

I feel fury rising in my rib cage. "I need to know you're all right."

"I'm all right," she parrots.

"Remember how you wanted to help *your* mother?"

"She was a very independent woman."

"She let you help her."

"I never knew one thing about her money. Wait! There's a knock on my door! Bye, darling!"

Click. And she's gone.

It is outrageous to say that if I trusted God, I wouldn't need any information. My mother has wheeled God out and positioned him as a roadblock between us. Poor God! What did he do to deserve being used that way? My mouth feels dry and my chest tightens and I think I might go haywire. I kick my shoes off and sit cross-legged on the cold tile of the kitchen floor. I am remembering the chaos in Mother's desk drawer, the hams in her freezer, the thunderclouds on the horizon.

## Chapter 9

# ONE RED CENT

Because I don't know what else to do, I begin to call Mother more frequently. She talks a lot about how expensive the world has become. "A dollar seventy-five for a package of gum!" she cries. "All right. They can charge whatever they want. I refuse to chew gum." She gives up steaks, candy bars, leather gloves.

A rift opens in my quotidian life and memories thrust up like prehistoric mountains—memories of the way she worried about the budget when I was a child. Sometimes it's as if I'm watching a video, set in our old house in Lincoln, Nebraska, set in the period right after my father got sick.

~

Memory One. We kids are sitting at the kitchen table, kicking one another and from time to time, pretending to do our homework. It's the late fifties. Mother is wearing her black wool coat and big black rubbers, with a scarf tied over her head, carrying bags in from our car in the rain. She opens the back screen door, wipes her feet on the mat, sets the groceries on the counter, and pulls a little notebook out of her purse. Bending over the book, she jots down how many pennies she spent. Holding her pencil, she presses down hard, creating a record in her perfect Palmer

Method penmanship. Drops of water from her hand speckle the
notebook.

*17 cents, cough drops.*
*56 cents, flashlight batteries.*
*1 dollar 33 cents, pie and coffee for 3.*

Memory Two. I stop practicing my violin and briefly go to
the kitchen for a drink of water. Mother is standing over the
counter, her woolly coat almost touching the linoleum. It's fall,
the weather turning sharply chilly, and through the kitchen
window the trees are rioting in scarlet and purple. My mother
is concentrating, holding a stack of five-dollar bills in one hand.
She peels off bills, one at a time. She deals them into four piles,
one for each week of the month, then paper-clips each pile, then
lifts the lid of the strawberry cookie jar, that green porcelain
stem, and pushes the bills inside. There. Grocery money for the
whole month. You can hold it. It's real. If you get to wondering,
you can pull it out and count it again.

At night Mother rubs Pond's night cream into her face and
winds her hair in prickly rollers with big pink plastic prongs
stuck in them to keep them in place. In that condition, once
a month she sits up in bed with her checkbook and pays bills,
adding up the numbers. If the sum is too big, it will swallow up
her paycheck and demand more. Toward the end of the month
she seems jittery and she shuts down luxury items like ice cream.
As a child, I try to imagine what debt looks like. It's a ferocious,
whiskered cat, a lion or a tiger I've seen snarling in a zoo.

When you walk into the cat house, the tiger is lying down,
but when it notices you, it sits up and yawns, showing its terrible
yellow teeth. It watches you with growing interest, standing up,
its powerful tail lashing back and forth. You can't stop staring

at it, but you try not to make eye contact. The tiger pads to and fro before the bars of its cage, gazing at you hungrily. Debt is like that. The numbers never sleep. The sum our family must owe—for my father's medical bills, for food, for our clothes—is awake and growing. At any moment it might escape its cage and devour us. Mother is like a wild animal trainer.

My mother is still trying to tame the bills in my memory when I realize with a shock that I need to teach a class at the university in less than two hours. I grab the texts. Heading out the door to the car, I grip a cup of coffee. I didn't buy it from Starbucks at $4.50 a cup, but I did brew it from gourmet beans. By contrast, Mother bought Maxwell House in bright blue thirty-six-ounce tin cans, which proclaimed the astonishing news in a circle around the top: MAKES 400 CUPS! Using coupons, she could get the price to under a dollar. At two dollars a gallon for gas, this year, I pay more for one round trip to the university than our family spent on transportation for a month. We took the bus a lot.

What a bizarre country the 1950s were. How odd it seems that my mother recorded the tiny numbers she paid for the few things she bought at grocery and dime stores. She must have been engraving the numbers in her muscles and memory, too. Now it seems fanatical, the attention she paid to pennies. The cent sign itself looks weird. How long has it been since I've seen an actual cent sign?

But worrying about money allowed us to enjoy vivid wishes. I longed for a brown heather sweater from the Sears catalog. My mother hoped that I would forget the sweater and just pass geometry so I could graduate from high school. My brother yearned for a shortwave radio. The longing beneath all our other wishes, like the bottom box in a stack of Christmas gifts, was the hope that our mother would stay healthy and keep working so she could pay the mortgage. We kids wanted that just as much as our mother did. Nowadays the theory is that you shouldn't let children worry about the big griefs afoot in the adult world. But it was probably better for us to know what was at stake than to have to guess.

We saved things, because we didn't have much. A tenth of everything we earned, we were supposed to give to the Lord. My parents gave more. After all, they figured everything they owned belonged to God. What was left over, they stretched as far as they could.

I had six skirts and four blouses. I knew them the way a person knows her pets. We kept orphan gloves and if one of us lost a glove, we wore two that didn't match. I nursed and tended my one pair of shoes, which Mother bought two sizes larger than my feet so I could grow into them. They flapped out ahead of me and made running complicated, the long unmanageable toes stuffed with cotton. The soles of one pair fell apart before they fit.

Our entire electronic paradise was a black-and-white television with a screen about the size of a *Time* magazine, a black phone with a rotary dial, a box camera, a hooded blender, a vacuum cleaner, and a massive walnut console radio.

We didn't throw away sour milk; we made pancakes. We wrapped the smallest dab of leftover potatoes in tinfoil and fried it for breakfast. I stashed cotton from aspirin bottles in my drawer and used it to apply face powder. We reused big margarine tubs to store leftovers. One of my Saturday jobs was to paste S & H Green Stamps in books; we went only to stores that gave Green Stamps. In fact, it wouldn't surprise me to find out that my mother had selected our piano teacher based on who offered Green Stamps.

I spent wonderful hours dreaming over the restricted offerings in the S & H catalog.

I ease my black Toyota to a stop behind a long line of stalled traffic. A police officer is waving his orange gloved hand to direct the cars, one by one, around a fender bender. Idling, I take out a small pad of paper from the pocket of my car door and write:

Turn off lights
Save string
Bring home packets of salt and pepper from restaurants
Reheat used coffee in an aluminum pan
Reuse waxed paper and foil
Reuse gift wrapping paper
Make quilts and rugs from old clothes
Pluck chickens—pillows from feathers
Fix cars. Keep them going 20 years
Save bacon grease to make dressing for cabbage
Darn socks
Fix mechanical pencils, tape together broken glasses
Boil down leftover soap for new bars
Stick chewing gum on your night table and resume chewing
    in the morning

I still have the list. Whenever I remember other things we saved, I add to it.

*Chapter 10*

# OH BONNIE, OH RAYETTE

There's a traffic jam driving into Newark, Delaware. Inching forward, I worry about being late for my first class. I hear an explosion of thunder. The street and sidewalks have turned dark gray from rain. Black clouds are rolling in from the west. I glance into the backseat, checking for my black umbrella, and then flick on the windshield wipers: *lock-heave, lock-heave, lock-heave.* I creep by a house with a panel truck parked in the driveway that advertises itself as a pool service.

We children didn't spend afternoons lolling beside swimming pools, the way I imagined rich people did in Lincoln, Nebraska. All summer our family tended a vast garden. We canned its phantasmagoric abundance: tomatoes and rhubarb, beans and corn. In August Mother bought bushels of peaches and apricots to preserve.

We knew people who went hungry. I knew kids who didn't have a coat or ten cents for the bus. They walked. They were not statistics, or friends of friends. We talked to and went to school with these people, though we didn't know very many of them, and the ones we knew tried to disguise their need. Oh, but we suspected. Their mothers were widows and took in boarders; or their mothers had died; or their father had been laid off. They wore shiny, frayed shirts with sleeves that stopped above their wrists. I add their names to my list. Douglas. Jo Ann. Anabell. The sisters, Bonnie and Rayette.

Oh Bonnie, oh Rayette! I remember that after their father died of throat cancer, their delicate birdlike mother offered herself around the city until she was hired as a secretary by a religious organization that barely paid her anything. Dark circles formed under her eyes. When I spent the night at their house for a sleepover, dinner was turnip soup and bread. Afterward their two renters showed us how to make plastic bags of pink and yellow frosting, how to force the frosting out into the rosettes that we first admired, then hungrily gobbled. When Rayette and Bonnie's house was repossessed, they took turns telling about it at school during circle time. I decided then and there that I would never tell something like that because, as my mother had informed us, there is such a thing as a Family Secret and you don't have to tell everything you know.

One morning Bonnie and Rayette told us that they were moving. We were surprised and asked where, but they didn't know. Maybe to their grandparents' house, Bonnie said, but maybe not, because their grandparents lived in a two-room apartment in some faraway place like Oxbow, Montana, and how would they all fit into it? That fall Bonnie pulled out all her eyebrows and eyelashes. With no eyebrows, Bonnie looked bald as a baby bird. I wondered whether her eyebrows would ever grow back. If they didn't, who would marry her? When my mother asked me what was wrong, I told her that if our house got repossessed, whatever that meant, I might pull out my eyelashes.

She laughed. "Don't be so melodramatic. I pay the mortgage first and buy food and everything else with what's left over." But I had nightmares long after Bonnie and Rayette disappeared from school for good.

Although Mother counted pennies and wore hand-me-downs from cousins in Montana, she was a proud woman. One Saturday afternoon during the winter of amazing snow, Julie and I showed her the Reddi-wip bowl full of money we had made selling hot pads door to door, colorful hot pads we had woven on our toy loom.

"Where did you sell them?" she asked.

"Around here," I told her, ambiguously.

"In this neighborhood!?"

"Yep," I said, stacking the nickels and dimes and pennies into rows on the dining room table. We had gone up and down our street in our oldest torn coats wearing our old shoes with no socks, hoping to work up a little pity in our customers. I imagined that I was the little match girl and would be sleeping under a bridge in the snow that night.

"You sold those hot pads to our neighbors?"

We pointed to the rows of nickels and dimes and quarters.

"We're not the Snopes," she told me gravely.

"What are the Snopes?" I asked.

"You take that money right back."

"Back where?"

"To the people who gave it to you!"

"It's snowing."

"That wasn't a problem before."

"It's snowing harder now."

"Give them their money back."

"Then we get the hot pads."

"Fine," she said.

We used those hot pads for years.

———

Luckily Mother didn't have much interest in accumulating new stuff. She preferred the past. She attended the auction where the hay rakes and wooden chests and the butter churn from her family farm were sold. She piled our blue Ford full of stuff she had rescued. In those days, it wasn't chic to furnish your house with antiques or to wear handmade clothes. It smacked either of privation or of bad taste. But my mother defiantly outfitted our house with nineteenth-century chairs and Depression-era glass dishes and her grandfather's spinning wheel, antiques her parents had abandoned in favor of knock-off Danish modern.

Mother also spurned au courant clothes sold in the stores. Handmade was sturdier. And if you wore homemade clothes you didn't meet yourself coming and going. As for me, I didn't even comprehend that styles change until I was about sixteen. Then I was smitten by fashion. Upward-inching hemlines. Puffy sleeves. Voluminous gathered skirts and crinolines. Madras. Seersucker. Waffle cloth. The textures and patterns thrilled me. So did the mystery of human form as it could be variously revealed and hidden by fabric stitched into different shapes. The nape of the neck showing this year, the calves, the next. I stepped up my babysitting jobs, for which I charged twenty-five cents an hour. I aimed for one chic dress in the fall. I would pick out a Vogue pattern and, like an architect, spend weeks modifying it. Finally, I would sink a fortune into fabric and create a one-off suit or dress.

It seems far away, the strange 1950s country where five dollars was a fortune and my life was worth twenty-five cents an hour. But the truth is, even now as I write this, it's the 1950s inside me, just as it was inside Mother. When I leave a room, I turn off lights. I wash plastic bags and hang them over the faucet to dry. I fold waxed paper and tinfoil for a second use. Clothes I haven't worn for years still hang in my closet. I love thrift shops. I relish giblets because as a child I learned how tasty they are.

Maybe some of this seems less radical in light of the new post-2008 frugality and the environmental movement. I would like to say I engage in these activities because I am a good steward of the earth. But that isn't why. Inside me lives the teenager who learned to save.

I have the wit, most of the time, to check the facts and rein myself in. Oh come on, I say to myself. Lighten up. Have a little fun. But I *do* have fun. Playing the game of pennies lends humdrum days a thrilling edge. It's a challenge to see how many hair washes I can get out of one bottle of shampoo. I'll drive a mile to save ten cents a gallon on a tank of gasoline.

I try not to get carried away. But what does it mean, *to get carried away*? One person's sanity is another's craziness.

As I park and walk into my office on the university campus, I begin to think that the difference between me and Mother is this: She is losing her ability to check the facts and ride herd on her 1950s self. Her old self lives inside her head and shouts through a megaphone that she's heading for financial ruin. Maybe the boss self inside Mother that governs all the other selves is not as strong as it used to be. I begin making up a cartoon to explain Mother. I make her Manager Self sit at a big switchboard, deciding how loud each of her other selves get to shout.

At home that night, I call Mother on our land line. It's the third time I've called her in a week. I ask myself, when did I get accustomed to the lavish pleasure of talking long distance any time to anyone I want?

As I listen to the phone ringing, I remember Mother's long-distance phone behavior when we were children. Every Sunday she made a phone call to her own mother. She talked for three minutes, timed with an egg timer or a minute minder. She let us kids talk to our grandparents, but a minute of conversation for each of us was the outside limit. Longer than that and she'd panic.

If you're eight, how can you have a decent conversation with your grandparent, keeping your eye on the clock like that? No matter what I said, it sounded stilted. Good grief, sometimes Mother would cut us off before we even had time to say good-bye.

Later that night, after I talk to Mother on the phone, as I'm brushing my teeth, it's as if I can see her sitting in her bed in Lincoln, Nebraska, paying the bills. She seems so real that I almost hear her calling to me as I walk by.

"Be back by ten!" And she blows me a kiss.

# FIELD NOTE 2

## WHAT IS MEMORY?

*Memories of my childhood begin to appear unbidden.
I marvel at their strangeness the way a deep sea diver
wonders at brilliant coral reefs and exotic fish.*

*I have zero understanding of why this or that memory
suddenly swims up from the murky depths.*

*I conclude that in spite of all the memorizing I have done—of
scripture, of music, of multiplication tables, of bus schedules, of
presidents, of facts for my Ph.D. exams—memory isn't an arm or a
leg, to be controlled at will.*

*Sometimes a memory leaps in like a big playmate who hasn't
booked a play date. It won't take no for an answer. I try to sit with it. I
try to give it my attention.*

*Then later, when I call, it won't come.*

*Chapter 11*

# HOW WE'LL HELP HER

Not long after I began worrying about Mother's finances, I had a dream.

We were all gathered for Christmas and I was cooking a goose for dinner. Everyone knows goose is about a third fat, which spits and sizzles as it cooks. I left the room for a minute and when I returned, flames were bursting from the oven. They quickly spread to engulf the walls. Daniel grabbed the land phone and called the fire department. The two of us worked with towels and baking soda trying to put out the fire, but it got ahead of us, eating up the floor, licking whatever lay in its path. One wall blackened and curled to nothing. The ceiling began to cave and heavy embers gushed to the floor, shooting bright red. I realized the room had become so hot we would soon be cooked alive.

Then I remembered that upstairs my mother and our children were asleep. I took the stairs two at a time, shouting to wake up Molly, who was old enough to know what to do. But Jack was sleeping at the back of the house and Mother at the front. While I was thinking about which to rescue first, a whole section of the second floor fell though and I could see the fire climbing the staircase. There might still be time to save one of them, but not both. It would be either Mother or Jack. I had to make a choice and if I didn't decide fast, I would die with them in the conflagration.

I woke up moaning, Ahhhhhhhhh. I sat up in bed in the dark, blinking at the blinds, where the streetlight seeped through. It doesn't take Joseph to interpret this dream, I thought. It's about how dangerous love is, how you can't save everyone you love, even if you want to, even when you're expected to.

And I remembered when I was six my father was peeling off his slicker in the dark garage, with Mother helping him, because he was weeping. He was gulping big ragged intakes of breath and his shoulders were shaking. I hadn't even known my father was capable of crying. I stood quietly, hardly blinking for fear of making things worse. I reached out to touch Mother, only to make sure she was still there, and my little sister touched me for the same reason. It was Good Friday and my father had been out fixing downed electrical wires after a thunderstorm to restore light to our small town, not knowing that his friend, Arnie Carlson, who got there first, had touched a live wire and been electrocuted. My father told us he found Arnie sagging from the line with his boots on, his face and limbs still twitching from the current as if he were alive. And he might have been alive, too, that's the terrible thing, but my father couldn't save him, or even find out, because Arnie's body conducted the electricity just like the wire. If Daddy had touched him, he'd have died, too.

If you love too much, my father told us, you try to save someone you can't save, and you get pulled under, too. Or maybe he never said that. Maybe I just understood it. I am thinking how if my father had touched Arnie, Mother would have rushed to my father and touched him, and Michael would have rushed to Mother to touch her, and I'd have rushed to touch Michael, and my little sister would have touched me. We'd all end up dead. And that just shows how deadly love can be.

Your mother is a conductor and even your children are. They might kill you.

But maybe it's wrong to try to save yourself. Maybe we're supposed to try to save everyone around us, and if we don't make it ourselves, well, that's okay. So what am I going to do for my mother, who is drifting into another country, a country whose name I don't even know. Old age? Poverty? Not Alzheimer's. At the time Alzheimer's didn't occur to me.

—

My mother and I are on the phone, discussing the woman who can't stagger through a day without consulting Mother several times for advice. "How's Bertha?" I ask.

"Poor Bertha! Remember her son, Robert? You know, the one who's divorced?"

I'm thrilled that I've hit on a question that has Mother jazzed (though she hates jazz, which she tells me was invented by musicians with sloppy rhythm).

"Well, her son Robert's moved in with his new honey," Mother tells me. "Her name is Candice. Candice has a pet alligator that terrorizes Robert's kids. Now they won't visit him on weekends."

"Bertha's life sounds like a soap."

"She hasn't seen her grandkids for two months."

"Maybe she should disappear the alligator."

"You mean Candice? Candice loves it," Mother declares.

"I mean Bertha should disappear it. Just warn her not to flush it down the toilet."

"For heaven's sakes. Who would flush an alligator down the toilet?"

"It's an urban legend."

"What's an urban legend?"

"A story. The sewers in big cities are crawling with alligators. When people flush them down the toilet, they breed."

"You're pulling my leg," Mother says.

"Yeah."

"Well, don't," she scolds. "I depend on straight talk from somebody in your family."

"Don't try to flatter me," I retort.

"I want to talk to that husband of yours," she tells me.

"Are you bored with me?" I ask, making my voice sound woeful.

"I want to bandy words with him," she replies in an impudent tone.

He's taught her to say that: *they bandy words*. I laugh and hand Daniel the phone.

———

Then I change clothes and drive over to our building to do some work. Daniel and I own a five-unit apartment house that we manage ourselves now, after professionals lost money managing it for five years. The building still doesn't run a profit. It was Daniel who bought this 1860s townhouse and renovated the third floor and moved into it. He planned to refurbish all the stately arched doorways and random width pine floors, turning the building back to a single-family dwelling. After we got married, we kept it as a rental property. We had to: it was something about the way capital gains taxes worked at the time. We'd have taken a bath if we sold it.

The building stands in a partly gentrified neighborhood, which is one of life's optical illusions. The neighborhood is either half run-down or half renovated, depending on your point of view. My point of view, as I wring out my sponge into a bucket of tepid water reeking of ammonia, is that the street looks pretty much the same as it did when Daniel bought the building twelve years ago. We're lucky if we make several hundred dollars a month renting five apartments. I clean the halls myself now and when a tenant leaves I place ads in the *Inquirer* and show the vacant apartment twelve or fifteen times before we find a tenant who can pay $450.00 a month for a two bedroom. We would sell the building, but the value of properties in this neighborhood is lower than it was when Daniel bought it.

I grab the bucket of dirty water, sloshing some on my jeans, climb to second floor rear, unlock the door, and stare at what the tenants have abandoned this time: a table set for breakfast with Cheerios and slowly curdling milk, a double bed with plaid, rumpled, stained sheets, shirts and socks and personal possessions strewn from one end of the place to the other. I climb down to the basement, grab a couple of cardboard boxes, lug them up to the second floor, and begin hurling stuff into them: one box for stuff we can use, such as a flashlight and an extension cord, and the other box for the roast beef sandwich that is going bad, the torn coloring book, the plastic figure of a circus barker with fluorescent wings.

You wonder who these people are, the ones who leave so fast, maybe on the run from a drug lord or the police. And these are the tenants who passed our credit check! We've hosted a pusher in first floor front, a prostitute and her john in third floor, a guy who set the building on fire smoking in bed in second floor front. We once rented to a guy who sold live roosters on Sunday mornings, displaying them on the hood of his rusty 1982 Chevy, parked in front of the building. We figured there must be a cockfighting ring somewhere in the neighborhood. Half the time the tenants don't pay the rent and Daniel has to file in court to get them evicted, after which they are treated to fourteen months free rent before the sheriff will come and toss them out. At the moment we have two vacancies and a tenant who is not paying the rent. As I start flinging stuff into a new box, sweating to beat the band, I'm wondering what we'll do if Mother really can't afford to buy shoes or glasses. How will we help her?

I can feel the tintinnabulation of my blood pounding in my ears as I work. I remind myself to think before I make any hasty offers to bail Mother out of money problems.

*Chapter 12*

# ACCOUNTING

When I get home from cleaning the apartment building, I have a talk with my sister and discover that Mother's accountant, Gwendolyn, has left a phone message for Julie. The tax documents Mother sent Gwendolyn are jumbled. Worse yet, Mother didn't send Gwendolyn any income statements. How can Gwendolyn do Mother's taxes without figures for her income?

When Julie calls Gwendolyn back, the accountant gives details. She has phoned Mother to ask her where the missing documents are, but Mother swears she sent them. So Julie jumps into her Honda and drives to Mother's house to investigate. She's determined to find Mother's missing records and deliver them to Gwendolyn.

This is what Julie tells me.

But things don't go exactly the way Julie has planned.

Julie discovers Mother scrubbing her dinner dishes. After a brief chitchat, Julie asks whether Mother is having trouble with her taxes.

Mother, who is swabbing the kitchen counter with a sponge, pivots around. "No," she snaps. "Why?" She is becoming irritable at our questions about her finances.

"Gwendolyn's missing some of your information," Julie tells
Mother.

"How do you know?"

"She called me."

"Why did she call *you*?"

"She's worried about you."

"About *me*?"

"She needs information to finish your taxes."

"Then let her call *me*!"

"She did."

Mother blinks her brown eyes. She's thrown off. "No she
didn't."

"She says she did."

"And you believe her instead of me?" Mother asks.

"Mom, you've been working with Gwendolyn ever since
Daddy Jim died. She likes you. She adores you."

"How do you know?"

"She does our taxes, too. Remember?"

Mother looks vacant.

"Gwendolyn needs all your numbers or she can't do your
taxes."

"She's always done them before."

"Because you gave her the numbers."

Julie gets up and walks toward Mother's study. Mother trails
her anxiously.

Julie suggests that they get out her files.

"I'll get them," Mother barks. They step into her study and
she opens a desk drawer. She peers in, then rummages around.
The files are not there. She's bewildered. She opens several
other drawers. Eventually she puts her hands on some of the
missing files.

They're mislabeled. And the income files are missing. Julie

helps Mother organize the statements she can find. They search for and discover a few others. As Julie sits at Mother's desk and tries to piece together her income statements, Mother grows increasingly silent. She begins to sniffle. Julie asks what's wrong. Mother announces that yes, she is in over her head. She says she's embarrassed, humiliated in front of her daughters. How will she ever hold her head up again?

Next time Julie and I talk, she explains what she and Rich have decided to do. They will:

1) Review Mother's income and outgo every month.
2) Simplify and rebalance her financial holdings, which still contain all the complicated income funds and bonds that my stepfather loved to manage.
3) Make sure Mother is paying estimated taxes to the IRS every quarter.

"Does Mother have enough money?" I ask Julie, feeling relieved, finally, to put the question so plainly.

"Enough for what?"

"To eat. To get new glasses."

"We have to sort that out," Julie tells me. "Her accounts are all gummed up."

"Will you have time?"

"We'll make time," Julie explains in a detached voice. She has clearly thought this through. She sounds certain it will work. After all, Mother lives a financially simple life. She owns her house. She has only a few bills: the electric bill, the phone bill, taxes.

I decide that in my phone calls with Mother, I will reinforce Julie's plan. If the two of us don't speak with one voice, Mother will not comply.

*Comply.* What kind of verb is that?

I hang up and sit quietly by the phone, staring out the window at the trees tossing in the spring wind. In one chop of the hatchet, the privacy that insured Mother's dignity is gone. The deed has been done. Part of me wants to protect her from our attack on her secrecy. Part of me realizes that's no longer an option. After all, Julie's news only corroborates the ominous foreboding I felt a year ago as I stared at the mangled heap of papers in Mother's desk.

It's comforting, at least, that my younger sister knows so much about business. She heads the Volunteer Center in Dallas, hub for all the nonprofits in the city. If Mother has to surrender her sense of privacy, at least she is lucky to be relinquishing it to Rich and Julie.

But I begin to feel left out. I feel like the unfortunate child who stands outside her family house, knocking on the door, which no one opens. I watch the trees shiver and bend in the storm, feeling a raw need to be closer to my family, feeling regret that Mother has now become dependent on my sister, not me, for financial advice. After all, I am her oldest child.

I walk to the kitchen, haul out the cutting board, withdraw a sharp knife from the wood block, and pick up an onion. First, I slice through the papery orange outside skin and flake it away. A piece flutters toward the floor. Grasping the naked, weepy onion with my left hand, I begin slicing it with my right. I try to make the slices so thin that I can see through them, chopping and crying, chopping and crying. When I dab my eyes on my sleeve, I smear onion sap on my face. I put down the knife and squeeze my eyes shut.

In the land of the free and the home of the brave, there are no rules about which child assumes what role in a family. We invent ourselves. It is Julie's role to take over Mother's finances now. My sister and I have always shared even-steven in our mother's life. Recently my role has been to take her to London and Vermont for long rollicking vacations, vacations she raves about and loves so vividly. And she tells me she adores visiting us in Philadelphia. You might say I'm the holiday kid. How did I, who so rarely ever takes a vacation myself, become the holiday kid? I wonder. And how am I going to help Mother, now that she may need something else more than she needs vacations?

# FIELD NOTE 3

## DOING RESEARCH

*I take so many books out of the library that I have to lug them in a large cardboard box. I search the Web. I read everything I can get my hands on about memory. Such questions I have. How do people remember? Why can I sometimes remember things and other times not? Why does Mother's mind keep lighting on some memories and not others? What is a human being without memory? Doesn't character itself depend on memory?*

*Above all, can a person without a memory still be human? Can I do anything to fix Mother's memory? Maybe there's some method or trick or system, some magic we can use to help her.*

*If only, if only! Et cetera.*

*I worry about Mother, mostly, but I also worry about myself, because I am beginning to get myself mixed up with her. When she forgets a word, I search for it, try to supply it. When she forgets where she is, I feel disoriented. When she pairs black and white polka dots with wildly flowered pants, I feel twinges of embarrassment. My vivid memories of scenes from my childhood begin to trouble me. What does it mean that, in company with her, I "live" in the past so much?*

*I ponder ways that schools teach us to remember: acrostics and rhymes and lists and adages, for example. I read Wikipedia and then, thirsty for more, I order used books on Amazon. They explain that memory is a capacity one develops with use. But who memorizes anything these days? Is our dependence on Wikipedia and our unwillingness to memorize related to our Alzheimer's epidemic?*

*Chapter 13*

# NAOMI AND RUTH

I book a flight without thinking about how I'll make time to go to Dallas or what it will cost. Let the pieces fall where they may; I need to find out where I stand in this new family landscape. I call three graduate students before I find one to take my Thursday classes and when I get to the airport I discover that my flight has been changed. I wait in line for over an hour to get a new ticket. Everyone else's plane has been canceled and rescheduled, too. At the American Airlines counter, I complain that although they had my phone number no one called to tell me about the change. I am facing a five-hour wait for the next plane, scheduled to go out at ten forty-five that evening. The woman with a jaunty red and blue scarf tied at her neck informs me, "This is the real world, sweetheart. Get adjusted."

Which world is the real world? I wonder. I wish someone would tell me.

———

On my first full day in Dallas, Mother and I shop for what she honest-to-God needs: underwear, rubber-soled shoes, closet organizers, an extension cord, a new bedside lamp. Now that Julie and I know how much Mother has in her retirement account, we worry that she might outlive her money. Her own mother lived to be ninety-seven. If our mother lives that long, Julie and I will need to support her. We'll cross that bridge when we come to it, we say. Meanwhile, we'll be careful. So when I discover the things around Mother's house that are falling apart, what she has not been able or willing to replace, or what she has not noticed needs replacing, I call stores and comparison shop.

This is something I can do to help Mother. But I hate to shop. Just before I left for the airport, I snatched George Herbert's collected poems, poems written in the calm voice of a rural, seventeenth-century parson. I hoped it might scatter a little fruitful silence into the hub of glittering, throbbing American commerce that is Dallas. So I take the book everywhere Mother and I go, as if it were a religious relic. Just looking at the cover reminds me there's a way to think about things that doesn't involve marketing. In the fourth store, while I'm strolling down aisles of electrical equipment, being hammered by edgy music and bleached by fluorescent light, I become so catatonic I have trouble putting one foot in front of the other.

As we're climbing into her car to drive home, Mother sees the book. "What's that?" she asks.

"Poetry."

"Oh, darling, is that your new book?!"

"It's George Herbert."

"Who's George Herbert?"

"He lived in the seventeenth century."

"But we're shopping."

"That's why I brought it."

"I will never understand you," she announces cheerfully.

Herbert's poetry also comes along with us the second day, when my mother drives us to an outlet mall. We walk into a vast, barnlike structure, lit by fluorescent lights. Strolling up and down the acres of clothes, Mother gets tuckered out and begs to leave, but I'm determined we will find a couple of blouses to replace the torn ones I put in the rag bag the night before.

"All right, have it your way," Mother says, "but I'm done walking!"

She sits in the dressing room while I run back and forth between her and the rows of dresses, pants, and shirts to find a better size or a different color. We select two shirts and a teal mohair coat. She's thrilled. I pay for them at the register.

The next day, on the way to the post office to buy Mother stamps, I stop at Julie and Rich's house. I'm thinking I'd better make this quick or Mother will guess I've played hooky from the stamp errand. No, wait! That's what Mother would have thought when I was ten. Now the reason I have to step on it is because she might guess Julie and I have been talking privately, which will make her feel left out.

So I decide I won't go into Julie's house and sit down. I ring the doorbell and Julie appears in her blue apron and big oven mitt, opening the door, allowing delicious smells to waft out, looking surprised to see me.

She invites me in. I tell her no, I need to make this fast.

"I just stopped in to give you the good news," I say. "I've been with Mother for two days straight. She gets tired, but she's really not that bad."

"Well, when you're here, she's different," Julie tells me.

"How?"

"She gets high, so her memory functions better."

Admittedly, I don't see her every week. Julie generally does, even if it's only for an hour at church. So I can't argue with her. I wonder how I will ever be able to gauge how our mother is doing. I can't tell over the phone, that's for sure, and when I'm here, apparently she's different than the way she usually is.

"Something's wrong with her," Julie tells me.

"What?"

"She forgets things. She can't keep the days of the week straight. We invited her over for dinner on Thursday and she came on Tuesday."

"Maybe her medicines are quarreling," I say.

"Or possibly she's had a small stroke. Or she could be verging into dementia," Julie guesses. "Don't you want to come in?"

"I'd better not," I tell her reluctantly, fighting my savage desire to step in and sit down and drink a glass of wine with my sister and really talk to her.

"We need a neurologist to give her a comprehensive exam," Julie suggests.

"A comprehensive exam, yes," I say. "But not a neurologist."

"But Jeanne," Julie says reasonably, "I've already made her an appointment with a neurologist."

"Then I think we should cancel it."

"Why?"

What's wrong with my sister, I wonder, that she doesn't remember the misery I've suffered at the hands of neurologists? They hijacked two years of my life. Do my sister and I know one another at all?

Julie looks at me, her expression blank. Before Mother's recent failures, we'd hardly been in touch. We've been overwhelmed with children at home and stressful jobs. It's possible that I never told Julie about the taxi that rear-ended my car on the South Street entrance to the Schuylkill Expressway.

So I tell her the story of being misdiagnosed by a neurologist after the accident and put on a seizure medication that made me crazy. When I tried to get a second opinion, the new neurologists confirmed the misdiagnosis of the first one. I grew stupid and diffuse. I couldn't walk straight. I began to believe I might be losing my mind. I felt more panic every time I saw another neurologist, and I saw many. I spent two years dizzy and nause-ated before our children's doctor, a family medicine specialist finally told me that I had a garden-variety concussion, which had healed, and took me off the seizure medication.

"Oh, dear," Julie says. "I didn't know that."

"Maybe I forgot to tell you."

"Goodness, I'm so sorry."

And she is. I can tell.

We smile at one another, two sisters, glad to be reunited and taking care of our mother together. Julie promises me she will cancel Mother's appointment with the neurologist. She announces that she will not pursue any health options for Mother that the two of us don't agree on.

⁓

When I get back to Mother's house, the kitchen smells like lemon, which Mother is slicing to arrange beside the fish she's just taken out of the oven. We devour dinner, both of us sleepy and lazy and peaceful, until we hear a sharp pounding on the door and excited voices.

Mother's eyebrows shoot up. She bounds off her chair and flings the door open. In tumble three children of various sizes followed by their parents. "Come in," she shouts. "You're just in time for dinner!"

"No," the father laughs. "You aren't going to feed this whole crew, Erna! We were just driving by and the kids begged to see you!"

Mother pivots to face the kids and claps her hands. "You didn't!"

"Yes we did!" the littlest one hollers, shrieking with laughter. The others nod solemnly. Their mother grins.

"They love you, Erna."

"Well, I'm the lucky one. I'm just thrilled that you want to see this old woman," Mother gushes. She opens her arms and hugs each of the family members, these people from her church. Then she goes down the pecking order, telling me their names, first the parents, then the children, right down to the four-year-old. I shake hands and we chatter for a while.

Then the father interrupts, "Kids, we need to let Erna and Jeanne finish their dinner."

"Just one more minute," Mother implores. "I've got something for them."

She pokes around in her louvered kitchen closet, where she keeps gifts of all sizes and descriptions. She dips and weaves, picking up this and that, putting things back, working up a sense of mystery. Finally, she hands a tonette like a wand to the blond four-year-old. She finds a red racing car for the boy. Then, grabbing her wallet, she pulls out five dollars for the oldest. The shy eleven-year-old with straight blond hair in a ponytail glances at her parents.

"It's for your college fund," Mother coaxes.

"It's okay, Meredith," her father says. "Mrs. Kelley wants you to have it."

Before they leave, they tell us the forecast is for snow. The four-year-old has never seen snow. She's jumping up and down in her pink sneakers. Mother squats down and ties one of her shoelaces. I, who live in Philadelphia, tell them about snowball fights and building snowmen and how every single snowflake is different from the others and all the great myths of snow. Then we send them out into the night. They'll come back to visit Mother again. Good, I think. Now I am looking out for her. For our whole lives she looked out for me, but now the hourglass has been turned over and the sand is running the other way.

After we finish dinner, my mother picks up her King James Bible with the gilt-edge pages. It's a ritual, something she's done after family dinners ever since I can remember. She flips it open and reads from the Old Testament. "Entreat me not to leave thee," she reads. "Whither thou goest, I will go."

I know this by heart. It's Ruth, talking to her mother-in-law, Naomi. Their men are both dead and there's a famine in the land. Naomi is moving to another country, where she figures one of her relatives will take her in. Ruth can't bear the thought of Naomi departing, so Ruth decides to leave her own country rather than to separate from the old woman.

When Mother finishes reading, she squints her eyes closed and prays, "Dear Heavenly Father, we just thank you for this time together. We ask you to bless us and keep us through this night. And Lord, give Jeanne a safe trip home tomorrow." She mentions missionaries in the Sudan, and Dana T, and several other sick friends, and Bertha.

My head is bowed the way Mother taught me to bow it. I'm staring at my lap, listening to her soft Midwestern voice. She's a prayer warrior. That's what her friends say about her. When I was a child, listening to long tedious prayers during family devotions, I would take apart my Cinderella watch and study the tiny microcosm of wheels that measured time. This steady measurement seemed a fraud. To me time either seemed to gallop or drag. And why is it, no matter how fiercely you watch a moment crawl forward, you can never get it to move in the other direction?

I'm thinking now of the jewelry box that rested for so many years in Mother's inner sanctum. On the milky glass cover, a woman in a floaty Edwardian gown grips the ropes of a swing, smiling with bliss as she feels the wind on her face, pumping further, faster. But the words on the box convey a different message: *Do not waste time, for time is what life is made of.* My mother gave me the box—which her mother had given her—when I was in my early thirties. She probably thought I needed it. I was the child who threatened to be out-of-whack with time.

"Amen," my mother chants. She looks up at me brightly and suggests, "Let's watch *Wall Street Week* !"

I glance at my watch. It's almost eight thirty. Too late.

"How about a little news?"

"I'd better call home," I say.

"Let's just talk a little more." She's wrapping leftovers for the refrigerator.

"I need to check in with Jack and Daniel." I remind her that our fifteen-year-old is scheduled to play the entire Tchaikovsky violin concerto with an orchestra in two weeks. And he hasn't memorized it yet.

"Oh, goodness, darling! Call him." She's flipped into crisis mode.

"I think he'll be fine," I reassure her. "I'm just worried."

"Now you know what it's like to be a mother."

When I was in my twenties, trying to break away from her, I once informed her that she was hovering and overprotective. I'm over fifty now and she's still digging back.

I laugh and say, "Remember when you told me *May your children do to you what you are doing to me.*"

She wheels around. "I didn't say that to you!"

"Yes, you did."

She looks at me tenderly. "Darling, I get so lonely for you."

"I know, Mom."

I will go home tomorrow. She will feel lonelier for me than she did before I came. I think about that a lot. I don't know what to do about it. I live thousands of miles away from her. She moved to Dallas to marry Jim. I moved to the East Coast to finish a Ph.D. at the University of Pennsylvania. And now we have an expensive, difficult commute to see one another.

And then, here in her kitchen, suddenly I am no longer the polite, independent adult I have been for twenty-five years. I am plunged willy-nilly into our past together, remembering—or maybe seeing for the first time—how Mother has always been able to bewitch those around her, to subvert all their logic and common sense. I know, for instance, that she chose the story of Naomi and Ruth to remind me that Ruth isn't even Naomi's real daughter, for pity's sake, but only her daughter-in-law, and *still* she picked up and followed the old woman out of her own country straight into a foreign land. Go thou and do likewise, my mother means. Dallas is certainly a foreign land, as far as I'm concerned. Could Mother actually be suggesting I should forsake my children and husband to move here? Well, it will be a cold day in hell before I do that, and she must know it. Why has she started me thinking about such a thing?

*Chapter 14*

# THE BEWITCHING

Mother binds you to herself so fast it makes your head swim, and by ties you can't see, either, until it's too late. Everything about me, including the way I see her, has been shaped by her. She is talking to me and I am standing in her kitchen in Dallas, answering, but I am also thinking about the strategies she used to bewitch us.

There were the holidays, family days, she called them, for instance, when she built an architecture of elaborate celebrations. Birthdays meant lavish chocolate cakes with seven-minute frosting, candles, marshmallows constructed to look like carousels, parties with games and prizes and presents and fame as the child whose mother dished out the best favors. She also allowed the birthday child to command our family's dinner menu. One year I asked for chocolate sprinkles on the mashed potatoes and chicken with twisty pink crepe paper streamers ascending from the cake to the light fixture above the table. Then there was the year my brother insisted on nothing for dinner but the vegetables I hated: cooked spinach, slimy kohlrabi, lima beans, and Brussels sprouts. I think Mother made it and we all ate it. I think I gobbled it up, secretly thrilled to watch

Michael trudge painfully through the dreadful vegetables. My parents must have snickered their way through the meal.

At Halloween Mother turned us into ghosts and pirates and vampires. She convinced Daddy to light a bonfire when we got back from trick or treating with muscley orange and yellow flames that snapped and licked the dark front yard sky. She popped corn while we sorted through our pumpkin heads full of Hershey bars and toffee and traded with one another until ten o'clock.

Christmas, oh Lord, brought caroling with "round yon virgin" and "O Little Town of Bethlehem" and "Hark the Herald." We drank warm cider with sticks of cinnamon and decorated the tree, which made the whole house smell like cedar. In the late afternoon we sat on the couch in the living room staring at the blue and white Christmas lights falling on the crèche under the tree. The Christ child in the manger turned his parents and the shepherds and kings and all the animals holy because there was a cardboard halo around his baby face.

Mother hid the presents she got us children but she wouldn't allow us to keep secrets from her. At night, after we went to bed, she unwrapped the presents we laid under the tree for her and then wrapped them again so they looked untouched the next morning—at least that's what my father told us. That's how excited she was about Christmas and Santa Claus and the eight reindeer on the roof.

And then there was the Fourth of July, the most famous holiday in the Midwest, with sunny lawn picnics for thirty-seven relatives and watermelon and sparklers and roman candles and singing "Oh say can you see" so fervently that tears welled up and prickled my eyes. Mother chased into and out of the house, screen door banging, carrying the hot dogs and hamburgers and orange gelatin salad with carrot shavings. She called, "Go ahead, eat, don't wait for me!" Someone at the crowded picnic table yelled back, "Not on your life, Erna, it's not a celebration without you." She was the spirit of the holidays and she knew, she must have known, that even when we were grown, in our thirties and forties, out there way beyond her, the weather would bring us back to those celebrations. On every holiday, beneath whatever lively caroling or lonely divorce or hubbub of our own children, she would have us again. We were tethered to her by holiday memories she had forged long ago.

In addition to the regular holidays Mother fashioned other holidays out of ritual and food and festivity. Those celebrations were tied to the seasons so that when the season rolls around, I think not only of them, but of her, directing the script. Take, for example, the fall arrival of the great-aunts. Every year while Mother stayed home and cooked, my father drove us through musky red leaves as dusk descended to the bus station in downtown Lincoln, Nebraska, to meet Great-Aunt Alma and Great-Aunt Irene. The year I was eight, Mother decided I was old enough to go on that ceremonial journey. Michael and I smelled the leaf fires all the way into the city, and I was sad for poor Julie because she had to go to bed before their bus got in. But there wasn't room in the car for all three children plus the aunts and their luggage.

We're driving through the dark empty streets of Lincoln, Nebraska, in our blue Chevy with the running boards. I feel triumphant at being allowed to stay up so late. At first I am spooked at the dark, empty streets, then riveted by the men in ties getting off a Greyhound bus, accompanied by women in coats and hats, met by relatives who exclaim in the fake voices adults use. They hug and go off in cars. In the deserted wood-paneled station my brother and I lounge like royalty, waiting for the next bus. Outside, shadows wobble across the pavement as blasts of wind swing the hanging light fixture. I see the outline of a specter moving across the shadowy tree line and I inch closer to Michael, who is rolling a red toy car down the arm of the wooden waiting room bench.

When the bus pulls up and the aunts climb off, looking wrinkled and stiff, we throw ourselves into group hugs. I rub my face in their fragrant, rough cloth coats. Daddy claims the aunts' luggage. He picks up the two leather suitcases, one in each hand, and we usher them to our car. Aunt Alma with the dry papery white skin sits in front with Daddy while Aunt Irene, who smells like lilacs, sits in back with Michael and me. Michael gets the window. I'm on the hump seat, clinging to my narrow slice of space, with Aunt Irene's pudgy leg touching mine.

"You've grown like a weed!" she enthuses. "What a big girl you are." I don't say anything because what does she think? Of course I'm growing. If I didn't, my sister would catch up with me and then what? But I don't tell her that because if you can't say anything nice, don't say anything at all. Besides, as our parents tell us every day, children should be seen and not heard.

At home, Aunt Irene enfolds Mother in a bosomy hug and then holds her off at a distance and then pulls her into a hug again and exclaims how beautiful she is. Aunt Alma shakes Mother's hand and says, "It's lovely to see you again, Erna." Behind the wall in the kitchen my brother and I are stealing bacon from the pan. He makes his voice deep as Aunt Alma's and intones, "It's lovely to see you again, Erna!" and we burst into giggles and fall all over the place laughing. We help ourselves to more bacon and Michael says again, "It's lovely to see you again, Erna," and we start laughing again.

As the portly aunts chatter, they take off their navy felt hats and stick the hatpins back in them, laying them carefully as wreaths on the dining room buffet. When my mother calls us to the table, we devour pancakes and bacon and eggs in the orangey kitchen light and the aunts regale us far into the night with stories of how many souls they have saved. They are lady evangelists, now in their sixties, just back from their revival circuit around Iowa, where every fall they preach the Gospel, gathering souls into the New Jerusalem. Though I am barely taller than the kitchen table, and have hardly traveled beyond the Carlsons' farm on the outskirts of Parkers Prairie, I imagine the Fall Holiday of the aunts is a festival Mother invented to give us something to celebrate between the Fourth of July and Halloween.

While we eat, Aunt Irene exclaims in a high, childlike voice, "Oh, Erna! What tasty bacon! Where did you get such lovely dishes? What a wonderful house you keep!" Aunt Irene is the singer. Her voice quavers and pulses with vibrato as if she might break into tears, even when she's commenting on bacon.

Aunt Alma, the preacher, says, "You're overtired, Irene. You need to go to bed." I turn to Michael, who is mouthing, "You're overtired, Irene. You're overtired, Irene," and I try to keep a straight face, but I erupt into snickers. Watching me, he can't maintain restraint either. He laughs so hard he falls onto the floor. I sneak a look at my mother, but our parents and the aunts are talking about bringing home the boys after World War II, and they pretend not to hear us. Or maybe they don't.

Aunt Alma and Aunt Irene talk to one another the way our parents talk to one another, confidentially, in low voices, without the kind of politeness people use when they don't know one another. They were roommates in college and this is their eleventh year of taking the bus to Clarinda, Iowa, and Davenport and Wichita and Omaha. They eke out their hair-raising maidenly existence on free will offerings, so my mother insists that they stay with us for a week every fall. We can do this for them, my mother tells us, give them a little break. After all, God has given us plenty and they are his servants, and my father smiles at my mother proudly because they're his relatives. He says to her, "Good for you, Cookie."

—

That night in Dallas, when Mother read the story of Naomi and Ruth, I recalled scenes from the past, how holidays tethered us to Mother with little invisible threads of longing. I saw her, not as an eighty-five-year-old woman, but as all the various mothers she had been during the years when I was growing up, when she was orchestrating our lives. "Give me a child till she's six," Mother used to say, "and I'll have her for the rest of her life." This sounds sinister, but I don't think she meant it that way. She simply believed it was a mother's duty to shape her children. Children need to know who's in charge, she'd say. It makes them feel secure. Till I was eighteen, she opened my mail.

And Mother never hesitated to tell me what to write about, either. She'd tell me the story of her father's bull chasing her and then sing out, *Now, there's something you can write about!* I would think, *Over my dead body.* But look, I have written about it. Our mother shaped the writer who is writing about her and there is precious little I could do to change that, even if I wanted to.

Standing there in Mother's kitchen after the Naomi and Ruth story, it came to me that I probably love my children the way Mother loved hers. Maybe I love them more than I love my mother. But that's not what I mean, exactly. I mean I know how she loves me, because I know what it feels like now to love a child. There's hardly a moment when I'm not aware of my children—where they are, how they're faring. I was put on earth to feed and defend them. I am the only mother they will ever have. If I don't stick by them, who will?

Then, sitting with my mother after hearing her read about Naomi and Ruth, I remember a time when I loved my mother that passionately. At the age of ten, when I left home for a week of camp, I felt such bittersweet longing for her that it literally made me sick.

Right there in her kitchen in Dallas Mother is telling me, "If you get hungry in the middle of the night, there are leftovers. And crackers. And cheese. I hope it's the right kind. I can never remember which of you girls likes cheddar and which likes American."

"Thanks, Mom. But you know I don't eat after dinner."

"It's all in there if you want it. Just help yourself."

"Thanks." I feel the need to wind down. The two of us have been together all day.

"Do you have enough light in your room?"

"Everything's perfect."

"Do you want me to help you make up the bed?"

Every night since I've been here she has offered to help me make up the pull-out couch. Every night I told her, thanks, I can do it. I suppose this is a delaying tactic on her part. I remember my children asking for another bedtime story, a drink of water, anything that would delay my leaving them at night.

Then I stop thinking about this because my mother can sometimes read my thoughts.

"I just hate it when you leave." She touches my arm.

"You have a zillion friends."

She drills down on the fact: "I hate it when you leave!"

"You'll be coming to Philadelphia in August."

"It's so long till August."

This is a side of my mother I rarely see. She is so capable, so popular, or maybe so cagey about hiding her loneliness.

———

I fall asleep reading. In the middle of the night, I get up, pull out the couch, make the bed, and change into pajamas. I doze off, then wake up, then doze off again. All night I hear my mother moving around outside the door. We are both insomniacs.

The next morning snow wraps the lawn and trees. I think of the children who came to visit her, how they're seeing their first snow. In the brilliant early light I can see honest to goodness stars glancing off the snow, sparkling like they do in pictures of the star above the manger.

My mother and I eat a leisurely breakfast together. Then I pack. At ten minutes to eleven, with the snow mostly melted by the sun, I tell my mother I need to leave for the airport.

We usually say good-bye at her front door. On the day I leave she's usually been eager to get back to her own life. She's planned lunch with a friend today. But this time she follows me out of the house. I wheel my suitcase over the curb, tuck it into the trunk of the white rental car, and pull the key from my pocket.

When I hug her, I can feel her jagged intake of breath. "Be careful, darling," she says in a choked voice.

"I will."

"Don't drive too fast."

"I've got plenty of time."

"Your mom will always stick with you," she tells me.

"Even if I end up in jail," I chime in.

"I'll bring you a chisel in a cake," she finishes, laughing. When I was a teenager and she didn't know how I would turn out, she often informed me that if I got sent to jail she'd smuggle a chisel into my cell so I could hack my way out.

"Thanks, I may need you," I say.

Suddenly her eyes are brimming.

I kiss her good-bye. Then there's nothing left for me to do but get in the car, turn the key in the ignition, and back away from her.

She doesn't budge. She remains there, standing, waving. Then she reaches her hands out to me.

I pull in again, turn off the engine, and go to her. I, who rarely hug anyone, give her a long hug. I have never seen my mother so undone. Even that grim December when my father died and she was left alone with three young children, she didn't cry. I back the car out for the second time. She stands at the curb watching me back away from her on an insanely beautiful spring day in Dallas. Tears start down her face.

I am struck to the heart. If I ever thought I'd lost my place in the family by moving to the East Coast, she has informed me that I haven't.

*Chapter 15*

# HOMESICK

As I drive under the steep blue Texas sky on the way to the airport, I can feel myself leaving the territory of adulthood, where my mother and I called a truce in our conflict, where we dwelled at a peaceable distance from one another, rarely mentioning our disagreements. In those days, I saw her once or twice a year, in the summer and maybe again at Christmas, when ritual could be made to stand in for intimacy. On this trip we have been thrown together at such close range that I am being flung back into my past. I don't understand what is happening. I am recalling a week at camp that I haven't remembered for thirty years.

I keep seeing the way Mother looked when I backed my rental car away from her, how she seemed to be fighting loneliness. Whizzing by strip malls and into the Dallas countryside, I relive a morning in 1954 in Lincoln when my young mother climbed into her car while I stood watching, and backed out of our driveway to go to work.

I was ten years old, already lonely, because that morning I was going off for a week of camp. But I was also thrilled, because I could see that Mother was reluctant to part from me. Little did I know then about the exquisite and terrible longing called homesickness that I would suffer all week.

And yet, bizarrely enough, during that week at church camp I fell in love with a necklace in the shape of a cross. It was the exact kind of religious image that Mother scorned. That was the first time I remember aligning myself against my mother's way of seeing the world. Eventually my fascination with images led to no end of trouble between us. But that trouble came later. When I was ten who could have guessed what that piece of kitschy jewelry foreshadowed about our future?

—

It's March and snow is piled on the windowsill. Frost has tooled lace on the glass.

I'm about nine, eating Rice Krispies, when my mother asks me whether I'd like to go to church camp. She pours corn flakes for my little sister and douses them with milk.

"When?" I ask.

"Next summer."

Next summer seems like an eternity away. First comes Easter, then my birthday in May, then summer. My brother is swinging his legs under the table. He kicks me accidentally and I kick him back. So he kicks me on purpose and I aim a hard kick toward his shin.

Before we could launch into the verbal insult stage, she says, "Kids from lots of different churches will be there. It lasts for a week."

My brother pokes me on the shoulder and I punch him on the arm.

"Stop it, you two," Mother commands. She pulls out a chair and sits down between us with her bowl of Wheaties. "Why don't you think about it for a while," she suggests shrewdly.

I didn't know it at the time, but my mother had an ulterior motive for wanting to send me to camp.

I had never been separated from my mother overnight. But church camp offered the fabulous and real possibility of life without my brother and sister and without my parents. No one would force me to pick the peas, or eat my slimy kohlrabi, or dry the ugly Melmac, or go to bed while it was still light. Six whole days of freedom stretched before me like a veritable midway of circus rides. I could swim whenever I wanted, including right after lunch. My reading reveries wouldn't be interrupted by my mother telling me to go outside and get fresh air. I could get by eating nothing but cookies. I could stay up all night if I pleased.

The Monday I set out for camp, my mother had to leave for work at St. Elizabeth's Hospital at seven. I was already up and dressed. I sat on my parents' bed watching her pull on her white nylons and adjust the seams. She powdered her chest above her bra and stepped into her nurse's uniform. My father handed her the brown bag lunch he had packed for her and then we walked behind her to the car. Her nylons made a reassuring whishing sound as she walked, but when she turned around to say good-bye, her face registered inclement weather. She hugged me for several seconds longer than normal, then got into the car and twisted the key in the ignition. The motor turned over, but she idled in the driveway, rolled down the window, stuck her head out, and said, "Don't forget your sweater."

She backed up the car a few feet, then stopped. "Give her a little money," she said to my father. He pulled out his wallet and handed me two dollars. "You'll be okay," she told me, flicking her head quickly. Then she hastily backed away, the motor whining. I felt delighted that she was going to miss me. It gave me a sense of power.

My father helped me fold and pack my Sunday dresses in our tan suitcase. I was taking dresses because I wanted to look cool at camp. Daddy had a heart condition, as my parents called it, which is why he'd sold his general store in Parkers Prairie, Minnesota, and moved us to Lincoln, where my mother could get work. In our new city he cheerfully scouted stores and vegetable markets for the family groceries, tended us kids, and sewed small cheesecloth bags of herbs to flavor his savory soups. That fall he had poured his energy into helping to establish the Lincoln Christian School in a church basement.

As I watched my princely, sandy-haired father latch the suitcase with his freckled hands and buckle a belt around it, I began to feel slightly queasy. I walked downstairs, carefully gripping the handrail. I stood in my favorite spot in our backyard, beside the tiger lilies. Closing my eyes, I tried to recover the reckless pleasure of running free without any parents for a week, but I felt seasick, as if I were standing in a violently rocking rowboat. The waves, pulling me farther from the shore, were not about to stop. I was going to camp.

A tenuous bunch of authorities ruled over us campers. There was a director named Pastor Ray, who looked slightly goofy in his tight rayon shirt and brown pants. A few parental volunteers stood around Pastor Ray, and a squadron of gangly kids worked behind folding tables. They looked about the age of the high schoolers I knew from church. We were standing in a clearing in the woods. Cabins were scattered around the edge, in the trees. Above their doors, on posters, fat, cloud-shaped Magic Marker letters spelled out: *The Purple Dragons, The Holy Ghosts,* and *Nancy's Storm Troopers.* One was called *Cabin Six.* I didn't want to be assigned to Cabin Six, which I believed must have something wrong with it.

Our counselors shoved one another, hooting and laughing as they checked off our names, allotted us sheets and pillows, and handed us our schedules. They ebbed and flowed like water, losing track of us briefly, retreating, whispering, buzzing, swarming in a group, then remembering their jobs, returning to their posts. I didn't know anyone except the severe and vertical Audrey Jones, the friend of our family who had driven me to camp with her daughter, Marilyn. She was talking with the other parent-volunteers.

Other campers went off with their friends, laughing and gabbing, holding their assignment sheets. I was on my own, literally struck dumb by the high jinks of the counselors. I didn't know which line to stand in and I was too shy to ask. Hoping I was right, I added myself to the longest line. When I got to the front, I faced a cute, tousle-haired high school boy. "Uh, I'm here for camp," was my brilliant opening. My words sounded far away and disconnected from me, like the voice of a ventriloquist. Woe is me, I thought.

⁓

I spotted the necklace on Monday afternoon, after unpacking my suitcase in my cabin. That moment comes back in the vibrant, present tense.

Walking around the tables in the camp canteen, I see a small box holding a greenish plastic cross. It's about the width of a table knife and the height of a Popsicle stick, and it is affixed to a rawhide string. I stand at the display table staring at it, keeping myself very still. I can feel my heartbeat in my wrists, which dangle at my sides. In the stifling Nebraska summer afternoon, a trickle of sweat runs down my stomach. I cannot believe how beautiful the cross is. A little placard explains that it glows in the dark.

Glancing significantly at the grown-up tending the cash register, so he understands that I am not stealing, I remove the cross from its box. I stoop and thrust it into the shadows under the table. It emits a minty light, which is entirely inexplicable to me, since the necklace doesn't contain any lightbulb or battery. Shining beneath the table, it appears to be cutting into the darkness with its sharp edges.

Mist clouds my eyes. I want this cross the way a person wants health. At Temple Baptist Church, where my family belongs, we believe it's wrong to keep images. Our sanctuary contains pews facing a plain oak communion table and a podium. We don't allow religious symbols in our houses, either. So I have never held a crucifix or looked at one carefully. My aching love for the simple fluorescent cross nestled in the palm of my hand is as electrifying as it is tender. I haven't the faintest idea that this attraction is the first step of a journey that will lead me to a radical separation from my mother. My problem at the moment is that the cross costs two dollars, and two dollars is the entire amount wadded up in the small red plastic coin purse back in my cabin, the amount my father handed me just before I got into Audrey Jones's car yesterday and drove away from him. I decide I cannot buy it.

It's Wednesday, after lunch. I've gotten through the first two days and we are all hidden away from the consuming heat, resting on our bunks in our cool, dark cabin. We can hear the sighing of the pines outside and a little breeze blows through the screened windows. Our counselor, Nancy, checks the door to make sure no one is eavesdropping, then motions us campers to gather on the bunks around hers. She confides in her hoarse, sensual voice that the Lord is leading her toward John. John has big shoulders and a beard. He buries the camp garbage and builds the bonfires. But just yesterday I saw John holding hands with Maureen. I am astonished. Does Nancy really think that God wants John to break Maureen's heart? My parents are intensely loyal to one another. It is just beginning to occur to me that people actually jilt and get jilted.

As a mosquito buzzes in the humid early afternoon air, we sit, hushed. Stunned by the magnitude of Nancy's confidence in us, I wait for her to unburden herself further. Nancy fishes in her purse and draws out a new lipstick. She breaks the seal and screws out its tongue. Then she passes it around, permitting us to test it on one another's lips. I am puzzled because my mother has taught me that wearing makeup is wrong. It seems odd to me that a counselor at Bible Camp is pushing lipstick, but I've never held a tube of lipstick, and when I get my hands on it I feel a joyful flutter in my stomach. I pass it to the girl on my left.

Before we resume Quiet Time, Nancy makes us hold up both hands, palms out, and swear to secrecy. She plans to put a frog in John's bed tonight. As an afterthought she makes us swear that we will not get into mischief while she is busy with the frog.

I was probably the smallest child at camp, and I had no inkling of the awakening that would befall me in a year or two. For me the curtain hadn't opened on the opera of adolescence. I didn't even know there *was* an opera. Not that I wasn't passionate. That summer I lustily sang four-part harmony: *I've got a home in glory land that outshines the sun. I've got a home in glory land that outshines the sun. Do Lord, oh do Lord, oh do remember me, way beyond the blue.* They were the songs of my Baptist people, earthy and rowdy, and I loved them.

Then there were the lyrics that actually were love songs, though I didn't yet comprehend that. *I come to the garden alone, when the dew is still on the roses and the voice I hear singing in my ear no other sound discloses. And I walk with him and I talk with him and I tell him I am his own. And the joy we share as we linger there, none other has ever known.* I warbled the words with a passionate urgency that I didn't yet understand as sexuality.

At night we huddled in a circle, mesmerized, as the bonfire licked the sky with its yellow and red tongues. I felt like a Neanderthal child: close, folded into her tribe, safe against the enormous, feeling dark. But during the day I walked around camp on the edge of tears, overwhelmed by the terrible facts I was discovering about the world. Naïve as I was, I could feel the undercurrent of pulsing adolescent sexuality. Everyone seemed to comprehend it but me. I knew enough to be aware that I was missing something, but what? And then there was the fierce competition between cabins. I began to wonder whether everything my mother had taught us at home as normal human behavior was actually deviant.

What brought on full-blown homesickness was a tactless remark from some older girl, some sarcasm, some condescension that made me suddenly aware of how young I was, how terribly out of place. The girl might have been Maureen, who by then had surrendered John to our counselor, Nancy. I don't remember.

It's mid-week and I am brushing my teeth in the rough-timbered, stinky bathroom. The windows have been propped open and sparky bright morning air flows above the row of sinks. Someone—say it's Maureen—is standing beside me at the next sink. She is a willowy high school girl with the power to decide what happens at camp. Her long, brown hair curls tastefully on her shoulders. I feel a presence, and I look up at her, seeing that she is watching me, appraising me. The glistening, hard black of her pupils in the middle of her blue eyes makes my heart stammer in my chest. I work to breathe. I feel like a fish flailing in a boat. I try not to betray my alarm.

"Hi," I say through a mouthful of Colgate. I have learned that much. You have to greet people in the morning, even if you don't feel like it. Even if you never greet members of your own family at home.

She tosses her hair back. "Are you old enough for this camp?" she asks.

"What do you mean?"

"I bet you're not eleven!"

"I'm ten."

"Honey, Jesus wants you for a sunbeam."

I'm not sure what she means by this, so I am unable to contribute a reply to the conversation she has honored me by starting. In our church they sing "Jesus Wants You for a Sunbeam" at the children's service. The last time I sang it, I was about six. It slowly dawns on me that Maureen must be telling me I am too young to be here.

I realize that she's probably been watching me observe and then imitate what the older kids do. I wonder whether I appear even more bizarre than I feel. I hear the water gushing from the faucet. Outside there is the sound of tremendous flapping, as if wet sheets are blowing in a gale. I see through the window a mob of startled crows taking to the sky.

Maureen is standing with her orange toothbrush in her mouth, staring at me, waiting for me to reply. I try to think of something, but my mind is blank and smooth as a bald gray highway going nowhere. I'm breathing fast. I turn and begin brushing my teeth again. She shuts the water off with a flourish and walks out. That seems to put a period at the end of the long sentence of my weeklong childish incompetence. Suddenly, after my conversation with Maureen, I long to go home. I want my mother. I begin to feel what I only later learn the word for. I feel homesick.

When I am done brushing my teeth, I walk to the canteen. I saunter around the tables, pretending to be interested in the pastel candy with Bible verses printed on it and then the fluorescent bumper stickers announcing that GOD IS LOVE. But the cross reels me in a slow circle around it. Finally I reach the table and pick it up. I feel calmer. Holding it in a shadow, I am comforted by its lovely green light.

———

Homesickness is a disease that rivets its victim's imagination on home so powerfully that nothing else seems real. I, who had read *The Boxcar Children* and dreamed about the pleasures of being an orphan, began suffering from an imagination entirely filled up with my mother. I pictured her stepping into her car the Monday I left for camp. I heard her voice calling my name over and over. I smelled her Tweed perfume and felt her hand lightly on the back of my neck. The very woodsy air I breathed stifled me. I couldn't eat. I cried. I vomited. My head pulsated. I feared talking to anyone, in case I might dissolve in tears. I was infected with self-consciousness. I watched myself like a homesick child in a movie who loses weight, dwindles, and slowly dissolves into the landscape. The next day, I stayed in my cabin during Hymn Sing and Bible Study. Pastor Ray didn't notice.

Even Nancy didn't notice.

Dutifully I went to craft time, where I lolled in front of bins of Popsicle sticks and clay and yarn strips and paper and sequins and glue and paints. I could not think of a single reason to pick up any of it. I needed to lie down. I wanted to sleep. The counselor in charge cheerfully tried to convince me to braid a lanyard, which he said I could use as a key chain. He suggested different colors, the bright gold, the royal blue, the forest green. The thing is, I didn't own any keys.

"Then give it to your mother," he suggested. I wanted to see my mother so desperately that the very syllables *mother* made me bolt from the tent.

My mother's friend, Audrey Jones, who had brought me to camp, drove up on Friday to volunteer. She must have noticed that something was wrong with me. She lured me out of my cabin by inviting me to the canteen. She bought me a Coke, and asked me whether I was all right. She meant well. But all I could see was how different she was from my cozy, black-haired mother. She was athletic and plain-spoken, with a square jaw. She had a habit of wearing anklets with heels.

Sitting across the table across from her, I couldn't talk, I was so homesick. I knew I was being monstrously ungrateful. Her only crime was not being my mother. But I was unable to stop feeling the mawkish longing that this woman could not satisfy. We listened to the rain *plink-plonking* on the canteen's metal siding. We sat together in raw silence, a generous, concerned adult and the broken child she was trying to help.

⁓

The week at camp turned so ghastly partly because there wasn't much adult supervision and our counselors were unprepared to manage a bunch of children. And maybe my mother should have foreseen that. But I need to explain. She convinced me to sign up for this camp because I'd spent the previous August roving our neighborhood with a juvenile delinquent named Junior.

Some afternoons Junior and I lurked around houses, sneaking onto porches and snitching whatever we fancied. We invoked the "finders keepers" rule. We figured that if people left toys and sprinklers out, our minor thievery might teach them a lesson. It might keep them from falling prey to even greater thievery. One afternoon we pillaged cookie samples from the garage of a Keebler salesman and ate them till we lay like fat ticks on his front lawn. Afterward, I felt vaguely guilty. That evening when I saw a man heading down the sidewalk for our front porch, I felt alarm. His lunging walk and balled-up fists tipped me off: I should not have taken the cookies.

He rang our doorbell. My mother answered the door. He told her that her daughter had stolen and eaten the samples he needed to make a living. He shouted loudly enough to attract attention from our neighbor, who stopped coiling his garden hose and watched.

My mother slipped into her confident nurse persona. "My daughter wouldn't steal cookies," she informed him.

The cookie salesman cursed and stomped his foot. He raised his voice. He exploded *fuck* and *good God* and other forbidden words like bombs on our front porch. In our living room, tense as if I were walking on a tight rope, I stood watching. Mother flipped the screen door lock to keep him from pushing into the house and bashing her. She summoned me. "This man says you went into his garage and took his cookies. You wouldn't do that, would you?" Her eyes evaluated me for any twitch that would hint otherwise.

I swallowed back terror. "No," I told her.

No.

But my mother was not a fool. Bible camp was her way of separating me from Junior. Maybe she thought at Bible camp I'd experience a programmatic change of heart. As it turns out, that week did set me on a different path, but not one she would have chosen; she was a Baptist and religious images gave her the heebie-jeebies.

On Friday afternoon, I made a final journey to the canteen to look at the cross. I'd taken that walk many times, even though I had decided early in the week that I couldn't afford it. Walking into the canteen tent, I saw they were having a sale. The price of the cross had been slashed to a dollar thirty. Noticing that I was eying it again, the man at the counter asked me how much money I had. I showed him my dollar ten. He took all my money, slipped the cross into a bag, and handed it to me.

For the first time during the entire week, I felt bliss. I crawled under the display table, where the cross illuminated the dark. Its light created a homey glow under the covers of my bunk. And that night it lit up the path when I traveled alone to the bathroom. Its Halloweeny radiance appeared transcendent to me, as it apparently did not to other campers. There were almost as many cross necklaces remaining on the commissary table at the end of camp as there had been at the beginning.

I don't remember what happened to that cross. During one of my many moves I must have given it away, probably because it bespoke a childhood I wanted to shed. But it signaled a beginning, too. It marks the first time I'd felt drawn to an image. It was kitschy, I confess. But now, as I sit here writing, I wish I could hold the cross again and look at it.

I would make it stand for something: maybe for the fact that our most crucial decisions are small ones that start as secrets inside us and find their way out. I'd let it stand for that mystery at the center of each of us and for the unpredictable, funny grace that can befall us—because it was grace, surely, that made me see the beauty of that cross. I'd let the cross mark the first time I remember feeling the bittersweet longing we call homesickness and the first time I departed from my mother's literal way of seeing the world.

# FIELD NOTE 4

## PAYING ATTENTION

*I give myself assignments, hoping I can improve my
memory. I try to recall what a dandelion looks like, for
example. Not approximately, but exactly. How it rises
from its leaves, how the head attaches to the stem, how
it gets from that full-blown loveliness to the fuzzy ball stage. It scares
me that I can't see an exact picture of a dandelion in my head. I talk
to a friend who's taking a sketching class. She tells me that sketching
has made her see more clearly. You have to pay attention to something
before you can remember it, she says. I realize that I've never looked at
a dandelion carefully.*

*The first week of April arrives, warming the lawn. I spy dandelions
out there. I open the door and stride across our front porch. In front
of me, my elongated shadow stretches absurdly, already crossing the
street a good twenty feet ahead of me. I plant my bare feet in our
succulent, cool grass where a crop of dandelions has sprung up. Each
is about the size of a quarter.*

*I lean over, feeling my weight shifting to the balls of my feet, and
gather the fingers of my right hand under one bright yellow flower.
The stem gives way with a tiny moist snap and I raise the fluffy yellow
button to study it.*

*Above me raggedy white clouds are racing through a blue sky.
The universe never stops its restless motion. No one can attend to
everything at once, the cornucopia of stars spilling from the heavens,
the subtle wind, the birds, insects, the rustling trees and clouds, the
secret motion of blood inside us, our own eyes as they blink. Too much
goes on. I try to block out everything but this one dandelion with its*

bruised stem and its tufted loopy yellow flower. I close one eye. Then I open it and close another.

One blink makes the dandelion appear to leap in my hand.

Remember this, I think. You need to pay attention to this one dandelion or you won't remember any next winter. I focus so fiercely that I extinguish everything from the morning but this one flower. It wheels like a sun through the spaces of my long-term memory onto this page.

*Chapter 16*

# SUBVERSION

Now that I have become one of the people my mother subverts, I begin to understand what a genius she is at subversion. On the phone with me she sounds like the woman I've known all my life, the one whose voice I listened to in the womb, the one who laid down mama-talk as she drove me to orchestra rehearsals or hung wet wash on the clothesline.

But now that her children are colluding against her, she's on guard. Like a quarterback on a football field, she dodges and weaves to avoid contact.

"What did you do today?" I ask her.

She considers briefly in silence. "You guess!"

"Marilyn took you to the grocery store."

"That's right!"

Marilyn, who lives down the block, loves to drive, but she doesn't own a car. Since Mother's cut back on driving, Marilyn sometimes ferries Mother to the cleaner, the bank, the grocery store, the shoe store, all in Mother's car.

I wonder whether Mother actually saw Marilyn today. Occasionally Mother narrates her day in such detail that I believe it. But often she tells me to guess. Then no matter what I say, she agrees with me in the festive voice of a game show host.

I wonder whether this allows her to avoid dangerous shoals of memory and language, where her ship might founder.

I change the subject. Recently she's been telling me new stories about her past. "Who taught you to drive the Model A?" I ask.

"It was a Model T."

"Okay. The Model T."

"Who said they let me drive it?"

"You did," I tell her. "You drove it to school."

"Did I?"

"Yes."

"You learn something every day." Her voice drips with irony.

I decide to ease out of that subject and head in a different direction.

"How's your back?"

"It's hurt all day."

"We should do something about that," I say.

"About what?" she demands.

"Your back pain. You want me to call Dr. Karp?"

"Who said anything about back pain?"

"You did."

"Dr. Karp is the raccoon in the chicken yard," she snaps. I'm alarmed by this screw-loose conversation. Then the old story floods back in a torrent, the way her mother shot the raccoon. Mother is speaking in code. It's really not so different from the way she's conversed all her life, talking about the present in terms of the past. She must be telling me there's something about Dr. Karp that she doesn't like. I make a note to quiz her about that later.

The 2000 elections are looming. "Who are you voting for?" I ask her.

"Oh, honey, if I thought about stuff like that, I'd have no room in my head to think about important things." This is one of her mantras. Her memory is like a suitcase into which she can pack a limited number of items.

I laugh, but I feel unmoored. After we say good-bye, I hang up the phone, and again consider the disadvantages of being the child who does not live in the same city as her mother. I'm floating eerily above her everyday reality as a balloonist floats above the earth.

Oh, come on. Don't be melodramatic, I think, aware that I am parroting my mother. You just talked to her. What difference does it make whether she went to the supermarket today? Even if she invented everything she said, you know the people and events of her life. She sounds fine, and now it's time to go to the vestry meeting.

I walk out the door into the late summer evening, and jump into my Toyota.

But facts matter, I think, stopping at the stop sign.

Hypersensitive though she is to people with power, she's always subverted authority and followed her secret voice. When she was a nurse at St. Elizabeth's in Lincoln she sneaked dead fetuses out of trash bins, wrapped them in diapers, brought them home, buried them in a row behind our garage, and marked the graves with their last names: Baby Larsen. Baby Wilkins, Baby Johnson.

Now Julie and I have become the authorities. Mother sidesteps me because she's leery of telling us the truth. Both of her children are now in positions of power over her. She depends on my sister for rides to the doctor and for keeping her finances straight. She depends on me for long visits, frequent phone calls, and leisurely escapes from Dallas. She can't afford to have us withdraw those favors. She has to play the game any way she reckons will keep her safe. Having the power to decide what happens to our mother has turned Julie and me into what our mother sometimes sees as the Other Side.

I do not like this.

*Chapter 17*

# THE FANNING OF A PEACOCK'S TAIL

On the phone my sister is bewailing our mother's downhill slide. Mother doesn't drive as much or as far. Instead of walking, she now wobble-de-wobbles. When she spends more than a whole day by herself, she feels blue. She's hit or miss about her pills. She mourns the activities she can't perform, but fails to look for alternatives. Her lists don't staunch her memory leakage; she misplaces the lists.

"I misplace lists, too." I laugh grimly.

"No! This isn't like us," Julie says. "It's dangerous."

"What shall we do?"

The solution, Julie believes, is for Mother to get her mind off her own troubles.

So the next week Julie gives Mother a pep talk, urging her to expand her world by helping others. She lays out volunteer options. Of the alternatives, Mother chooses reading to the blind. Then she doesn't lift a finger to pursue it.

Two months later, Julie and I plan a super-duper checkup, which we hope will diagnose our Mother's strange behavior. Julie calls her internist, Dr. Karp, and they have a heart-to-heart.

They settle on a date. If this checkup were music, it might sound like the flashy ending of a late Beethoven symphony. If it were a painting, it would look like the fanning of a peacock's tail in final afternoon sunlight. Julie and I believe it will put a period at the end of a yearlong, dangerous chapter in our mother's life. Finally we will know. We will finally be sure.

After the checkup Julie writes me a three-page single-spaced e-mail. The day did not go as the two of us planned.

⌒

When Julie picks Mother up at her apartment, Mother is flaunting three different ropes of costume jewels against her purple blouse. The more she adorns herself like a Christmas tree, she knows, the better she looks. Her feet are bedecked in new suede black pumps with rhinestones. On her wrist, slender silver bracelets jingle. She has tastefully blended rouge into her cheeks. All her nursing life she has alternately worshipped doctors for their power and despised them for their arrogance. Now a doctor has the power to decide whether she's crazy or sane. She's ready to fight. She's outfitted herself for her most important battle yet.

On the way to Dr. Karp's office, Julie reminds Mother that the purpose of this appointment is to discuss her memory problems. Julie goes down the list. Maybe Mother's pills are arguing. Maybe she has early dementia. Or possibly some other progressive disease. "Maybe you've had some small strokes," Julie says.

Mother sits in the passenger seat, nervously running the edge of an envelope under the nail of her right thumb.

"But Dr. Karp won't be able to help you unless you're absolutely honest with him," Julie points out. "You have to help him."

"Help him with what?"

Julie pulls into the hospital parking lot. "You want Dr. Karp to be able to diagnose you accurately, don't you?"

"Well, yes." Mother says without conviction.

"Because if he *can* tell what's going on, we might be able to stop the progression."

"Progression of what?"

"Of whatever is wrong."

"Well, I guess that makes sense," Mother equivocates.

"So will you tell him everything?" Julie nudges.

"I always tell him everything." This is so outrageously false that Julie doesn't even bother to contradict her.

—

Dr. Karp walks into the examining room, wearing a white lab coat over his tie and starched blue shirt. He's six five, a massive piece of mahogany furniture, and he's reading a folder. When he sees Mother, perched on a chair beside Julie, he sticks out his hand. "Good morning, Mrs. Kelley," he booms, shaking heartily. "It's so good to see you!"

"Hello." Mother ducks her head and smiles up at him flirtatiously.

He shuts the folder, leans against the wall, and gazes at Mother. "I bet you can't tell me what the date is!"

"It's October!" Mother blurts out like a bright kindergartner.

"Good! And the date?"

"The sixteenth, I think."

"That's close."

"Well, if you know, why don't you tell me?"

"It's the fifteenth," he announces.

"That's not a bad date, either." She laughs.

He looks amused. "You like that date okay?"

He picks up her arm and applies a blood pressure cuff. "So who's this, sitting beside you?"

"You know her!" Mother counters, worrying for his sanity. "That's Julie."

"Do you have any other children?"

"I have a daughter who lives in Philadelphia."

"What's her name?"

"Jeanne. Why?" Mother is puzzled by the erratic behavior of this doctor she has seen many times.

"And grandchildren? I bet you have grandchildren."

"Four," she tells him. He glances at Julie, who nods affirmation. Mother is reaching for her purse to get out pictures. She's ready, ready, ready to show off her astonishing, prize-winning family at a moment's notice.

But Dr. Karp pulls out a step stool and motions for Mother to climb onto the examining table. She rises. When she falters, he gracefully takes her hand and helps her up. She's a Southern belle at a cotillion.

During the physical exam Dr. Karp asks Mother more questions. Most of them she answers easily. If she doesn't know the answer, she parries and thrusts with him. Her wrong answers are so clever that he gives her partial credit.

Then the doctor excuses himself. He needs to make a phone call, he tells her, but he wants her to remember three words till he comes back. Ball. Dog. Car. He tosses the words toward her as he bolts out the door.

After the door shuts, Mother blinks at Julie with big brown hopeful eyes. "What did he say?"

"I can't tell you."

Mother's eyes narrow. She doesn't believe it. In the past it's always been us Murray girls against the authority. Mother wants desperately to be pronounced healthy and good. "Why won't you remind me?" she asks.

"Dr. Karp wants to help you, Mom," Julie explains. "Remember, we talked about that."

"But this isn't fair! He just dropped those words in the middle of a bunch of other stuff. And then he asked me to remember." Mother's bracelets jingle-jangle with emphasis.

Dr. Karp cracks the door and sticks his head into the room. "Mrs. Kelley, can you remember the words?"

"Not a single one of them!" she scoffs in a feisty voice. "Julie started talking to me the minute you left and she made me forget."

"I bet you can remember one."

"Nope."

"Well, don't worry about it," Dr. Karp tells her, stepping back into the room. He hands her a legal pad and asks her to write a sentence. She can choose the topic and say anything she wants.

She seizes the paper and scribbles. Then she hands him what she's written.

He reads it and guffaws.

Mother has written that her children think she is losing her mind. Mother and her doctor laugh together. Mother glances at Julie, who hasn't seen the sentence. Julie obliges her by looking clueless, though she can guess what Mother has written.

Dr. Karp turns to Mother. "Okay. I'd like you to read these directions. Then do whatever they tell you to do." He hands her a sheet of paper.

She studies the sheet. She looks up. He's gazing tactfully toward the door. So she looks down and reads again. A minute passes. Then three minutes. She glances at him and back down at the paper. Her gaze is a mouse, trying to find a way out.

"It's okay," the doctor says. "It's just fine, Mrs. Kelley." He takes the sheet from her. "Why don't you come across the hall to my office and we'll talk."

On the walls of his spacious office hang sports trophies and on his desk stand pictures of his beautiful wife and handsome children. The place reeks of cigar smoke. Dr. Karp leans back in the overstuffed chair behind his desk and says, "Mrs. Kelley, if you have any impairment, it's very slight."

Mother peeks at Julie as if to say "I told you so." She is put out at Julie, at me, at whoever engineered this exam. A person never knows when or which one of her children will betray her. This is all conveyed in one withering glance.

Dr. Karp goes on. He's taking Mother off her heart pills and increasing the medication she takes to control bleeding in her colon. "Are you taking these pills three times a day?" he asks her.

"Yes," she says in the voice of a good girl.

"Every day? Three times?"

"Well, sometimes I only take one."

"How often do you only take one?"

"Well, maybe most of the time."

"Why?" he asks her.

"When I start feeling better, I lay off the pills," she tells him. This is a principle she's taken away from nursing school.

"No! You feel better because you're taking the medicine," the doctor explains. "If you stop taking it, you'll get worse!"

Mother winces and shies away from his strict blast like a scolded puppy.

Dr. Karp repeats sternly that she must take every morsel he prescribes the exact number of times per day he tells her.

She blinks her large brown eyes at him. The heels of both rhinestone slippers are hooked on the lower rung of her chair now. She nods gravely. But her eyes are darkening with deceit. Deep inside she believes her intuitive ability to diagnose and administer medications is superior to the mechanical, scientific methods of a physician.

"All right, Mrs. Kelley," Dr. Karp booms. "Do you have any questions?

"I want you to know that I'm just fine," Mother informs him in a formal voice, made friendly by her sense that she might still win the match. "My kids worry about me. They don't realize this, but people a lot younger than me have worse problems."

"That's right," the doctor replies. "I see them every day. They're my patients."

Mother casts Julie another I-told-you-so look.

"But you probably should get a formal assessment, Mrs. Kelley," Dr. Karp says. "Here's the name of a neurologist." He jots a number on a pad and hands it to Mother.

Julie, who has tried to stay out of the discussion, breaks in. "Mother has two daughters who are devoted to her."

Mother beams proudly.

Julie forges on, "We're taking care of her together. And my sister has had bad experiences with neurologists. She wonders about a gerontologist instead."

Mother casts a poisonous look at Julie. Dr. Karp shrugs and nods. Sure. That's fine with him.

Then Julie asks whether Mother might benefit from an antidepressant. Since she's cut back on driving, Julie explains, Mother is often lonely and depressed.

Mother casts her eyes down, blushing.

Julie bravely presses forward: she understands that depression is related to short-term memory failure.

Dr. Karp shrugs and writes a prescription for an antidepressant.

Mother and Julie leave the office.

Game over.

Mother is glowing, triumphant, jazzed. At eighty-five, she has just played a game of wits with one of the most renowned internists in Dallas. Alone, she has subverted the standard Alzheimer's exam. She has dodged a diagnosis.

———

In the next seven years before Mother's death, no doctor ever succeeded in diagnosing her with dementia. Various doctors administered the standard test at various times. Sometimes she approached the test indignantly, sometimes with a sense of one-upmanship. She was Houdini, handcuffed and locked in a trunk and thrown into a river. She always slipped out of the shackles and emerged smiling, her head bobbing above water.

I'm guessing the test became a less useful measurement every time Mother took it. But to say that is surely to admit that she was still learning. If nothing else, she was learning how to pass the test.

On the day we moved Mother to the Alzheimer's unit, we still had no formal diagnosis of Alzheimer's. We moved her because we worried that she might get lost when she was taking walks with her friends. They would wander around the campus of Christian Care and when they got tired they would plop down on a curb with their feet planted in traffic until someone rescued them.

To get a formal diagnosis of Alzheimer's back then required a postmortem autopsy. After our mother died, Julie and I didn't request an autopsy. We didn't see the point. She was the point, and she was gone.

The evening after Mother subverted the Alzheimer's test in Dr. Karp's office, Julie and Rich loaded her into their car and drove her to Abilene to visit one of her grandchildren, their daughter, Eve, and her husband, Lance. Although this visit had been planned for months, to Mother it probably felt like a reward for passing the test. She chattered happily in the backseat all the way to Abilene.

# FIELD NOTE 5

## The Human Brain

*I doubt that I could pass an Alzheimer's test. This worries me.*
*I start practicing how to remember random words as they flash past:* Ball. Dog. Car.
*I look up* memory *and* brain *on Wikipedia.*

Distinct regions of the brain, it turns out, must work together to recall even three small words, even for a short time. Connections fire between 1) the occipital lobe and 2) the temporal lobe, linking information from sight and hearing. Other regions kick in, too, for instance 3) the part that remembers habits, called the basal ganglia, and 4) the cerebellum, which is important for motor control, attention, and language. The connections are organized by the prefrontal cortex. This is the brain's front office.

I write down all these terms and try to memorize them, as if scientific terminology were a prophylactic against forgetting. Short-term memory, I learn, can hold only about seven items. Even these few decay and disappear after a day or so.

Knowing fancy terms for the regions of the brain doesn't help me remember better. What helps me remember ball, dog, car is telling myself a story about them. It gets the 5) amygdala to kick in. My amygdala makes me feel emotion. To put it another way I start caring about the words.

I tell myself a story. I imagine driving through our neighborhood, where a ball is chased by a dog under my car. Good thing it isn't followed by a child! I think. Switching off my car, I jump out and toss the ball onto the neighbor's yard where it belongs.

When I tell Mother about the regions of the brain and how they work, she gets very quiet. She looks like she has no idea what I'm saying.

113

*Chapter 18*

# LEARNING SUBVERSION

Given that I was over fifty when I began taking care of my mother, how could anything I learned about her have been news to me? But her adroit performance in Dr. Karp's office was a bombshell. To think that my mother, who had masqueraded as a pious, obliging woman for years, could be as defiant as any revolutionary! Maybe the reason I had not understood this earlier was that she was the authority I needed to subvert. All my life I'd seen her from a child's perspective. Suddenly I was being forced to see her from the vantage point of an adult.

Looking back as I write this, I understand the story this way. As Mother grew more addled, as she needed more care, I had to decide how much time I could give and how much love I could afford. I had to figure out who this woman was to me.

The more time I spent with her, the more my childhood flooded back. I remembered a summer at church camp. I recalled ransacking my brother's bedroom for *Lady Chatterley's Lover*. I remembered defying my mother over a pair of long stockings. The memories jutted up, thrusting through my everyday life like new-formed mountains on the plains. They arrived with no respect for their actual sequence. They came attached to no particular meaning.

To put it another, better way, the steps my mother and I repeated now seem like a dance. Her homesickness for me as I backed my rented car away from her in Dallas made me recall a younger mother who could hardly bring herself to back away from her daughter on the morning I left for camp. As Mother and I moved together through her Alzheimer's years, we repeated many such patterns. I began to track connections between us and our earlier selves. Standing there, talking to me, Mother was never just an eighty-five-year-old woman tipping into dementia. Something she would say or some look she would toss me could reel us both back to the past. There she was, in her mid-thirties, my mother, young again.

These childhood memories helped me to see that I cared more about my mother than I knew. For twenty-five years, after I left home, the two of us had shopped and played with my children and cooked and celebrated holidays together a couple of times a year. We were rather distant adults, each with a house and a man. We lived a thousand miles apart in very dissimilar regions of the country. I knew how different we were, but until her Alzheimer's years, when her younger self came back, I hadn't begun to grasp how powerfully she had affected me.

I'm eight. My father has been diagnosed with a heart condition and can no longer run his general store in Parkers Prairie; therefore my parents devise a new adventure. They take a road trip through the Midwest to find a city, and we move to Lincoln, Nebraska, where they know no one. That fall, instead of taking us to public school, my parents drive us to the radically dissident, fledgling school they have helped to start with a group of new friends in Lincoln.

As we float through traffic, my parents go over the facts again.

We will feel weird at first, but we'll find new friends. My lucky sister, who is too young to go to first grade, sits over the hump in the backseat, swinging her legs, which don't reach the floor. My brother sits on the other side of her, quietly looking out the window. I push one shoulder through the two front seats and touch my mother's sleeve to make sure she's still there, and still my mother. She twists to smile at me and spits on her thumb. As she rubs dirt off my cheek, I protest and squirm.

We park and descend concrete steps into the basement of a church. The ceiling appears startlingly close and when I glance up I see aluminum heating ducts and wires and insulation. Dirty sunlight shines through the small, rectangular, high windows. All I can see is a slice of blue sky with raggedy clouds scurrying by. Kids stand awkwardly askew all over the basement. I don't know any of them. My chest feels hollow, and I hold my breath the way I do when we drive by a cemetery. I don't like the stale, dusty smell down here.

I grasp my mother's hand while she talks to another adult. "This is Mrs. Tinderson," my mother tells me, squeezing my hand. I look up. Mrs. Tinderson is a vertical woman with pointy features who wears a nice, flowing wool plaid skirt and a rust-colored hand-knit button-up sweater. I would like to touch its braided pattern, but I know enough not to. She smiles and says hi. I am surprised at how deep and commanding her voice is. Scrunching down to my height, she shows me a book with bright pictures, letting me turn the pages at my own speed. Her skin is a beautiful walnut color.

When Mrs. Tinderson strolls to the front of the class to welcome us, the room quiets, as if she had twirled a dimmer switch. One of the fathers prays, asking the Lord's blessing on this first day of school. Then the parents begin moving toward the door.

Seeing tears swim in the eyes of the shorter blond girl beside me, I think, *I'm not crying! Not me. But oh boy, oh boy, is my mother leaving me here alone?*

"We'll have fun," Mrs. Tinderson announces. She invites us to sit at the tables, then sits down in a small chair like ours, opens a book, and begins reading a story about a girl called Heidi. She flings her happy voice like a bright scarf on the air. I forget that my mother is gone until it's almost time to go home.

———

We kids learn subversion by watching our parents resist the mass education system in Lincoln. It may not have dawned on my mother and father when they helped to start that school that reading and math were not all we'd learn there.

On cold fall days Mrs. Tinderson requires her daughter Ethel, who is also in second grade, to wear exactly the same kind of garter belt and long brown stockings that my mother makes me wear. When we sit in our desks, the garters press red indentations in our thighs. In the girls' bathroom Ethel and I compare our angry red marks. We hate the way the stockings slow us down when we run. We are the only girls who have to wear them. We think our mothers are unfair, that possibly they are mistreating us.

When Ethel suggests that the next day we should refuse to wear our stockings, I am enthralled by her defiance. I agree, and we make a pact. The next day the temperature is below thirty, the sky is spitting snow, and we both show up at school wearing stockings. Now we have something else in common: our mothers are both dictators, we tell one another. We begin practicing how to subvert our mothers.

I begin to spit out the cod-liver oil my mother makes me take to prevent rickets and bowed legs and I'm pleased that it might be making our philodendron grow faster. At least the plant is not dying. On below zero days when my mother sends me to school with two pairs of mittens, I rip off one pair at the bus stop and stash it in my lunch box.

I thought at the time that this subversion was taking me to an untamed country my mother had never entered, but now I know differently. Our whole family, including our mother, was subversive.

To get to our new school, my brother and I take a city bus into the heart of town, walk a couple of blocks, and hop on a second bus. My parents warn us not to talk to strangers, to stick to our business. After a couple of weeks, I think I could do the route with my eyes closed. One morning my brother and I duck into a corner store to buy sunflower seeds and Mary Janes, candy cigarettes, and bubble gum.

We begin to stop in every morning. What our parents don't know won't hurt them. Mrs. Tinderson doesn't allow us to eat candy in school, so we devour the sweets before we get off the bus, but I hide sunflower seeds in my desk. All day I sneak them into my mouth, cracking the shells open one by one with my teeth, lingering over the savory nuts. I am learning new facts. That the teacher doesn't know everything. That I can go anywhere I want if I have a dime for the bus. That people my parents don't know can be interesting.

———

The Lincoln Christian School subverted the larger culture, by virtue of its very existence. The city and state had set up, accredited, and supervised primary and secondary schools, of course, and the rule was, everyone must attend school. The goal, I suppose, was that America could achieve a kind of mass culture. But my parents and those of the other kids in the Christian School didn't want any part of mass culture.

Not that they knew how to set up a school. My mother had

a three-year nursing degree from the University of Minnesota and my father had dropped out of North Dakota State in his junior year. There were a few other Christian schools around the country in the 1950s and maybe they served as inspiration and models for our school. But our family couldn't afford to make long distance phone calls or pay consultants and we didn't travel. If my mother and father were part of a national independent school movement, they didn't think much about it at the time. They were on their own in the middle of a large country with a handful of other parents. What they didn't have in information or institutional backing, they made up for with chutzpah.

My parents helped to invent that school out of nothing. They had no idea what a curriculum was, and they didn't know where to find teachers. The first years they calculated what to ask for tuition, guessing at expenses. They networked to find students. Every year they tried to set the tuition low enough to attract new students, but high enough to cover expenses, and when they fell off on either side, they went into debt. They made mistakes, nearly lost the school, recovered, and survived to open the following fall. It must have felt to them like building a bridge across the Grand Canyon. To look down made them feel dizzy, so they didn't look down. They just nailed one plank in place at a time. Then they trusted their weight to that plank, while they nailed down the next.

—

My father sits at our dining room table filling out stacks of papers requesting accreditation for the school. Before Christmas, the Nebraska State Board of Education plans to send out an examiner. This man will decide whether the school will be accredited or shut down. I don't even know exactly what we're supposed to pass, but my parents tell us kids that the outcome will depend partly on us. The man will try to find out what we've learned by talking to the students. "Volunteer to show him your papers," Mother coaches my brother and me. "Be friendly." In morning circle at school and evening devotions at home, we pray that God will make the State Department of Education give us a passing grade.

After lunch one day in the spring, Mrs. Tinderson welcomes the corpulent, mild-mannered man from the Board of Education. He takes off his rubbers at the door, wipes his feet on the mat, and sheds his raincoat. He's clad in a gray suit and he keeps a pleasant look fixed on his face. He lowers himself gently into an adult-size chair that a sixth grade boy has lugged to the back of the room. As the three third graders troop up to the front of the class for their reading group, he looks on amiably.

I turn around and spy on him over my shoulder. His eyes are closing. I suspect he's bored. I'm tempted to feel offended. Hasn't he seen our miniature African twig huts? Moreover, taped to the wall are tracings of our own hands—which we have brilliantly converted into pictures of zebras and fish.

I raise my hand and request permission to show him these things. When he asks me easy questions and smiles good-naturedly, looking a bit like my father's oldest brother, I know, I just *know*, we have him on ice. Several weeks later our School Board gets a letter saying that the Board of Education has tentatively accredited the Lincoln Christian School.

Since my mother during those years took off every morning for her nursing job, my father did the most work for our school. After he died, my mother was elected by acclamation to the School Board. I now suspect that she was the only woman on the board during those early years.

Soon I ran out of grades and moved on to public high school

and Lincoln Christian School faded from my memory; that is, until I was asked to read my work at the seventy-fifth anniversary celebration of a literary journal published at the University of Nebraska called the *Prairie Schooner*. That was about ten years ago. I hadn't set foot in Lincoln since the day we drove out of town, just after I turned eighteen. I assumed the school had gone under, but before I flew to Lincoln I checked the Web and was surprised to find a site with the phone number. When I called, the baby sister of my best friend, Carol, answered. Now the mother of a high school student, she was volunteering in the office. We nattered away like long lost buddies. She invited me to visit.

So that's me, sitting for almost an hour in front of the Lincoln Christian School in my gray rental car. I'm gawking at the contemporary, rambling brick building that sprawls across acres and acres of lawn.

Before I go in, I call my mother to tell her where I am. "You're calling from where?" she shouts.

"Lincoln. Remember? I told you I was flying here."

"I never know where you'll turn up next, darling," she tells me.

"Mom, the school has a huge building! You should see it."

"It's a miracle," she chortles. For a moment she's bedazzled by what she and my father accomplished.

Inside, I introduce myself to the intense principal, the lively librarian, and the young drama teacher. The school has dozens of teachers now, they explain, more than a thousand pupils, miles of halls. An hour later, sitting cross-legged on the gym floor with a class of theater students, I tell the story of how the school got started.

I just open my mouth and it spills out.

My father had been dead for more than forty years, and, truly, I had never told anyone this story. I never understood it as a story, much less as a triumph. I just assumed the school had perished, because I saw it wobbling on the brink so many times.

Now, suddenly, as I write this, I feel ashamed of predicting failure for my subversive parents. What kind of daughter am I? At least I brought a picture and biography of my father to the school. I handed them to the librarian. She led me into one of the long turquoise-tiled halls and pinned it reverently in the founders' display cabinet, which houses the long-term history of the Lincoln Christian School.

Rediscovering the Lincoln Christian School transformed my view of my parents. Fragile as their experiment was, it was also brave and farsighted. They were experimental, defiant people. I found out that if you subvert the culture and start a school and it succeeds, you're not a dissident anymore. You're a visionary.

You could say my subversive mother and father are no longer subversive.

They've both officially become founders.

## Chapter 19

# THE ARCHANGEL GABRIEL

Soon after my visit to the Lincoln Christian School, Mother detonates a small explosive device. She tells me she isn't driving her car anymore. I exhale into the phone. "Why?"

"My tires look soft."

"The Saturn dealership is half a mile from you. They'll check your tires."

"They'll tell me I need new ones."

"I thought you liked the guys over there."

"I'm not as naïve as I look, honey."

I'm used to the way Mother invents pretexts, but soft tires is a doozy of a pretext for giving up her car.

She counts on driving. She started on a Model T (or was it a Model A?) when she was fifteen. She is by nature restless, and driving gives her a small way to exert control over circumstances she can't change.

I refuse to believe she's stopped driving because her tires are soft.

I believe she's afraid she'll get lost.

She's been lost more than once. A month ago, for instance, when she was driving back from the shopping mall, she panicked. Nothing looked familiar. She couldn't remember where to turn. So although she hates the feeling of ice against her teeth, she stopped at a Rita's Water Ice.

Carrying her lemon ice to a table, she sat, watching customers come and go. Eventually she zeroed in on a pleasant-looking couple. Approaching them, she explained that she was lost. When they asked where she lived, she showed them her driver's license. The man helped her into the passenger seat of her own car. He drove her home while his wife followed in their Chrysler.

I listened to her tell this story, alternately worried and awash in admiration for her. "I'd have panicked," I confessed.

"I wasn't a school nurse all my life for nothing!"

Thank God the couple at Rita's Water Ice didn't turn out to be ax murderers. He might have been the archangel Gabriel disguised as a middle-aged Dallas businessman. But next time might turn out differently.

I call Julie for a dose of candor.

"What will she do if she doesn't drive?" I ask.

"Oh, she'll still take her car out in her own neighborhood."

"What about garden club?"

"Her friends will have to pick her up."

"She was always the one who gave people rides."

"I know."

"It made her feel important."

"It's the end of an era," Julie says sadly. "And my life has just gotten significantly harder."

"Yes," I say.

But the truth is, Julie will not be able to take Mother where she needs to go. Julie leaves for work at seven in the morning and doesn't get home until after five. Mother will have to find friends who can give her rides. I spend an hour and a half researching taxi services in Mesquite, the suburb of Dallas where Mother lives. I jot down numbers.

Then to gain a little perspective, I stand at the window and gaze out at the birds flitting around the feeder. I feel bewildered and orphaned. The woman who built my identity is losing her own. One by one the struts and timbers of herself are falling away. How will she live without driving? She'll dwindle away like a sweet potato vine in October, one leaf browning at a time, sinking into the earth until finally she will become invisible. It's intolerable, unthinkable. I dig my fingernails into my palm and walk around my study like a zombie, fiercely focused on how to halt this.

I learned from Mother the fact that when a person is distressed, she should make lists.

I will start calling her every day.

I will visit her three, no, four, no, five times a year.

I will find her rides (though I don't know how).

I will. I will. I will.

I don't even know what all I'll do for her.

Why? Why do I care?

Because she raised me. Because after the preacher chanted earth to earth, ashes to ashes, and they lowered my father's casket into the black Midwestern soil, my mother, who was wearing a red-and-black houndstooth hand-me-down suit, squared her shoulders and walked away from his grave, calling her children to follow, and we did, we followed her down that hill into the rest of our lives. Because she stood in our living room, one hand on her hip, and glared at us and said, I will never make you live in this house with a stepfather! Because she sent us to college with every last dollar she had. Because she told us we could do anything we put our minds to. Because half of what she said was wrong, but I believed it, feeling lucky to have timber to build a world. When I stopped believing what she said, and told her so, she stuck by me but still fought for her own truths like the

Champion Mother of the Earth. She stood so firm that I could measure the distance I had traveled from her.

Yes, all that. But I have a husband, a job, children, a house, neighbors, a church. I live half a continent away from my mother and maybe it's sick, maybe I'm sick in the head to worry about her the way I do. Why do I? Maybe because I can't imagine doing anything else. I'm like a duck flying south for the winter without knowing the way, without guessing how long it will be or how hard it will be to find food. I worry about her as naturally as I worry about myself. However strangely she acts, whatever weird things come out of her mouth, I know her life and her stories. I am remembering more all the time, and who else, besides my sister, does? What if we who know and love her desert her? Who will she have?

—

I go upstairs to wrap Christmas packages. I'm wild with too much to do. I have spent hours and hours trying to help Mother. I need to finish designing two courses for a month-long teaching stint in London. Tomorrow I have a mammogram, which is always unsettling. And Molly is coming home from Virginia. Before that, somehow, I need to grade thirty-five final exams. And there are holiday cards to answer and e-mails and calls to return. But all evening and most of the night I rack my brain for a way to help Mother. Unable to drive, sitting around her house, she'll get depressed, I know.

Rinsing a pint of beautiful raspberries for dinner, I feel a wave of peace wash over me. It seems to come from nowhere. It is a gift. How surprising, to be alive, I think. How improbable. What a miracle to be able to see the yellow winter light tingeing the rhododendron in the backyard. To smell the wine I've just uncorked.

And then a brilliant thought comes to me. What I would want if I were Mother, if I were abruptly grounded and waking up to days of boredom. I would want to read. It's true that Mother has never been a reader. But she did push her children to read. She must understand the value of books. I decide to use all my wiles to convince her to start reading. As I think about this, my enthusiasm picks up momentum. It's the most valuable thing anyone could do for her. And it's not such a long shot. Lots of people begin new projects after they're eighty. Mrs. Guthery took up cross-stitching and Mable Hendron fell in love with bridge. Mother can take up reading. Since I'm the child she empowered as the reader, I am the very child who should— who *will*—convince her to read.

I pour the raspberries into a brilliant blue pottery bowl. I am aware that reading rises like Mount Everest between my mother and me. It is so big we don't even fight about it anymore. I am Darth Vader and she is Luke Skywalker. Or maybe it's the other way around. I have always wanted my mother to read. When I was young, I wanted her to read whatever I was reading. Then I loosened up, shifted to other kinds of books: cartoons, coffee table books, *Our Daily Bread*, romance novels. I still give her books occasionally. She politely thanks me and avoids opening them.

But now, I think, I will talk openly about it with her. She'll see the genius of reading. If she gets bored enough, she will switch from adventures in her car to long wonderful trips of the imagination.

That night on the phone she laments the tedium of her life.

"Okay," I say to her. "What would make you really happy?"

"Getting in my Saturn and driving to the mall."

I feel alarmed. "But you won't."

"You asked what I wanted to do."

"Oh, Mom, you don't want to drive," I reply in a light voice. "Think of the trouble—dealing with the insurance company, comforting parents of the children you kill."

"What do you know about it?" Her tone is venomous. "When you get to be eighty-five, you'll want your car back, too."

She knows what she is doing. It is terrifying to imagine being eighty-five. But I can't act out of terror over my own impending old age. It's apparently not safe for my mother to drive. She needs a substitute.

"Here's an idea," I say. "Tomorrow I'll stop at Barnes and Noble to buy you a good novel."

"I'd rather get my Christmas shopping done." She protests, "I can't even go to garden club tomorrow."

"Can't Donna pick you up?"

"Donna has the flu."

"You want me to call one of your friends to come and get you?"

"They all live across town."

"Call a cab. I'll find the number for you."

"I'm not doing that. It's too expensive."

"If I were there, I'd drive you," I say.

"You're not here," she counters. Then, plaintively, "I just want to get out of here for a while."

"When I read, I always feel like I've been away."

"Well, I don't!"

She pauses.

"I want to get away in my car!"

She's the one who made the decision not to drive. I begin to feel guilty for withholding my mother's car—and happiness—from her.

Mother is King Lear and I am Goneril.

Of course I can't tell her this joke. She doesn't even know

who Goneril is. In that way she's like most of the other people in the world. But I want to share this joke with her.

I see more clearly than ever before that my mother needs reading. She needs it the way a sick person needs medicine. "I could order a book by your friend," I offer. "What's his name? The guy who leads tours in Israel?"

"Don't ask *me*. I'm the one with memory problems," she counters.

"You know, the one who brings you stones from the Holy Land."

"Charlie Dyer."

"I could find you one of his books."

She's suspicious. "Where would you get it?"

"Amazon."

This shocks her. "From the jungle?!"

"It's a website."

"What's a website?"

"They sell books. They would send you his book in the mail."

"Not on your life," she says. "I'm not ruining my eyes!"

I can see she's becoming entrenched, so I move on to other subjects.

The next day I buy and send her a gorgeous coffee table book featuring flower gardens. Now that her resistance is down, I hope she'll go for it. It's just a matter of time. She'll be sitting in her living room, listening to Mozart's greatest hits, feeling the blahs. Then she'll glance at the magnificent cover and pick up the book. She'll start reading it. She has to. For the first time in her life, I think, she may be forced to read.

*Chapter 20*

# THE READING WARS

All the next week a pale song hums itself inside me, the slight hope that my mother might begin to read interesting, challenging books. I will be the child who orders books for her and the two of us, mother and daughter, will read together. Finally, at our age, we will hang on the phone exchanging witty, pithy insights.

But even if Mother starts reading, I know that I won't stop feeling guilty about reading, because that's what she drilled into me. If you spend so much time reading, she argued, you'll never get any real work done. *Ha!* I think. *I'm a professor in a university where most of what I do is read and write.*

I am, nevertheless, the child of that young mother who rarely read herself and who told me that reading would destroy me.

—

It's 103 degrees in Lincoln, Nebraska. My mother is in her late thirties and she is sitting at the kitchen table, twisting the elastic steel arm band of my dead father's big watch around her wrist. She is paging through a book as massive as the New York telephone directory. It contains all of Shakespeare's plays. The letters are the size of midges, written on paper so thin you see print from the other side as you read. She gets up for a drink of water. She washes out a few dishes. She combs her foamy black curls. She checks to see whether the mailman has delivered anything interesting. She stops by my chair to mention that I might want to go out and weed the garden. She sits down to study. A dog barks outside and she immediately jumps up to look out the window. She goes back to Shakespeare for a minute and turns two or three pages.

"This is so dumb!" She twists a black curl around her index finger. "It's about a handkerchief!"

My mother is trying to support three children on the salary of a nurse, which is minuscule. And gnawed down every year by inflation. Before she can get a raise, the State Department of Education requires that she pass a Shakespeare course. Why Shakespeare, I don't know. She has no time to indulge in culture. But it is clear that without a raise, she will no longer be able to support us.

I have just turned fourteen, and I feel Mother's attention is like a big basket that holds my concerns easily, with plenty of space left over. She is a widow, but she is not a victim. She is so smart that the principal of the junior high where she is the school nurse phones our house after school to ask her advice. She's the one who decides whether we can keep more stray dogs, and she knows what to do about bullies. She laughs and gossips like a teenager on the phone with her girlfriends. She can cook a mean spaghetti sauce and she's pretty. Everyone, as far as I know, admires her.

So I assume my mother is right about Shakespeare. That summer the running jokes in our family go like this: Q. How many Shakespeare characters does it take to change a light-bulb? A. They used candles.

If Shakespeare's plays are that stupid, I think, why does he

have such a big reputation? But, oh well, I am beginning to discover the adult world can be bizarre. We lock our ridicule of
Shakespeare into the vault of Family Secrets.

Every morning my mother drives off to class at Nebraska
Wesleyan in her ancient, chalky blue Chevy. She chugs back
home in the stunning heat, sets up an electric fan, and tries
to settle down to Shakespeare at the kitchen table. She is kin-
esthetic as her own hair, coiled and springing. She prowls the
house, waters plants, organizes drawers, washes a dirty window,
throws vegetables into a pot for soup. She is in love with the
life of the body. When the leaves darken into August, she has
not accomplished that mysterious feat that no one can really
explain. She has not changed the little black squiggles on the
page into mental images of kings and clowns and lovers. The
truth is, my mother cannot read Shakespeare.

If she realized that, she must have been alarmed. Much of her
vitality and pleasure came from her confidence that she could
support us. Maybe she felt like a passenger watching an in-flight
TV news channel when the anchor reports an impending plane
crash. The flight number is hers.

She grows tense and grouchy. The Shakespeare professor, she
tells us one night at dinner, could never operate in the "real"
world of broken legs, severed fingers, and stolen cars—the sorts
of crises she manages weekly at Irving Junior High School.
After all, the poor guy thinks the pretend handkerchief and
the love-juice in Shakespeare's comedies have the same status
as an actual leg broken on an actual trampoline. Shakespeare,
my mother points out, isn't going to pay our mortgage or keep
our shelves stocked with spaghetti. My mother never understood how well Shakespeare sells. Or why. I realize that now.
But under her influence, I firmly categorize her professor and all
other intellectuals like him as ineffectual. I believe my mother,

that they can function only because they have secretaries who keep track of their pencils and help them find their cars in the parking lot at night.

My mother's Shakespeare paper comes due. This paper involves not only writing, of course, but reading. And how can she write about plays she hasn't read? God knows she has plenty of imagination—more than enough to invent plots and characters. But she is aware that if she made up the plot, she would be found out. She absolutely must pass this course. So she sits down at the kitchen table with blue-lined notebook paper and a pencil, and she whips up a confection of ornate prose, picking up what she thinks of as the flowery style and diction of Shakespeare without divulging anything about what she has read. Her argument spirals around and around.

When my mother finishes the paper, she asks me to critique it for her. The year before, critiquing her paper would have been my father's job, but he died in December, and now we are alone and she is trying to support us. The confidence she has placed in me is thrilling. I am just beginning to get a reputation in the family as the Child Who Reads. None of the drawbacks of that role have manifested themselves yet.

With the conviction of an unwashed subversive who feels she needs to defeat the councils of the washed, I read my mother's paper. I have begun to imagine Shakespeare as a football field where my mother's team is being mauled by the opposing team of her professor. I know who I am pulling for. I am gripped by the spirit of a cheerleader. Hit 'em again, harder. Harder. When I can't follow the argument in my mother's paper, I explain to myself that, after all, I am only fourteen. A person has to ease into the works of such a big-deal author. I point out a few piddling punctuation problems, but then I tell my mother that her paper is great, which is what she wants to hear.

I know there is something wrong with what I am doing. I know my mother's paper is impossible to read. I don't quite understand why. The truth is, I don't want to understand. I could think about it. I could probably figure it out. But that would take a lot of time and I don't feel like working that hard. *Do whatever you can get away with*, as Flannery O'Connor once said in a different context.

My mother's professor awarded her a C on her paper. The threat of welfare passed. She received college credit and a salary increment. Rather than being grateful to him, though, she pointed to her passing grade as evidence of just how inept he was. And I agreed with her. Now I believe something very different. Maybe reading Shakespeare strengthened her professor's insight into character and enlarged his empathy. Shakespeare can do that to a person. Maybe the professor saw my mother as the protagonist of a tragedy. Maybe he gave her points because she was turning the script into a good play.

Trying to please my mother about her Shakespeare paper initiated my descent into duplicity about reading. When I signed off on the paper, I knew I would be celebrated as the kid who had helped her defeat her teacher. My mother acted grateful and proud, and she wasn't faking. She took me to get a strawberry ice cream cone. I soaked up her gratitude without feeling responsible for the consequences of a judgment I understood was faulty. And then I forgot it. That fall I became fiercely involved in defending a certain hedge fort on the playground against boys at recess and I began seriously practicing the violin. I thought little more about my mother's Shakespeare paper for the next thirty years.

But the sides were drawn after that. I thought of life as offering two choices: my mother's active world or the corrupting, imaginary world of her Shakespeare professor. Ironically, that summer I had begun to devour books. I had learned the trick. I could slip the collar of everyday life and follow fiction anywhere it beckoned. I read books by Paul Hutchens about the Sugar Creek Gang, which I imagined joining. I failed to notice the gang was made up entirely of boys. But then, I failed to notice almost everything. I spun a cocoon of reading against the madness of a world where my father could disappear with no warning. The chair became my habitat. I camped there for whole days at a time, cradling one book after another—books that ignited breathtaking scenarios lit by magic neon lights. Occasionally, nagged by my mother, I would get up from the chair and step into the sweltering Nebraska afternoon to pick beans for dinner.

During those years my mother's creed was my creed, at least officially. She believed that if a person feels grief and horror while watching the fictional Macbeth murder Macduff's children, that person has not stayed sufficiently alert to the demands of "real" life. That person is caught up in vain imaginings. That person may be lazy and bound for life's trash heap. I was failing my mother, I realized, because I secretly suffered and triumphed with characters in books. In public I defended and sided with her. I didn't want the family to go under. And besides, she had a lot of power. On a hot afternoon she could decide whether or not to take us to the swimming pool.

In the reading wars, I was a traitor to my own side. My mother's professor wasn't the main person I betrayed, of course. When Flannery O'Connor said to do whatever you can get away with, she went on to say that she usually couldn't get away with much. I violated a human principle so deep that it has roots in the beginning of time. I betrayed what I knew was true. It has affected my relationship with my mother ever since. Eventually I had to reverse myself and openly honor books, or I could never have lived a free, happy life.

For me reading is a sacrament. As I write that sentence, I imagine ghostly theologians pulling up in a ring around me, shaking their hoary white locks and muttering curses on me. But a sacrament is an outward and visible sign of an inward and invisible grace. And isn't that what language is? God tells Adam and Eve to name the animals and plants. Once they had words, they could make great leaps. They could explain crows and trees and radishes. And they could articulate what they felt, what they imagined. Because of language they could embark on the journey of their own lives, learning and remembering and passing on their experience. Without language, it would be hard to tell humans from brutes.

*The Story of My Life*, Helen Keller's autobiography, describes reading as a sacrament. Helen Keller was blind, deaf, and dumb, and by the age of eight she still hadn't learned to speak. She wrote that she felt imprisoned in a state of perpetual, savage despair.

> *I was without compass or sounding-line, and had no way of knowing how near the harbor was. "Light! Give me light!" was the wordless cry of my soul. . . .*

Then one day Annie Sullivan tapped the word *water* on one of her pupil's palms while she poured water over the other. Helen Keller's world cracked open—*water*/water—and the connection washed over her. The world was no longer without form and void. Water became itself, air became itself, her hand became itself. "Everything had a name," she wrote,

> *and each name gave birth to a new thought. As we returned to the house every object which I touched seemed to quiver with*

*life. That was because I saw everything with the strange, new sight that had come to me. On entering the door I remembered the doll I had broken. I felt my way to the hearth and picked up the pieces. I tried vainly to put them together. Then my eyes filled with tears; for I realized what I had done, and for the first time I felt repentance and sorrow.*

Learning to read ushered Helen Keller into the moral order.

And reading did the same thing for me. In 1950 I stood beside my mother in our kitchen, holding a worn Dick and Jane reader, sounding out the words, knowing I was faking as usual; that is, remembering the story rather than reading it. But then the story took off like a jet from a runway. I read pages and pages beyond anything I remembered. My mother stopped mashing the spuds, frowned with pleasure, and told me that I had learned to read. I understood that somehow—I had no idea how—I was vacuuming the story off the page into myself. I did not merely feel a sense of accomplishment. I felt set apart. It was one of my earliest encounters with grace.

I don't know why I didn't bookmark that day in my mind and honor it afterward. Well, I do know. Although I felt it deeply, I didn't understand how significant it was. There are no cultural markers for learning to read—no public celebration, no religious ritual. By the time I was fourteen, I had forgotten the essential holiness of that moment. I was a cracked cup. On the one hand, I couldn't stop reading. On the other, I couldn't stop believing that reading was a dangerous habit that would leave me passive and unable to support myself.

This rift was not helped by the fact that I picked up two diametrically opposed signals about reading at school. The teachers hyped reading. In first grade children who couldn't read were segregated into groups called "Blackbirds," while those of us who flew through the primers were called "Bluebirds." We avoided the eyes of the "Blackbirds" as we passed them on our way to the front of the class. And the division between readers and nonreaders persisted. As teenagers, we were led to believe the nonreaders among us were marked for lives of crime and addiction. Looking back, I wonder that we didn't stone those kids publicly at the end of the year.

Or they, us.

But in spite of public declamations of support, high school was actually not designed for reading, either. We filled the building with restless activity. The teachers nattered on and on. Students passed notes, carried on experiments, banged lockers, sprinted and screeched through the halls. We were always on display. There were no quiet nooks for hanging out with a book. No one admitted to liking books, even "smart kids." I thought they must have gotten A's without reading.

My mother sent mixed messages, too. She ridiculed readers like her Shakespeare professor, but she urged us to succeed at school. She was smart enough to know that in America learning to read was the way to thrive. However, she didn't expect any of us to *like* reading.

—

At home, I developed a reputation for being the reader of the family, which means being a dreamer, someone who can get lost in any fog that happens to roll in. As everyone knows, in a family, a person grows to resemble her reputation. A grandmother might say, *You drive just like your great-uncle Elmer.* Or, *Good grief, listen to her. She's getting funny, like her father.* When you're young, the aunts and uncles who haven't seen you for a while will stand around and make these comments in your presence—as if you were a piece of used furniture, or an African violet they're thinking about purchasing. What they say about you makes you think about yourself that way. Which in turn pushes you further in that direction.

My mother often sent me downstairs to find a jar of canned plums or rhubarb for dessert. When I forgot what she wanted and came up with a jar of pickles she became eloquent in her annoyance. *Mankind could have evolved in the time it's taken you to find that. Go down and get it right!* I obediently climbed down and spent another ten minutes looking around, trying to remember what I was there for.

My mother blamed this lack of practicality on too much reading. She worried that I was so easily ensorcelled that I would not hear the sirens during one of our summer tornadoes, for example. They might find me wrapped around a street sign. Late at night she sat on my bed, her face and hands stippled by the waving shadows of trees under the streetlight, while she pled with me to change. But I couldn't figure out how to change. I had failed my driver's test because, the agent said, I was dreamy. I forgot my purse in school. I lost coats and boots. Reading carried me farther and farther downstream from Mother, standing on the dock, calling me toward responsible adulthood.

My mother might have been right—that there was something slightly sick about my inarticulate reading. I suffered from a lack of critical distance. Whatever happened to the main character in a book happened to me, and I was helpless to extricate myself or make judgments about what it meant.

Ironically, part of what brought me out of my inarticulate reading stupor was another Shakespeare teacher, a bull-necked former marine who made us read *Romeo and Juliet* in eleventh grade. He blurted out in sweet, clumsy words why he loved the story. I thought I would die of joy. Someone else had dreamed a story exactly the same as the one I had read the night before! He made us read *Julius Caesar* out loud. Oh man. We were terrible. Even I knew that. But the brilliance of the language lifted our clunky, illiterate little voices to heaven.

That year, my junior year in high school, I discovered a second, better, more active kind of reading—hauling the glittering jewels from the cave into the sunlight and exclaiming to one another—*look at this! Isn't this amazing!* In that class we talked mainly about plot. But simply to know that other human beings had the same story in their minds felt like the miracle of the loaves and fishes. This giant awkward sergeant made the Shakespeare play into bread we passed around and shared in class. And I began reading in a different, more self-conscious way. I was gathering food for the table. I had a premonition that I might do something useful with my life, however crippled my mother thought I was by my addiction to reading.

Nevertheless, I was determined not to study any more Shakespeare than necessary. Even though I majored in an undergraduate English Department where Shakespeare was a requirement, I successfully petitioned to avoid my mother's old nemesis. It was the Jesuits in graduate school who finally forced me to read Shakespeare for my master's degree. And it was watching Professor Stan Clayes leap from the floor to the top of his desk in his virtuoso performance of Henry V that finally converted me to Shakespeare.

Since then Shakespeare and I have been through every stage of love—astonishment, infatuation, disillusion, jealousy, worship. I've lived for periods of time in London and seen his plays at the Globe, where he may have acted. I've spent days in Stratford, where, as a boy, he ran the earth into his feet. I can picture him strolling around the market after he dropped out of school, as it teemed with horses and herbs, vegetables and flowers. He must have studied people, bewitched by their charm and their evil. He probably helped in his father's tanning business, out behind his parents' half-timbered house. The day would dawn, bright and cool in the summer, the stink of lye floating on the air. Quick as a wink he had a wife and three babies. He was probably desperate for money. Maybe he wrote couplets to sell for two pence with the gloves his father made. At the age of twenty-one, standing outside his house in Stratford, listening to three babies wailing, he must have glanced down the road toward London. He was looking for a way to become Shakespeare.

Sometimes I think I understand Shakespeare better than I understood my mother.

—

I wonder now whether my mother realized that she could not read Shakespeare. I remember one night in college, climbing into bed early to read a translation of Kant's *Critique of Pure Reason*. I opened the cover of the book and fell into a deep hole. I climbed out, thinking I had made some bizarre mistake, like forgetting to put on my glasses. I started over. I kept feeling the ground shift under my feet. After a couple of pages, I couldn't remember what I had read. I calculated rapidly. If I'd spent an hour and couldn't remember what I'd read, I definitely wouldn't finish the assignment before morning, even if I read all night. In fact, I realized I might never finish reading *The Critique of Pure Reason*. It is bewildering and humiliating to discover that you are holding in your hands pages of an English translation that you, as a native speaker, cannot read.

In fact, my mother read very little besides the Bible. Oh, sure, a cake mix box and our report cards and Mother's Day cards and sometimes she picked up a *Reader's Digest*. Once in a while she would read a how-to book. But she didn't read novels or nonfiction. I am still trying to figure out how she could read and understand the King James Bible every day, on the one hand, and yet pick up so few other books. In fact, no one I knew as a child talked about reading. Well, I think of one young married couple who read for pleasure, books about spirituality published by religious presses. My mother occasionally bought these but she didn't read them. She kept them on our coffee table.

Since my mother so rarely read, there was much we couldn't talk about. I would like to share the questions and the humor of reading with her. Once I was trying so desperately to read a nineteenth-century French novel that I invented things no one else in class recalled, because, of course, they weren't there. I laughed about that with other readers. But never with my mother. She might have felt the loss even more keenly than I did. She must have seen her teenage child paddling away from her in the canoe of reading, on a journey she either couldn't or didn't want to take.

But my mother was by no means storyless. It is a great irony that though she didn't read, she taught me to love stories—her own, and my father's, and those of her parents. With the verve and style of a fine soccer player dribbling and passing the ball down the field, she narrated the old tales. The past defines us, she believed, the story of God dealing with his people. Remember it. Write it on the tablets of the children's hearts. The story of Abraham's faith. The story of my mother's parents nearly losing their farm to hail. The story of how one winter midnight just after my parents were married, they seized their playing cards, carried them down to the furnace in the basement, hurled them in, and watched them burn.

My cagey mother aimed her stories directly at me. Maybe that's because I was the child who asked to hear them. I might read myself into ruin, yes, possibly, but my mother understood that if I wasn't ruined, I was the child most likely to hand down the legacy of the past. She fretted over my brother; she loaded her practical concerns on my sister. She handed me her stories more frequently and with more urgency as she recognized what I was becoming.

My mother is standing over the navy blue tub, lifting one dripping, steamy mason jar after another from the noisily boiling water. The kitchen thermostat registers 103 degrees. A mist hangs above the stove, encircling her. I am leaning over the sink, sliding skins off peaches. My vision blurs as salty sweat drips from my forehead into my eyes. In the living room, George Beverly Shea is rumbling, "How Great Thou Art." My sister, who stands at the kitchen table drying the scalding jars, is, like me, stripped down to her underwear. Our faces are flushed. Our wet hair clings to our heads. Then we hear a chime.

One of us shouts, the doorbell!

"It's Pastor Garland," my sister jokes.

We explode into laughter, three women who have been toiling since six a.m., loony from brain-numbing Nebraska heat. Julie scoots behind the living room drapes to spy on the caller. We wait, silent, jumpy as frogs on a griddle, hoping the caller doesn't walk around to the back of the house, where he might see us through the kitchen windows.

"It's a salesman," Julie hisses. "He's walking away." We relax.

"Girls," my mother begins. "I remember."

I remember. The powerful locomotive that pulled the boxcars of her stories behind it. She kept her family in the dairy business by washing the separator every morning before school. She watched as her parents' soybean crop was wiped out by hail. She went off at thirteen to board at a strange family's house so she could attend the new high school in Slayton, but she felt ashamed because the night before she left, her father cut off her hair above her ears. She ate nothing but chocolate bars for six weeks and developed boils. At fifteen she drove her brothers and sisters to school in a Model A. At sixteen she became the lone teacher for thirty-two kids in a one-room schoolhouse. By the age of twenty she was staffing a hospital ER alone during the night shift. One night a couple of cops came in with a man's arm wrapped in a bloody army blanket. They thrust it at her and announced, *The body's coming later.* In surgery she was the one who managed the eminent physicians. Her job was to hand them instruments from the autoclave: the scalpel, the forceps, the scapular retractor. If they felt irritable they would swear and fling the instrument across the room and demand another as she tried to calm them down. She was the recipient of half a dozen marriage proposals, most of them from doctors. She spent half a day stuck in an Otis elevator with a dead body. As the school nurse at Irving Junior High, to hear her tell it, she regularly threw herself onto the bodies of students and teachers to stop geysers of blood from shooting out of wounds. It was her coaxing that persuaded an unhappy junior high math teacher to come down from the far edge of the school roof, where the woman was munching a piece of cheddar and contemplating how far it would be to the ground.

I wonder now whether swapping stories might have healed the split between my mother and me. When she told her stories, what if I had reciprocated with stories from the books I read? Maybe there was a moment when, because I failed to act, we forever missed what we could have had in common. But I didn't know how to talk about the stories I knew. I usually couldn't remember the plots. They felt locked away in a dark cave. And anyway, what my mother wanted was not reciprocity, but an audience.

*Whatever you can get by with*, as Flannery O'Connor said. My mother didn't get by with her contempt for Shakespeare. I didn't get by with my duplicity about reading. Mother passed her Shakespeare course, but then watched her older daughter become increasingly more estranged. Reading laid its sword between my mother and me. Even if she were still with us, I know full well she'd never read this book. She would crow about it, maybe, and advertise it to her friends, but she wouldn't crack it open. I will never get over the irony that her stories started me down the road that took me so far away from her.

Sometimes now that Mother is gone, I imagine that we're all in heaven. After I've asked my father a lot of questions and he's given me the best answers he's got, I will go over to the booth where Shakespeare is sitting, signing his folios and answering questions. There will be a long line. I'll stand there gossiping a little in the warm breeze with other readers who adore the Bard. When I get to the front of the line, Shakespeare will look up at me and say, *I hear your mother's got some good stories. How about an introduction?* He'll get up and we'll go find her. The three of us will swap stories. My mother will stick around—not because she needs a bigger paycheck to support her children—but because she finds out that she really likes the man.

*Chapter 21*

# REMNANT

In August, after Mother all but stops driving, we plan to take her with us to Jack's music camp, Kinhaven Music School, in Vermont, where we will soak up the final weekend of concerts. We've done this with her every August for years. It is one of the pleasures we can still offer her. I pick her up at the Philadelphia airport a day before we're scheduled to drive to Kinhaven. As she walks down the runway from the plane, she's sporting a snazzy new plum-colored knit suit. When she catches sight of me, she gasps with pleasure, puts down her purse, and throws her arms around me. "Thank you, darling," she gushes, "for coming to pick me up. Imagine! Driving all the way from Dallas!"

I say, "No, *you* came from Dallas, remember?"

She, who could once locate a straight pin on a football field, frowns, thinks about it, and changes the subject.

On the way to the car, she plucks at my coat. "There's just one little problem," she tells me.

"What?"

"I forgot two carry-on bags on the plane." She ducks her head, looking abashed.

We return to the airport and slog around, trying to recover

the bags. We fill out forms, file documents, and speak politely to clerks. Then she remembers that she didn't bring those bags in the first place. We laugh about it.

It's Thursday afternoon when she arrives in Philadelphia and that evening as I'm scraping carrots and tossing the salad for dinner, she shows up with her purse and stands by our back door.

"Where you going, Mom?" I ask, trying to sound casual.

"Prayer meeting."

"We don't have prayer meeting at our church," I tell her.

"No, I mean my church. They're expecting me." She checks her watch and yanks the door open. A gust of wind blows across the kitchen counter.

"I thought you had prayer meeting on Wednesdays," I say.

"We do."

"Today's Thursday."

"It is?" She wrinkles her nose in puzzlement.

"All day."

"I thought it was Wednesday."

I don't mention that she's in Philadelphia, that in order to attend prayer meeting at her church she'd need to fly back to Dallas.

"Why don't you take your coat off," I say. "In a minute I'll put on some Mozart."

She sits down on a kitchen chair and describes the close little group of people who meet for prayer at Lake Ridge. They couldn't bear to give it up when the minister reluctantly concluded that with both parents working in most families and neither able to go out on Wednesday night, there weren't enough people to continue prayer meeting. So it's no longer an official church function. A seminary student took over and the small band slogged on, borrowing a room in the church basement.

Mother says the word *remnant* and pauses, not knowing exactly where to go from there.

I wouldn't have the faintest idea what my mother was talking about if I didn't remember Wednesday night prayer meetings from childhood. Not that it was ever mobbed, because it wasn't one of the more glamorous services, but Mother would bribe me to go with her whenever she wasn't drop-dead exhausted from nursing. While we chattered on the way to church, I would silently dare myself to pray out loud, the way I dared myself to do a back flip off the high diving board. The night I finally did, hearing my teenage voice flickering on phrases I'd never before uttered, I panicked and quickly doused the prayer. So it turned out to be very short, a fledgling petition, the appeal of an apprentice. But I felt proud of having the guts to try it.

No, Mother, I thought, looking over at her, you don't have to explain to me what prayer meeting is. You don't have to tell me why you love it, or why you forgot what city you're in and what day it is, in the hope of going to prayer meeting. I remember.

## Chapter 22

# KINHAVEN

Kinhaven is a music school located in the rolling Green Mountains of Vermont, just outside the town of Weston. Every summer for more than fifty years it has gathered first-rate music teachers and young musicians to practice during the week and give concerts on weekends. That's what the brochure told us, the brochure Jack brought home from school one spring day when he was nine. There were pictures showing Kinfolk, as the kids are called, running around in bare feet. There were pictures of teenagers practicing together in the rough-board rustic practice rooms, giving concerts in the beamed old concert hall, building boats to sail on the lovely pond, block stamping T-shirts, shaping pottery, eating s'mores, and staying up until all hours singing or folk dancing or watching movies. The children who go to Kinhaven grow up and send their own children to Kinhaven, where they discover they're not the only teenagers in the world who love and play classical music. No wonder Kinhaven feels like a family. The brochure offered pictures of scrumptious-looking meals with homemade pasta and bread and ice cream.

When Jack was ten, gazing at the food in the brochure, he announced, "I'm in!"

During the eight-hour drive to Vermont the day after I picked up Mother at the airport, Molly and Mother and I tell jokes and sing campfire songs. Molly is in graduate school and I don't get to see her very often. She worships Mother, since she went to visit Mother every summer for two weeks until she was thirteen. Those were the Daddy Jim years, the years Mother had money and leisure and she squandered every minute on Molly from rooster-crow in the morning until the stars came out at night. She arranged tea parties with our child as the guest of honor and took her to the swimming pool. They baked cupcakes together and Molly played hopscotch with the grandchildren of Mother's friends. Mother treated Molly to ice cream cones and root beer floats and pizza. Every day she gave Molly a new present. She walked Molly to the playground and drove her to the toy store and at night when Molly was finally tired, Mother gave her a bath and curled her hair and planted a garden on her back, which involved a ritual with rhymes and scented oil and a gentle backrub. She did for Molly everything she thought of doing for her own children, what she didn't have time or money to do the first time around.

Driving to Kinhaven, we are in high spirits. Molly starts songs in a brave, ringing voice, and I chime in. *There was a farmer had a dog and Bingo was his name-o. B-I-N-G-O, B-I-N-G-O, B-I-N-G-O, and Bingo was his name-o.* My mother adds her wavery treble whenever she can remember the words and when she can't, she invents them. I'm on guard, but I say to myself that she's made up lyrics all her life. And she has. Some of them are better than the real lyrics.

*Make new friends*, Molly sings, *but keep the old*, swapping one melody for another dexterously as a train switching tracks at a hundred miles an hour. *One is silver and the other, gold.* Mother and I follow her, singing *Make new friends* over and over. We like that one. We believe it.

Then we go into rounds. *Are you sleeping? Are you sleeping? Brother John, Brother John, Morning bells are ringing! Morning bells are ringing! Ding, dang, dong. Ding, dang, dong.* Molly is emitting light. She is radiant. My mother blissfully starts another round. We are the vacation kids, jubilantly traveling toward the hills of Vermont, as we have done so often in the past. A sense of peace descends on me. This is what we were made for.

When we're all sung out, Molly starts a game of I Spy with My Little Eye.

"Something starting with C," she announces.

"A cow," Mother guesses brightly.

"No."

"A cream puff."

"It has to be something you can see," Molly explains.

"I can see a cream puff," Mother says. "In my mind's eye. And it's making me hungry."

I think she is telling me she wants to get something to eat. So we pull off at the next plaza, where the choices do not include cream puffs. She's lucky to get a bowl of vegetable soup and a cup of hot water. The waitress keeps asking her whether hot water is really all she wants. The young woman probably thinks Mother plans to pull a tea bag out of her purse, but she doesn't. She favors hot water.

The sun is setting when we turn into the parking lot at Kinhaven, just as Jack is cutting across the lawn toward the rehearsal building with a cadre of barefooted friends. I honk. He turns, waves, leads them over to us, and makes introductions. He looks an inch taller than when I last saw him and brown as an oak in his T-shirt and jeans. I know better than to touch him in front of his buddies. His grandmother steps forward on her uncertain legs, then lunges for him, and buries her head in his chest. Looking embarrassed and paternal, he hugs her quickly. Then he announces that they need to go get their instruments and tune up. It's ten minutes till concert time.

At the concert, exhausted from the long car ride, Mother nods off. I think of waking her, but why should I? She's older than anyone in the hall, probably older than the hall itself. She's come all the way from Dallas. She sleeps though a particularly slow piece by Darius Milhaud. As Jack begins playing the "Musical Offering" by Bach, she wakes up. As his mother, I think her choice of when to sleep and when to wake up reveals her good taste.

"Mike's better than he was last year," Mother whispers to me, pretending she's been awake all along.

"You think so?" I murmur. Then I remind her. "It's Jack."

"I'll tell him how good he is."

"He'll like that."

She claps fervently, raising her hands up so Jack can see how much she appreciated his quartet.

"You have a pen?" she asks as the next group comes on.

During the rest of the concert she scribbles notes on the Xeroxed program beside the names of the students who are playing.

"HERE LAST YEAR," she writes by one name.

"MEDIOCRE," she scrawls by another.

"NERVOUS," she prints by another.

By the name of a young, geeky boy, "A BORPLE."

By one string quartet, "WATER RUNNING UPHILL."

And by another name, "LOVELY GIRL."

At intermission we all wander into the warm Vermont night and stand on the grass talking. The sky is lit by a big full-cheeked moon. Clouds that look like shadows of continents sail across the heavens. People we met at past Kinhaven concerts join us, other members of the board, parents of Jack's friends.

When we return to our seats for the second half, I am horrified to see that Mother has left her annotated program face up on her seat. I wonder how many parents have read her comments about their children. She would not have made a slip like this...when? A year ago? Two years ago? If she knew, she'd be appalled. All her life she's so desperately wanted to be good. She was expected to be upright, not to injure others, not to make a fuss, not to put herself first.

Maybe it's all right, I think, that she's no longer trying so hard to be nice. And frankly, her comments are less cruel than a lot of what passes for music criticism in our newspaper. Besides, I agree with many of them.

At the end of the concert, before the clapping has died away, Mother staggers to her feet. "Where's Mike?" she asks me sharply. Her eyes are alert, scanning the concert hall.

I pull her gently down. "I don't know."

"Won't we see him?" She sounds panicked.

"Tomorrow morning."

"Not tonight?"

"The kids work hard. They like to have fun after the concerts."

"Where do they go?"

"I don't know, Mom."

"What are they doing?"

"They eat pizza, I think, and watch a movie."

"Oh." She sounds disconsolate.

The clapping is over and the audience, here and there, is popping up.

"I want to see Jack," she says, sounding alarmed.

Maybe she's thinking about Michael, her lost son named Michael. The pace has been too fast for her, the dislocation too abrupt. She made the jump from Dallas to Philadelphia with difficulty yesterday. Today we pushed on, from Philadelphia to Vermont. No wonder she doesn't know where she is.

Daniel helps her climb down the risers. He takes her arm and guides her toward the door. Molly is holding her other hand. Her eyes are still combing the hall. "I'm looking for Mike," she tells Molly.

"You mean Jack?" Molly asks.

"Yes."

I spot Jack talking to friends on the other side of the concert hall. Molly darts off to fetch him.

He comes over.

"That was just wonderful," Mother coos at him.

He bends over her politely. "Thank you, Grammy."

"Music runs in our family," she tells him.

"I know."

"You're so lucky to have this camp."

"I am," he agrees.

"I lived on a farm. There were no teachers. I wanted to play in the worst way. I begged my mother for piano lessons. So she ordered them by mail and paid for them with her egg money. Can you imagine? Every month the mailman delivered lessons and I sat at the piano and taught myself."

Jack listens to her story, smiling. But he keeps glancing toward his friends.

"I have something for you," my mother tells Jack, wiggle-waggling her hand. He pretends to chase it the way he did when he was a child. Then she presses a quarter into his palm.

"Thanks, Grammy." He sounds courtly.

"Just keep it up, Mike." She beams at him.

"Okay," he says, frowning. "Only I'm Jack."

Maybe Jack doesn't remember who Michael is. I've told him, but he's eager to rejoin his friends. His father and I release him with thanks.

All night that night I hear Mother packing and unpacking her suitcase. Molly, who is sharing a room with her, gets no sleep.

At breakfast at the inn the next morning Mother asks brightly, "Wasn't the concert wonderful?"

"It sure was, Grammy," Daniel says.

"Jack is getting better."

"I hope so." I say, thinking of our long drive to lessons every week, the many performance classes and auditions.

"I miss him every day of my life."

Molly glances over at me.

"Michael," I explain to her. "My brother."

Molly gives me a knowing look.

"I miss him, too," I tell Mother.

—

The next day I grope for a way to explain to Jack why his grandmother can't remember his name. I grope for a way to understand it myself. Jack seems spooked by Mother's mistake and I don't want him to conclude that she's just a crazy old lady.

Mother is riding back in Daniel's car and Jack, along with his camping gear and clothes, is riding with me. On the way home I start in. "Grammy's son was named Michael."

He looks at me skeptically.

"My older brother. He died when he was eighteen."

"Hmm," Jack says.

"When she calls you Michael....well, you look like Michael to her."

"Okay."

"I'm sorry she forgets your name."

"It doesn't matter, really. It's fine."

"I think she's kind of...it's her former self talking."

"That's a little crazy, Mom."

"No it isn't."

"Yes. It's bizarre."

"We carry our younger selves with us," I tell him.

Jack: "When are we stopping for lunch?"

"I mean, think of when you were five, Jack."

"It's twelve thirty and we haven't had lunch."

"No, really. You were five once."

"Okay."

"You remember what it felt like?"

"Sort of."

"When you got that award at camp."

"Yeah."

"Your younger self."

"Okay."

"You carry your younger self with you. Just like Grammy does."

He folds his arms and gazes at me, trapped in the car, wondering how long this explanation will go on.

"So you want lunch," I ask him.

"Yeah."

"Which of you? You or your younger self?"

"My younger self." He grins.

So we pulled over at a diner.

*Chapter 23*

# MICHAEL

After Michael died, Mother talked about him every bit as often as she talked about Julie and me, her living children. All her life he haunted her memory. But until one trip to Kinhaven, my dead brother had rarely crossed the threshold of my mind. I had children of my own. My life was hectic and they needed my attention. I wondered occasionally why my brother still appeared so often in my mother's conversation.

Then after watching Jack one summer at Kinhaven, I recognized Michael's retorts. I felt the heat of his smoldering intensity. In the instant it takes a bell to ring, I understood what it might be like to lose a teenage son.

It was then I began to think about Michael, to see how he taught me to travel. It was travel that ultimately allowed me to separate from my mother. I don't mean that Michael ever really got very far from home. For most of his life he could barely breathe and the more he panted for air the more fiercely our mother watched over him. That was all the more reason for him to renew his efforts to escape. The task became a life and death struggle for him. Watching my brother, I learned how to battle for my own independence.

But during one summer at Kinhaven Michael began to

haunt my memories because I dimly understood that my own son was probably bent on separating from me.

—

When I was six I would rush in from school, hot and sweaty, the screen door banging noisily behind me, my vision spangled from the afternoon sunshine. If the smell of Vicks VapoRub assailed me—then I knew. He had been laid low by asthma again. In the corner of Michael's darkened bedroom loomed a cylindrical green oxygen tank with a nozzle on the top and a tube running to his nose. Walt Schamber, our town doctor, would be sitting on the bed, perplexed and frowning. On the other side, my mother would sit, cradling her chin in one hand, her elbow propped on her knee. They murmured *heart rate adrenaline injection* over Michael, who lay there laboring to breathe. If it was really bad, no one even noticed I had entered the room, because they didn't dare lift their eyes from him. No wonder Michael could be grouchy and exasperated. Even when he wasn't in bed, he lived in the center of my mother's full attention. He had a much harder time getting away than I did. I mean getting away from her.

—

The year Mother took us to the Badlands of South Dakota I began to learn what it meant to travel, in part because Michael had become more discriminating. By then he was seventeen, I was fifteen, and our sister, Julie, was twelve. We shouted out Burma-Shave signs to one another: *His face / Was smooth / And cool as ice / And oh! Louise! / He smelled so nice!* We swam in a shallow, warm pond and licked ice cream cones that dripped down our arms. In a roadside park we climbed halfheartedly on jungle-gym equipment that was too small for us. We stopped at what promised to be a wild animal petting zoo boasting a litter of gray kittens, two belligerent baby goats, and a balding donkey with calluses on its behind. After that Mother stonily passed up a sock museum. But I nagged until she relented at the billboard: STREAM FLOWING UPHILL!!

With hushed reverence, the guide led a half dozen of us through the sun-brindled woods to a hillside overgrown with ivy and scrub pines. Occasionally turning to caution us about our footing, he climbed ahead of us in his brown shorts and heavy boots to a place where a stream cut through the under-brush, squirting and pulsing over rocks. Uphill. Well, kind of uphill. Working to believe it, I could imagine that the bed tilted up. Around the glade, several hills came together at different angles, so it was difficult to tell what was ascending and what was descending.

The guide removed his hat reverently, as if introducing us to his own personal favorite Himalayan mountain, and waited for our response.

Because this was my idea, I felt I needed to comment. "Amazing!"

Michael took off his tortoiseshell glasses and squatted down to get a better look at the angle of the stream.

"It's a trick," he announced, standing up.

The guide's face turned flinty.

I could feel my cheeks flushing with embarrassment. We had given the guide our fifty cents, which seemed to me like a pledge that we would be a sympathetic audience. Moreover, I relished the idea of a miracle far from church. The stream might not look exactly as the billboard pictured it, but it was better than anything we'd seen so far on this trip.

"That water isn't flowing uphill," Michael growled.

"Take as long as you like," the guide said stonily. "Just watch your step when you go." He turned, jingling our coins in his pocket, and walked down the path.

Not to be taken seriously must have hurt Michael's pride, which had already been battered from two years without a father, a period of steady attrition. No father to take him to baseball games, no father to help fly his model planes, no father to teach him to fight. Two years of watching his friends take their fathers for granted. Michael was blond and slight and he had a temper, which sent him into asthmatic fits.

He wheeled aggressively to follow the guide. He was beginning to wheeze. Mother trailed him and laid her hand on his shoulder. Michael whirled on her with a look of savage irritation.

"Don't," she pled.

He glared at her.

"Please."

He hesitated. The guide's brown shirt disappeared into the trees.

—

Michael must have known he couldn't win a fistfight, but maybe he didn't think it would come to that. He had a fast mouth. And he didn't like to be fooled. But, more important, I think, even as a teenager, he grasped the difference between novelty and travel. Travel involves getting into someone else's point of view. It requires empathy. When you see water flowing uphill you don't feel empathy. Either you feel tricked, or you feel astonishment of the kind that doesn't do a thing for your soul.

By the next day, the whole water-uphill experience seemed tawdry to me.

Michael turned his lethal irony against whatever hemmed him in—Mother's increasingly careful, frugal, Midwestern habits, our church's literal way of reading, the romantic notions of the mother and sisters he lived with. He had to answer to the mother of three teenage children, a young widow. She was often weepy, sometimes supine on the couch, hyperventilating, with fluttering eyelids. She feared for his life, quite literally. But she also feared for his soul. Michael ridiculed the arrogant, color-blind Mr. Sampson for wearing one red and one chartreuse sock to church. He joked that sunlight bouncing off Mrs. Pringle's fillings as we shook hands with the preacher was as flashy as the Second Coming. He railed against Pastor Garland, who got the order of the planets wrong in his sermon. How could you believe what a preacher says about the Revelation of St. John, Michael demanded, if he didn't know high school science? Michael mocked the notion that he had a Christian duty to carry his Bible to public school on top of his books. He chafed at my mother's ten o'clock curfew on weekends. Sporadically he exploded at her, but mainly he smoldered in a long, sarcastic burn.

Michael's physical activity was so restricted by his asthma that becoming a ham radio operator was his only way of getting out. Always geeky, he hit upon the radio idea at fifteen, soon after my father died. He sent for the parts. He paid for them out of his allowance, stringing the wires, and rigging the thing himself. For once Mother let him do what he wanted. In fact, I suspect she helped subsidize the project, though she never admitted it.

In the middle of one night about six months after he got the radio working, I woke up in the bedroom that I had painted a sweet, hideous lavender, and heard static floating from Michael's bedroom. Outside, the night was utterly black, because we lived on the outskirts of town, beyond streetlights, next to farmland. Through my window I could see a cornucopia of stars spilling across the sky and the scent of lilacs drifted in. I threw my sheet off and stood up to get my bearings, then crept past our chairs and the couch, which bulked like young elephants in the dark next to the large split-leaf philodendron in our living room.

I knocked at Michael's bedroom door. Knocking was a rule Michael invented; the rest of us barged in on one another. When he opened his door, I edged in the several inches he permitted visitors, and slouched against his door jamb. He was a thin outline in striped pajamas sitting before the big, black contraption, jiggle-jaggling his bare foot up and down. His blond maverick curls were illuminated by the radio's faint light. On his head he wore a huge black headset, which made him look like an aviator. Human voices, sparks and splinters of words, shot from the machine.

"Come in, come in!" Michael called into the mike. He moved the dial slowly, as if casting a net to see what he might pull in from the darkness. The machine squirted light. Logging on to the radio, Michael had found people all over the world who talked to him in English at prearranged times of the night. He craved their voices. He told me he was planning meeting some of them.

—

That same restlessness lay behind our family's dreadful *Lady Chatterley's Lover* episode. In 1959 D. H. Lawrence's novel was considered pornography by many people in Lincoln. It became a cause célèbre, with ministers and moralists railing publicly against the novel until it became famous in our town.

One Sunday our minister, Pastor Garland, preached against it. The book was pornography, he said, and reading it would contaminate us.

I wondered whether he'd read it. If so, then why wasn't he tainted? And if he hadn't read it, how did he know it was pornography? I wasn't eager to be polluted, but by fifteen, I knew that not everything I had been told by adults was true. A person had to investigate. The trouble was, I knew that exploring could get me into trouble. I tried to assess the risk. What was the worst thing that could happen if I read *Lady Chatterley's Lover*? Surely reading about something couldn't be as dangerous as *doing* it.

Still, it seemed like a slippery slope.

While I fretted, Michael bought and sneaked a thirty-five-cent paperback copy of the novel into the house. I can't imagine where he found it and I don't know how Mother discovered that he was reading it. Maybe he taunted her with it during one of their spats. But my mother talked my younger sister into rooting the book out of our house before it corroded Michael's soul. Enflamed with mission, Julie recruited me to help her.

When Michael was away one day, Julie and I ransacked his room. I yanked open the drawers of his desk. Julie went through his bureau. As I opened his closet and stared at his shirts and shoes, I realized for the first time that my brother might have a sex life. He didn't date much, so I'd thought very little about it. As I pushed back his trousers, I was punished by lurid, Dante-esque visions of a deviant, monstrous, alternative brother feeding the furnace of his passions with smut.

I don't remember where we found the novel, but the cover pictured a raw-boned, good-looking male servant, reaching toward a lovely, pale, formally dressed woman. He was in the act of stripping away her chemise. I concluded that Pastor Garland had been right. Clutching the novel in my hand as my sister and I spirited it outside to the trash, I could almost feel its sensual throbbing. It was not until years later I learned that cover artists rarely ever read what's inside the book they're illustrating, and if they do, they always exaggerate the sensuality.

Now I think that reading *Lady Chatterley's Lover* was a way for my brother to hack open some space beyond Baptist youth group meetings, beyond our clean and bookless split-level family. The year he bought the novel, which used the word *fuck*, the nation held its breath as the Supreme Court decided it was not pornography, but a work of literature with significant ideas. That didn't convince anyone in our church. The novel describes an upper-class woman, whose husband is paralyzed and impotent, going mad with frustration. She begins a long, slow affair with their gamekeeper. The two of them come to realize that sex is not debasing, but a way two people can mingle their souls.

I don't imagine Michael ever got to the intermingling part. As far as I know, he never bought another copy. And he couldn't have found the book in the Southeast High School library. He never even mentioned that his book had disappeared. Maybe he didn't want to dignify our violation with a response. Or maybe he'd gotten what he needed from the book, a way of traveling, a way to find himself in a larger world.

Although I felt guilty about rummaging through Michael's things, I suspected that he'd have been happy enough to rummage through mine. That, I sensed, might have been a lesser violation, because I did not protect my privacy as fiercely as he protected his. What I knew was that we were rivals. He was our mother's first child, the chosen son, the sick one, the one our house belonged to before I arrived.

As soon as I could walk, Mother relied on me for help with her problematic, profoundly male oldest. *Honey, can you reach Michael's medicine? Could you get him a drink of water?* She would meet me at the door after school and warn me, *Mrs. Gifford sent him home from school and Dr. Schamber will be here in a minute. Can you play quietly?* I knew that Michael was smarter than me, but I could make friends more easily, and I was not as prickly. I worked to become useful, not only to my mother, but to others. I played the violin well enough to be featured in the *Lincoln Journal*. I sharpened my wit against Michael's repartee. Then, with a precocity that utterly outflanked him, I began dating, fell in love, and learned by experience about sex.

My brother often loudly claimed to pity the men who were snagged by my female tricks. He referred to me as "the brawling woman" and quoted Proverbs 25:24: *It is better to dwell in the corner of the housetop, than with a brawling woman and in a wide house.*

"So go live on the roof!" I would yell at him.

"Kids!" Mother would shout from the kitchen. "Don't drag the Bible into it!"

My mother could not bear the idea of Michael going off to college after he graduated from high school. She had lost my father and that was enough. But Michael was brilliant. Her friends, the teachers who had plenty of trouble with Michael's probing science and math questions at Southeast High School, told her so. What was she doing, holding him back? they wondered. He might be the next Jonas Salk, who had recently defeated polio. For all they knew he might be another Einstein. So that fall we piled our Chevy with Michael's hypoallergenic pillow, his physics books, his Adrenalin, and nonallergenic snacks, until the undercarriage hung low in our driveway. Then all of us climbed in and my mother drove us from Lincoln to a suburb west of Chicago, where Michael would be starting Wheaton College. We carried his things into the dorm, and made his bed, and stocked his shelves, while he paced and scowled and grumped to get rid of us.

Then Julie and Mother and I drove several blocks to a room

my mother rented for $15 a night in the basement of a professor's house. That evening I gazed out the window at moonlight on the lawn, at the moon itself, which was so large and round and perfectly white that it might have been a sheet-music illustration. The night was flawless. My stomach fluttered. I had seen freshmen talking, laughing, swarming on the quad, and I wanted to go to college, too, instantly, and eternally.

The next morning we left for home.

Michael, presumably, had gotten out.

The phone call came at seven a.m. the next Friday. I could hear my mother clinking breakfast dishes in the kitchen. It was a warm, sticky September morning, my windows flung wide open, and I could see a few reddening leaves in the crowns of the trees. I was just pulling on my pep club sweater, the heavy black knit with a big wooly gold letter S on the back. As my mother talked on the phone, something in her tone alerted me. I stepped out of my room, glanced toward the kitchen, and saw her sink to the floor. She didn't faint. In a real crisis my mother was never anything but composed and practical. She crouched like an animal in the corner, looking stunned, but asking questions. And I knew.

I knew.

It was her birthday.

We never learned the cause of Michael's death. My mother had been required to watch four autopsies in nurses' training, and she had vowed then that none of her loved ones' bodies would ever be ravaged that way. Over the years people who learn about my eighteen-year-old brother's death have wondered that my mother didn't need to know what killed him. But I've carried two children for nine months, kept them from running into the street, applied Band-Aids to their cuts, watched their bodies change in puberty. I understand why she didn't want to have to imagine for the rest of her life the knives plunging in, the sinews hacked, the heart torn out.

Still, without an autopsy, I have no barricade of facts to keep questions from swirling like angry floodwater. Michael was always pushing boundaries. About a decade ago, I began to wonder whether he committed suicide. By then the records were long gone, of course. But Chaplain Evan Welsh, who called that morning to break the news of his death to my mother, reported that the night before Michael died, he was having trouble breathing. He had checked himself into the infirmary.

His asthma was profoundly worsened by anxiety. And he must have suffered the same nerves all freshmen feel. *Will anyone like me? Can I do the work?* For all his independence, Michael reacted to every nuance of the emotional weather around him. He must have felt both elated and threatened by the campus, which was so different from his uneventful life at home. He had been rescued from death many times by our mother's gifted, intuitive nursing. This time she wasn't around to save him.

But the irony of his dying on her birthday, was that coincidence? In the early morning, while it was still dark, he must have found himself in a strange bed in the infirmary, fighting to breathe. That kind of struggle would distort his face, turning his lips and fingernails blue. Like a woman in labor, he would get caught up in the battle, lying motionless, with a faraway look in his eyes, acknowledging no one in the room. He couldn't. I remember the hiss of the oxygen, the buzz of a fly, the mustard-colored afternoon light filtering through pulled shades. That morning in the infirmary if he even remembered that it was my mother's birthday, I doubt that he cared. He was eighteen. He had been so bent for so long on separating from her. He was battling for every breath. And although I habitually attributed my own sentimentality to him, Michael was not sentimental.

As his body traveled on the train from Wheaton toward Lincoln, I drank my first cup of coffee. More than my first alcoholic drink, this was my entry into adulthood, the bitter, hot, aromatic taste of a new country. I was the oldest now; I was taking my brother's place. It now seems odd that I felt so little guilt about it.

Before we buried Michael, I felt him return briefly. Standing outside our church on the grass beside the hearse, I felt like I was losing my balance. The trees swam. I felt my brother moving beside me the way you feel the wind moving through a valley, and then I sensed him departing for good. I felt a great release, perhaps Michael's release as he left his body, which had always given him trouble. But I was sixteen and I thought mostly about myself. I experienced it as my own release.

Michael's funeral was, they said, a celebration of his home-going. As was typical of Baptists at that time in the Midwest, the family, what was left of it, his mother and younger sisters, arrived at the church early. We spent a few minutes with his body, which was lying in an open coffin. Michael's lips had been rouged and his blond curly hair was parted rather than swept straight back with Brylcreem, which was how he did it. As I looked at him in the close, sickly perfumed air, my hands began to shake. I trembled all over with fury at the men from the mortuary. All his life he had so easily felt violated. Even though he was plainly dead, I expected him to sit up and smash in the faces of the impudent morticians. In spite of their fake solemnity I suspected that for them this was just another pleasant fall day. I wanted them to choke and clutch at the air as he had. I wanted to see their faces turn blue as his sometimes did. I wanted to yank up the bitter dark root of death and make them swallow it one piece at a time until my mother forgot her grief.

I know now, as I didn't know then, that these men are lightning rods for grief and anger. When my mother requested that they make an adjustment to Michael's hair, one of them gravely complied. In the last moment before we were ushered away from the casket, my mother spotted a fly, stepped over, and waved her hand above my brother's cheek, brushing it from his face. It was her last attempt to protect him. Shortly after that, they closed the lid.

—

After the funeral, our stunned friends kept stopping by to bring hot dishes and pay their respects. My mother answered the door, ushered them in, offered them food, and talked quietly with them. I was sitting in a corner of the living room trying to understand how my brother could be gone, trying to comprehend that I would be taking my brother's place as my mother's oldest child. I spent that afternoon and evening learning to play cards with the guy who had escorted Michael's body home from Wheaton. Cards were not allowed in our family, but this was a game called Rook, a shadow version of Hearts. And after all, we had just buried my brother and my mother was not thinking about me. As I practiced shuffling and cutting the deck, as we played game after game, I came to believe that if I could learn to play cards, it would be a sign that I could do anything I needed to do. The game felt ceremonial, like a rite of initiation. My brother's friend knew that, too; we didn't need to talk about it. We had both been raised with religious ceremonies. When he said good-bye several hours later, he left his cards with me.

—

That summer at Kinhaven, when Mother watched our teenager, Jack, playing music and hanging out with his friends, she must have been seeing Michael again. The tilt of his head, the quick retort, the fascination with technology—I saw with surprise that Jack was, in some ways, yes, like my brother. And I began to put myself in my mother's place. I could do that for the first time because I had this teenager. What would it be like to lose him?

So it was twenty-five years after Michael died, because of Mother's slip of the tongue, that I began reflecting on who Michael was to me. I began recalling scenes and episodes of our lives together. His most important legacy to me, I now understand, was his brave search to find other cultures, ways of seeing human experience through the eyes of others, even though sometimes he could barely make it out of the house.

Ironically the child who didn't even travel safely to college and back taught us all to travel. I have been writing this as though I have known all along how smart my brother was about getting out. But the truth is, until that night at Kinhaven it didn't occur to me that Michael was the one who triggered my urge both to leave my mother and to travel to places on this earth that are strange to me. Often now I think about how precocious Michael was, how difficult, how perceptive.

It wasn't until I had a child myself that I understood what a great tragedy it was that he lived to be only eighteen. It was a tragedy for him and it was a tragedy for Mother, who wanted so desperately to protect him. Most of us are still pathologically confused at the age of eighteen. If only he'd had time to sort things out. If only he'd been able to shake hands with the strangers he met on his radio. How did he know, after our father died, that he needed to practice traveling? Maybe he had some sixth sense. Maybe he realized that he would be taking a long journey. Maybe he was trying to imagine inconceivable distances, a little at a time. Maybe he was getting himself ready to go.

# FIELD NOTE 6

## MEMORIZING MUSIC

*Then I'm the Mother shredding my Kleenex in the audience while my fourteen-year-old, Jack, stands onstage and plays the entire Tchaikovsky violin concerto from memory with a professional orchestra.*
I know if he forgets, the maestro will have to stop the orchestra. Someone will bring Jack the score. They will confer about a place to start again and his humiliation will probably beget more memory problems.

In those days, I was Jack's violin mother, the one who knows how to play a fiddle, the one who practiced with him, the one who feared memory loss. I feared it so much partly because his grandmother was losing her memory.

What will you do? I asked him. How will you memorize this?

Oh, he told me, muscle memory helps. Your right hand knows whether the note is up or down bow. Your left hand feels patterns, where its fingers go on the fingerboard, how the tailpiece fits against your palm in fifth position. And then there's the melody, the ongoing musical story you can remember and hum any day of the week. The orchestra has a different musical story. The orchestra's story gives you something to hang your own story on.

That wasn't a good enough guarantee. Driven by need, I chopped the Tchaikovsky violin part into hundreds of musical phrases based on its structure. I numbered the phrases. I told Jack to memorize each separately by number. Then we rehearsed. When I called out #67, he played the phrase. I'd call out #115 and then he'd play that. It was as close to a memory guarantee as I could imagine.

*The Saturday night of the concert he played the phrases in perfect order. He played magnificently. I've never watched the video because I can still see him. How do I remember him standing there onstage? I don't know. But we've invented language for it.*

*Just say that I see him in my mind's eye.*

*Chapter 24*

# LLOYD

Every other summer for a decade while Molly was growing up, the two of us flew to Sioux Falls, South Dakota, rented a car, drove to Pipestone, Minnesota, a three-stoplight town of retired farmers, and met Mother at the house where my grandparents once lived. That house had become Uncle Lloyd's after our grandmother died. There for three or four days we entered an orgy of cleaning and painting. On alternate years Julie and her daughter, Eve, came to help Mother save Uncle Lloyd. She pressed her children into service because she was desperate to keep that bungalow up; it had belonged to her clean and orderly German parents. She had comforted her beloved mother: not to worry, she would take care of her hapless oldest brother, Lloyd.

In that house, long before my mother showed signs of Alzheimer's, I first witnessed a foreshadowing of what I saw at Kinhaven the summer Mother called my son by my brother's name. That summer at Kinhaven was the first time I had thought about how my mother was really a composite of many selves—selves I recognized, selves I was familiar with. It made sense to me that surely, as I told Jack, each of us carries our history with us. We're all multiple in that way. But we steady ourselves in the present moment so we will seem predictable and sane to our friends and family.

When Mother was in the company of her older brother, Lloyd, maybe she didn't ride herd on those different facets of herself quite so stringently. I remember how she could morph from character to character in that house, or at least present different versions of herself, depending on what she needed in order to cajole her brother into doing what she wanted. Of course, at the time I didn't think much of it.

So here we are, performing the summer cleanup. After a preliminary tour of the house Mother announces fiercely, "This refrigerator goes!" She summons her brother from the basement. He climbs the steps in his ragged leather carpet slippers and stands humbly on the landing, gazing toward her in the kitchen. Her hair is wildly curly from the moist heat, but she wears dangly earrings and she's drawn her lips in audacious plum. Always mindful of her dignity, she's scrubbing the kitchen in a gathered skirt and a turquoise blouse with rhinestone studs on the yoke.

Molly and I have already dumped the dozens of ancient white Styrofoam Meals on Wheels trays from the refrigerator and all the leftovers they contain into black plastic trash bags. Mother is grubbing around with a rag inside the freezer. She ducks out to glance at her brother, who has climbed the steps slowly and is now gazing with longing toward huge garbage bags filled with his lost leftovers. "Lloyd," Mother says in an exasperated voice, "the door is falling off this thing!"

"It is?" His watery tone makes clear the fact that the refrigerator and its door are beyond his pay grade, either to fix or to understand.

"You're the one who uses it, Lloyd! You must know that!"

"I haven't had any trouble with it," he claims.

Mother hurls herself into a harangue. "Why, Lloyd, if our mother saw this refrigerator, she would be so ashamed! I'm calling the man next door to take it to the dump and we're getting you another one this afternoon."

"I'll call Halverson to come and fix it," he negotiates.

"It's twenty-five years old, for Pete's sakes. You need a new one anyway. Look at this!" She yanks a broken plastic egg case out of the door and holds it up.

He stares at it noncommittally.

"So are you willing to pay for another refrigerator?" Mother persists.

"I suppose I have to."

"That's right," she proclaims. "You do. Go get your checkbook."

He turns obediently and climbs downstairs for his checkbook.

This is the man who earned a master's degree in chemistry at Northwestern University, the oldest of my mother's five siblings, the one who never married, who retreated to live with his parents when he was in his late twenties and dwelled under their roof ever afterward, except for the six months he spent living in our basement in Lincoln and helping Daddy build our house. Mother swore that her brother had suffered a nervous breakdown in his early twenties after some floozy broke his heart. Julie and I liked to swap guesses about how much he was worth. He owned a farm twenty miles out of Pipestone, and Julie figured he had a lot more money than any of us, and who could tell where he kept it?

I grabbed one of the bulky garbage bags and headed out the door on my way to the Pipestone Paint and Tile Store. "What color paint shall I buy for the living room?" I asked Mother.

"Oh, good grief, he doesn't care what color it is," she said, emerging from the cupboard she was cleaning. "Get whatever's cheapest." Flushed and triumphant from her recent victory over her brother's lassitude, she plunged her head back in and went on scrubbing, sending the smell of ammonia wafting through the kitchen.

I pushed open the back door, set the bulging, shiny garbage bag by Uncle Lloyd's beat-up silver trash cans, jumped into our tiny rental car, and backed down the driveway into the street. It was August and the sky was a fathomless turquoise known in Minnesota only in high summer. Driving at ten miles an hour down the wide street of two story homes, shuttered and silent in the temperate sunshine, I muttered the names of the families who live there: Persinger, Tillinghast, Connolly, Reinquist. I drove slowly out of respect for the sleepy town I had visited every summer of my life and because I knew sometimes children played baseball in the street. Down the block a red fire hydrant spouted a glittering, arching geyser that dropped to a bright running stream beside the curb. Three children in colorful shorts held their hands out toward the water, averting their faces from the spray. The boy gripped a big plastic dump truck till it filled and then splashed it on the girls, who squealed and leapt. When I smiled and waved, they froze and stared at me.

That night at dinner, Mother raised one of her favorite topics: teeth. "Lloyd, have you been to the dentist?"

"No," he admitted, concentrating on digging Limburger cheese out of the jar and spreading it on his bread. He ate Limburger cheese, not because he liked it, but in order to honor his mother and to perpetuate a place for Limburger cheese in his parents' house. Grandmother adored it.

"You have to go to the dentist, Lloyd!" Mother commanded.

"I'm thinking of having all my teeth pulled."

"What's gotten into you?" she screeched. "I still have every single one of my own teeth! And I'm proud of it."

"You're only seventy-five," Lloyd retorted calmly. "Wait till you get old."

"Lloyd! You are not having your teeth pulled!"

"They're a lot of trouble," he contradicted her in a reasonable tone. "It'll be easier to have a store set. Ma and Pa had their teeth pulled when they were in their sixties. They ordered matching sets of false ones and they never had to go to the dentist again."

"People don't do that anymore, Lloyd. You keep your own."

The next morning Mother made an appointment for Uncle Lloyd with the dentist and scribbled a note in large letters that she set by the phone, reminding him of the date.

"He won't go," she told me. "But what are you going to do? We have to try."

———

The last time I saw Uncle Lloyd he was wearing his wool helmet with the ear flaps down, sitting in his bib overalls in the living room of his dead parents' house with his knees together and his gloved hands clasped on his lap. Mother had just hollered him up from the basement. It was three days after Christmas. Julie and the kids and I had washed dishes after a turkey dinner with all the trimmings, which we had flown there to bestow on Uncle Lloyd so we didn't have to think of him spending the holidays like a hermit alone in his house. As we settled into chairs in the living room, I exhaled a long beard of fog into the room. I could see my breath because Uncle Lloyd kept the thermostat at forty-eight degrees, that is, while we were visiting. It was higher, he told us meekly, than when he was alone, because he wanted us to be comfortable.

"Lloyd!" Mother shouted.

He jumped. "What?"

She was holding out a plate of date bars and brownies and Christmas wreaths with Red Hot trimmings. "I said do you want a cookie?"

He kept his gaze on the floor in front of him, which is why he hadn't seen the plate in the first place, and shook his head quickly, ever so slightly, as if to rid himself of dizziness or water-on-the-ear.

Mother tossed me a look that meant you can never tell what this man is going to want. We had spent the whole afternoon baking cookies for him. "These wreaths are delicious," she coaxed.

"Then you eat them," he suggested in his foggy voice.

"Lloyd, you need to eat to keep up your strength."

"I feel good."

"You hardly ate any dinner."

"I liked what I ate."

"We flew a long ways to make a nice Christmas for you," Mother reminded him. "Don't you want to participate?"

He fell silent, with his eyes pinned to the flowered pattern in the rug.

"We're flying back tomorrow and with all those leftovers in the refrigerator! It's a shame, Lloyd."

He stared doggedly at the floor.

So Mother said, "Okay. Then, how about a little singing?" She peered at him. "What would you like to sing?"

Uncle Lloyd cleared his throat. "You do the singing."

Mother put the plate of cookies down and reached for Grandmother's old hymnal on the rack of the piano. Grandmother's blond Danish modern furniture and knickknacks and tatted tablecloth and Japanese figures standing on the wooden moon-shaped wall decoration remained exactly where they had been on the day she died fifteen years earlier at the age of ninety-seven. I could feel her there, still. Maybe it's not surprising that Mother sounded like her mother, Henrietta, when she talked to her brother in that house.

"Do you have a favorite Christmas carol?" Mother queried him.

"Well, uh, no," he said equivocally.

"Okayyyyyyy, then," Mother crooned in her warning voice, "we'll just sing whatever we like."

Uncle Lloyd steadfastly watched the floor.

"You want to play for us, Jeanne?"

I hadn't played the piano for years, but I moseyed over and handed Molly another hymnal and we took turns singing our own personal favorites: "What Child Is This?," and "It Came Upon a Midnight Clear," "Once in Royal David's City," and about five others, while Uncle Lloyd sat with his head bowed, encircling his right wrist with his left thumb and third finger.

After we finished, he said cheerfully, "Well, that was nice," and got up and wandered off through the dining room to the dark basement, where he slept on a narrow iron monk's bed under the joists and water pipes and heating ducts, surrounded by his three drip-dry shirts on hangers that he attached to a rope clothesline.

———

Pipestone was a town of many Mothers. The way she assumed the gestures and voice of our grandmother seems now almost like an intentional impersonation. But I doubt that she was aware of doing it. It was a practical matter. How else could a person deal with the apathy of a man like her brother? Consider this: he was over eighty, she was in her mid-seventies, and she was still trying to change him.

Sometimes, to achieve that, she would lapse into another character. Mother was in the basement one afternoon, for example, where Uncle Lloyd spent most of his life. She tried to reason with him about keeping his bathroom down there clean—the bathroom that consisted of a bald spigot for a shower and a clogged floor drain and an ancient sink stained with many colors of paint from the brushes he had washed out. Mother approached him as a vulnerable, pleading little sister.

"Lloyd, don't you want to keep things nice?" she beseeched in a miniature voice.

"Well-ahhhh, I need to pick up some Dutch cleanser at the Piggly Wiggly to scrub the sink," he replied gruffly, "I've been meaning to do that."

"I don't like to think of you living in this kind of mess."

He ducked his head with embarrassment at being thought of at all.

"You've always been so smart and wonderful," she wheedled.

Uncle Lloyd ambled across the room to my grandfather's workbench where he got busy sawing a board so he wouldn't have to look directly at Mother. She shook her head tragically and tossed me a troubled glance and bit her lip.

And then there was Mother, the Irving Junior High School In-Charge-Wheeler-Dealer Nurse, who would call to get his trash picked up or to arrange delivery for a new washtub. I also remember the charming Mother, the beguiler, the flirt, who, the night before we left, phoned every friend and relative she could think of who might consider stopping by the house during the next winter to visit her brother.

Mother's family of origin—what was left of it—this single male elderly sibling, could in a moment turn her into any number of different selves that became a clue to understanding her. I suppose, my mother had always been far more than she appeared on the surface. As she sailed into Alzheimer's, her multiplicity just grew more evident. To outsiders she may have appeared in her late eighties to be an animated, gregarious old woman. But all the earlier Mothers lived within her.

## Chapter 25

# MOVING MOTHER

Less than a year after Mother announced that she'd given up driving, she tells me she's renouncing her Symphony tickets. After all, how would she get to downtown Dallas, to hear the orchestra? She can't navigate to the cleaners, and the bank is almost outside her driving range now. The only time she gets to her beloved Arboretum and Botanical Garden is when I'm in Dallas. She hasn't stopped by McShann's Nursery for months to pick up flowers for an arrangement. What's the point of making arrangements if she can't show them to anyone? When one of her friends phoned last week to tell her about a new shoe store in the neighborhood, she was too proud to ask for a ride, even though she needs shoes with lower heels. So she let it go. Half the time she can't find a way to her garden club meetings. And still, I don't think she has opened a single one of the books I've sent her. They all look new.

Then what on earth does she do? I wonder. She cooks meals for herself and lounges on her sofa, watching Fox News. She listens to the same Mozart over and over. Even Mozart must be getting sick of his greatest hits. She raises basil and thyme on her patio. When she walks with friends, they bump into other friends on the Christian Care campus and sometimes have coffee together. And she pours over her Bible like a conscientious child, getting ready for her Sunday school class and her Bible study group. Some weeks Julie takes her grocery shopping or a friend treats her to lunch. That's about it.

That night in a dream I see a girl running for dear life in a green meadow, her black curls springing wildly. Her face is panicked. She glances over her shoulder at an amoeba-shaped shadow pursuing her. I try to climb into the dream to help her, but I can't unlatch the gate to the meadow. So I stand outside, watching. I open my eyes. I'm lying in my own bed. In the dark street, a car alarm is honking, beeping, wailing.

———

The next morning I suggest to Daniel and Jack that we move Mother to Philadelphia.

"Okay," Daniel says, flicking me a cautious look, then checking the clock on the stove. "We should think about that."

"Where will she sleep?" Jack asks.

"Maybe in the room where she stays when she visits," Daniel suggests, grabbing his keys.

"Then what would we do with all her stuff?" I ask.

"You mean what would *she* do with it." Jack corrects me.

He's right. The stuff is hers and there's a massive amount of it. But somebody other than Mother will have to sort through it, pack some of it, and then find a place for the rest of it.

Jack and Daniel exit for work and school.

I stand contemplating Mother's formidable amount of stuff. Into her two-bedroom bungalow she has managed to squeeze as many first-aid kits and envelopes and Jell-O molds and watering cans and bowls and sheets and place mats and wrenches and family records and spatulas and cleaning products, as most people could wedge into a five-bedroom split-level. Mother became more efficient at packing than anyone else in the universe, because whenever we visited her parents, they gave her as many groceries as she could fit into the trunk of our car. Then they stood cheering her in the Minnesota sunshine as she worked out the jigsaw puzzle of the picnic hamper and frozen ducks and wall paint and kitchen gadgets and suitcases.

Now she can't sort or organize. Now she wants to keep everything.

I grab a pen and paper and climb to our second floor.

The guest room smells clean, like nothing, not like moth balls, not like cedar, not like furniture polish. For three years only an occasional house guest has slept here. Bookshelves I nailed together twenty years ago in our backyard with one of my best friends hold our sprawling collection of yellowing paperbacks. Good books, profound books. If she moves here we'll need to box these books and move them. Maybe we will have to give them away.

We never repainted these walls. Their color belongs to another family, a neutral off-white, which nevertheless strikes me as lovely. I've left the elegant, recessed windows bare so we can enjoy their simple milled woodwork. The hundred-year-old pine floor glows red, as though the sun were rising through it. We've thrown only a couple of small Oriental rugs over the boards. But Mother doesn't like wood floors. She got so many slivers in her feet from the bare floors in their farmhouse as a child that now she luxuriates in her wall-to-wall carpets.

Standing in this no-man's-land of a guest bedroom, I can hear the radiators tick. Tiger Lily, our calico cat, is bounding upstairs toward me. She pauses in the doorway, cocking her head quizzically. I suppose she wonders what I'm doing here, where I so rarely come.

"How do you think Grammy would like this room?" I ask Tiger.

She knows enough to answer, though her reply is merely polite. She's not taking a stand one way or the other. "Meeeyowwfffff," she says, stalking in. Tiger adores Jack, but her point of view on the rest of us is intelligent skepticism. At six weeks of age, Tiger was the runt of the litter, practically dead from battering by older cats at the animal shelter. They stepped on her head in their frantic eagerness to be adopted. Molly and I took Jack to the shelter because we figured the only way to cure his fear of animals was to adopt a pet. We settled on Tiger because she was the one kitten sick enough to continue sitting on Jack's lap when he leapt up in terror.

Tiger settles her warmth on my right foot and begins licking a paw.

I pretend that I'm Mother, that I've just moved into this room. Jack's room is just down the hall. He's sixteen now. Today he's at school, so his door is shut. I imagine him in there, at home with his Marilyn Monroe poster and his computer games and his science fiction books and his violin etudes.

Mother would share a bathroom with him.

That wouldn't work. Not in a million years.

The third floor would be better for her, anyway, away from the family, but close enough to join us whenever she feels like it. I excavate my foot deftly from Tiger, who tumbles sideways. She scrambles to recover her balance, casts me a bummed-out look, then sits down and goes back to cleaning her face. This is why she doesn't trust me, I think. I lean down and pat her, hoping for brownie points.

Sprinting to the third floor, I glance around. Daniel uses both our third-floor bedrooms for his office. I wonder whether he could manage with one. Mother could have the other. She might like the pert little bathroom up here, under the eaves. Of course we would have to install a tub, since a shower is too violent for her. I wonder whether the bathroom is big enough for a tub.

I imagine Mother getting ready for bed up here. It's small, but not much smaller than her current bedroom. I love the roof lines, the tilting ceiling. Is there room for her double bed? Maybe that, and a dresser. Not enough space or furniture for her. She'll need both rooms. We could ship enough stuff from Dallas to Philadelphia to furnish a small living room for her next door to her bedroom.

Then where would Daniel work?

Daniel could take over my office on the first floor.

Then where would I put my desk and files?

I open a window. The smell of pine pitch wafts in. Outside in the maple tree blackbirds are chattering like raucous sixth grade girls at recess. The phone rings in Daniel's office, down the hall, and his answering machine clicks on. His voice tells the caller to leave a message.

I feel forlorn, suddenly, in our big, empty house with everyone but me gone and a robot answering the phone. A train clacks in the distance. The insistent chirp of a bird outside the window starts getting to me, like a knife sharpening itself on a whetstone. I step to the window and glance out. It's a robin as big as my fist, less than two feet away, perched on a gutter. He looks reptilian, a dinosaur with feathers. He swivels his head and holds my gaze with his cold black eye. I look away.

Mother would be up here alone with the birds.

I walk down to the guest bedroom and stand at the window, staring out at the moss that has begun fuzzing the sidewalk in this early, soggy spring.

How much time could I spend with her? I wonder. When I visit her in Dallas, she has my attention full time. That's probably what she will expect here. She has no idea what a crazy life I lead.

I check my watch. In ten minutes I need to leave to teach and I'll be in one meeting or another at the university until after six. I drive down to Delaware three days a week. And after the publication of a new book, I've been flying around the country to give poetry readings. I teach in London most Januarys. I still ferry Jack two hours to violin lessons, sometimes several times a week. I'm away from home for vestry meetings at church and once a month I spend several afternoons editing poetry for a journal.

And then there's writing.

I'm supposed to be a writer.

Maybe I could offload the editing. And soon Jack will learn to drive. But I have to keep teaching. We have to pay our mortgage and Jack's college tuition looms on the horizon.

If Mother moves here, who will she spend time with? She doesn't know our neighbors. We don't even know them well. It's a suburb. Nobody in the neighborhood stays home all day. Can Mother still strike up new friendships? Who would drive her to places to find people her age? Where are those places?

But hold on, I think, hold on. She loves us. And she's never liked living alone. Maybe being here, even if we weren't with her all day, would feel better to her than living by herself. At least we could give her the choice. I vow to check into health-care providers and senior centers. I will find train and bus schedules. I'm not bad at this kind of thing. We might be able to make it work.

Then I think of church. Where would Mother go to church? Since she swore off driving on big roads, Lake Ridge Bible Church in Mesquite, Texas, has become the sun around which her solar system revolves. She lives about two blocks from the church and three or four times a week friends pick her up for a meeting there. Sundays when I'm visiting, she proudly drives the two of us over, her head barely reaching above the steering wheel. Lake Ridge may be the only place from which she can find her way home these days.

The last time Mother was here, she visited St. Mary's Episcopal Church in Ardmore with me. She followed my cues, standing and sitting when I did, with the congregation. I opened a prayer book to the right page for her. *Almighty God, unto whom all hearts are open, all desires known, and from whom no secrets are hid: Cleanse the thoughts of our hearts by the inspiration of thy Holy Spirit. . . .* But then she got lost and started paging randomly through the book. When she put it down, I shared mine with her. But her trifocals made reading difficult. She gave up and stood looking confused while we repeated the ritual for the Eucharist. She didn't go to the railing for wine and bread, which is the whole purpose of the liturgy. I wonder whether the entire Episcopal service feels pointless to her.

And then there are the sermons. "Boy, darling, you sure get off easy," she told me after one of our services.

"What do you mean, Mom?"

"You don't even bring your Bible to church." It's true. We read the Old Testament passage and the Epistle and the Gospel from a leaflet we're handed as we walk in. To feel like she's been to church, Mother needs at least a half-hour sermon, delving into Bible passages, crisscrossing texts all over the Bible. She swivels through the pages, jotting loopy notes in the margins.

She isn't at home with the culture of my church, either. We gather quietly in the sanctuary, kneeling or sitting with our eyes closed. We read the ritual from the prayer book rather than making it up as we go along. And the service is soaked in silence, which feels to Mother like empty space, like nada, zero creeping in at the edges. It makes her nervous. Women in her church are not allowed to lead anything, so our woman priest blows my mother's mind. Moreover, Mother doesn't attend the theater and disapproves of playing cards. Drinking alcohol and dancing, considered by Episcopalians to be normal human activities, are taboo for her also. Above all, my mother doesn't have any time for statues or crosses. To her they seem like pagan idols.

I attend Lake Ridge Bible Church with Mother four or five Sundays a year. We slide into one of the long wooden pews on the right side of the contemporary, red-carpeted, sloping auditorium. We take turns reading the newsy bulletin. Around us people chat quietly. When the service starts, we share a hymnal and belt out the lyrics. Or we read the words from the big screen down in front. After the service, her friends stop by to welcome me. I'm getting to know them. They are splendid people. We greet one another warmly. We share Mother as if she were a plot of land where we are all camping together.

One Mother's Day, Julie and Rich and their kids and Mother and I sat in a row and sang lusty praise songs to Jesus. Then the senior minister sprang into the pulpit. "Today we want to pay tribute to all our mothers," he announced, "by honoring the oldest mother in our church." The congregation stirred. People glanced at one another. Who was he talking about?

He grabbed the mike, stepped off the podium, and walked down the aisle. Pausing at our row, he asked Mother to stand. She tottered to her feet. As he pinned a corsage of red roses on her coat, the congregation burst into long applause.

Mother ducked her head. She beamed and bowed slightly all around. "Thank you," she murmured with self-conscious pleasure. She opened her mouth to say something else. The minister moved the mike to her mouth and leaned down to listen. But she couldn't find words.

"Thank you," she repeated softly.

After the minister returned to the pulpit, Mother grabbed my hand and entwined her bony, trembling fingers with mine. A dozen people stopped by after the service to wish her happy Mother's Day. They told me how lucky I was to have her for a mother.

"You're right," I said. "I know."

Mother will never leave Lake Ridge, I realize as I stand listening again to the ringing phone in Daniel's office. No wonder. As driving and flower show judging and friendships drop away, leaving horrible silence, as it becomes harder for her to make sense of what she means, her church has welcomed her more deeply into its heart. Even as she falls further into memory loss, the people there will love her more.

But wait, I think, if she moved here, maybe the two of us could find a church *like* Lake Ridge, a church where she could still bask in that kind of spontaneous service, that kind of noisy and outspoken worship. The church would be an adjustment for me, but surely I can bend to make her happy. She's in her mid-eighties; I'm only in my fifties.

So I try to imagine what that kind of church would feel like. I put myself in a pew in Mother's church and try to leave myself there for fifty-two Sundays. I sing the praise songs, listen to the long made-up-on-the-spot prayers, the announcements, the sermon, the altar call. But my imagination keeps sneaking out of the pew. There are never any women helping to lead the service; it is hard for me to fathom why anyone would want to keep out a whole gender. Then there's the language, the same language I heard when I was a child in our Baptist church. A long time ago I realized I couldn't make heads or tails of it. A long time ago I began to squirm and sweat during altar calls. At the heart of my own faith lies, not certainty, but mystery, and not a little doubt. What faith I have depends on silence and reverence before the Force that moves the sun and stars. It has very little to do with cheerfulness or with inviting Jesus into my heart.

But to tell my family this would hurt them. We were fundamentalists. The term *fundamentalist* was coined as a badge of honor by early twentieth-century Christians who militantly opposed modernism and liberal theology. As the country entered World War II, my young parents proudly embraced both the name and the ideas. After the modernists sent cultural shock waves through art and culture, my mother and father joined with Christian conservatives who fought to preserve a small number of central religious ideas: the virgin birth, the bodily resurrection of Christ, and his literal return.

The word *fundamentalist* isn't used much anymore, except to ridicule and denigrate conservative Christians. I don't use it that way, either here or ever. Fundamentalists were my first people, the kin I loved more instinctively than I have loved anyone since: our friends at Temple Baptist Church, friends of all ages who picnicked with us, went to school with us, and brought us food whether we were celebrating or grieving. We knew they were quietly, constantly praying for us. My mother, who was loyal to the core of her being, never abandoned the fundamentalist ideas she and my father chose when they were in their twenties.

I am the one who changed. Not that I planned to. I just discovered one day that I was incapable of believing what I had been taught. The road I traveled away from Christian fundamentalism was long and thorny and lonely and dangerous. I had no idea where I would end up. No one helped me. I'm not sure I can even explain the stations along that road. What I know is that I can't imagine a way back. To go back would unfasten who I am. I would get there and find I was no longer the person who started the journey.

I am standing in our guest bedroom watching specks of dust jump around, jostled by atoms. They are dancing in a chute of sunlight that's falling on the bed. This is where, if my mother moved in with us, she would sleep. I sit down on the bed. The truth is, we can't move Mother here. Even if we could overcome all the practical problems—which we probably can't—our churches would divide us.

*Chapter 26*

# GRAVEN IMAGES

The division between Mother and me began the summer I went to Bible camp and fell in love with the kitschy fluorescent cross. By the time I was nineteen, my mother's fundamentalism was driving me bonkers. One night I marched into Mother's bedroom, where she was sitting in bed reading her Bible, and announced to her that I was leaving her church.

"What have I done wrong?" she lamented.

"Nothing," I said. That was the truth. It wasn't anyone's fault. She had done nothing wrong.

"Where are you going?" she asked.

"I don't know."

"You're not going to church anymore?"

"I don't know."

In my mother's household a person was supposed to *know*. The answers were more significant than the questions, and, in fact, often produced before the questions were asked. Mother was always preaching the advisability of having what she called, *Direction*. Until a person started moving toward a goal, my mother would say, she couldn't see the goal clearly. No wonder Mother regarded me with alarm.

"Darling, it's your *soul* you're gambling with."

But it was too late for her to reason with me. I was only acting out a choice that I had been making for years, a choice that started with my love for a greenish fluorescent cross and graduated to questions about our Welch's communion grape juice. It was a decision that began as a secret, even from me, a secret that had finally worked its way to the surface.

In my mid-fifties, when I found myself worshipping at Lake Ridge Bible Church, our old Baptist services sprang to memory again. We carried actual black King James editions of the Bible to church, to work, to school, in our cars, everywhere, in order to symbolize the status of the Bible as the foundation of our faith. We thought God dictated the words of the Bible in the same way a businessman might dictate a letter. We hung copies of the Sallman *Head of Christ* in our homes, a picture I believed was an exact likeness of Jesus. To know God, we were told, is to be happy. Our church taught us to sing, *I'm inside, outside, upside, downside happy all the time!* We blasted out, *Jesus wants me for a sunbeam.* We shouted to the rafters, *I've got the joy, joy, joy, joy down in my heart!* Of course this was before therapy and before sharing. It was before Catholics and Protestants visited one another's churches, before we made pilgrimages to synagogues and mosques. It was before sensitivity training, before encounter groups.

Most mind-boggling to me was the literal way our preacher read the Bible. He argued, for example, that the earth and everything on it was created in one actual week. If you read the first chapters in Genesis the way they're written, he claimed, Darwin's theory of evolution can't be true. Frankly, I didn't give a rip how long it took to make the world. As a teenager I wasn't evolved enough to care about something that theoretical. I had been taught to worry about my own soul first, which, I had been warned, could easily be doomed to eternal damnation. Not that I understood what that meant. In fact, I didn't understand the most apparently simple sentences I heard in church, not really. By the time I was fourteen, because my own salvation depended upon it, I was madly trying to figure out how to read. Meanwhile, my mother hung on for dear life to her church's literal, cheerful fundamentalism. Believe me, I thought twice before I threw it out. In fact, oh Lord, I've ruminated about it for most of my life.

—

One Sunday noon, just after communion, my mother and the other deaconesses are talking and laughing in the church kitchen while they wash two hundred glasses only slightly larger than thimbles. It's way past lunchtime and my stomach is growling with hunger. The deaconesses store great glass jugs of grape juice, which we use for communion, on the shelves in the church kitchen. So I edge one off the shelf.

"What are you doing?" My mother's eyebrows arch.

"Having some grape juice," I say, reaching for an ordinary plastic tumbler.

"You can't drink that!" my mother shouts, lifting her hands out of the dishwater. Her arms are covered with long gloves of bright soap bubbles. She steps swiftly toward me.

"Why not?"

"You just *can't*," she says in a matter-of-fact tone of voice.

Before she reaches me, I push the jug back onto the shelf.

I know better than to challenge her in public. The other deaconesses beam indulgently at me, turn back to the communion cups, and pick up the gossip where they left off.

The minute we get into the car to drive home, I ask Mother, "Why wouldn't you let me drink the grape juice?"

"Because it's off-limits."

"Why?"

"It just is." She meant *Period. That's it. End of discussion.*

I am aware that Mother has never been into discussing aesthetics or theology. Occasionally she brings Welch's home from the grocery story, though only a small bottle and only as a special treat, because it's so pricey. So I wonder for weeks about the difference between the Welch's in church and what we drink at home. I am plagued by my awareness that this obsession is weird.

I know better than to ask our minister. He possesses little interest and less language for discussing such issues. He regularly warns against too much "head knowledge."

This is the beginning of my apostasy. I'm on my own.

—

The dusty summer streets of Lincoln, Nebraska, spelled themselves plainly, from First to Fifty-fourth running north to south, and from A to Z east to west. The levelheaded, practical city fathers didn't bother with names like Symphony Road or Country Club Highway. And there were no curvy subdivision streets with lovely unfolding vistas. The town was reliably perpendicular and parallel. The simplicity of my early belief was like that small Midwestern city, its square houses, its Saturday afternoon Cornhuskers football play-by-plays blaring from open windows, the sweet-smelling smoke of burning leaves. When my parents selected the town, took it to their hearts, picked up their belongings, and settled there, it became our promised land, literal, plain, and true.

Early in May my mother would pound stakes in the ground at either end of the garden and run strings between them to mark off rows of carrots, sweet peas, corn, tomatoes, all the familiar crops. Every year we would plant something exotic like kohlrabi to expand our palates, because that's what my father had done. The straightforward, blunt seasons brought us hard, drenching rains, heavy snows, and punishing heat.

I picture myself climbing the steps to Temple Baptist Church in a quiet residential neighborhood in Lincoln, walking past the planter of English ivy, and through the modern glass doors. This is the church my Mother picked out for us when we moved to Lincoln from Parkers Prairie, Minnesota. I stand at the back, where we sat with my mother for my father's funeral when I was thirteen. I look toward the altar. But there is no altar. Not of the kind I expect after decades of worshipping in an Episcopal church. There is a plain rectangular, oak communion table. Above the table, on the platform, stands an unadorned pulpit with a practical-looking pulpit light.

There is nowhere in this church to fix my eyes. I have been told why. Our eyes are supposed to stay fixed on Jesus. And Jesus is God, who cannot be trapped in an image. This truism seems obvious. But on reflection, what does it mean? If He can't be mentioned or pictured, how can we know anything about Him? This becomes a knot I can't pick apart. I am fourteen and I want to ask questions, but every question I formulate sounds dumb or smart-alecky. *How can my eyes be fixed on something that isn't there?* My Sunday school teacher tells me that our inner eyes are supposed to be fixed on the *idea* of Jesus. *Why not a picture or a statue?* I ask. *Easy,* he answers so effortlessly that I imagine him whipping his Superman cape around himself. We're commanded not to worship images.

I know that. I've memorized the Ten Commandments, including the one against graven images.

My mother, who is very popular, has been elected a deaconess again, so she's laughing and gossiping in the church kitchen with other deaconesses while they wash the communion glasses. We kids are supposed to be collecting the tiny cups, but instead we explore the sanctuary. We climb onto the platform with its choir benches and oversize wooden thronelike chairs, where the pastor and music director sit. We unlatch tiny doors on the preacher side of the podium and discover breath mints. We hear running water and stealthily check out the baptistery behind the choir benches. It's a large, square metal bin that reaches approximately to the middle of my chest. Upon investigation, we discover that the water in the baptistery is . . . well, *real*. It shimmers in the light. I can smell the chlorine, and when I thrust my hand into the water, it's bitingly cold.

Of course I have known it was water all along. But the tub is being filled from a metal tap that looks exactly like our outdoor faucet. The janitor, who stops by to check on it, tells us the water has to stand all afternoon so it won't be too cold for the evening baptism. Such practical details about what goes on behind the scenes in church strips mystery from our familiar rituals and sets me wondering.

I climb down the steps, face the baptistery, and stare at it analytically. The metal tub is hidden by the blond wood paneling on the wall behind the choir. The baptistery doors have been swung open on their hinges to reveal a painting of an outdoor scene above the tub of water: a river, the sky with fake-looking scalloped clouds, fat flying birds, and some trees. Whenever Pastor Garland baptizes a candidate—that's what they are called, candidates for baptism—this picture creates the impression that the water is not tap water and the event is not happening in a church, but outside.

This strikes me as odd.

I've seen dozens of baptisms. The candidate steps down into the water where Pastor Garland is waiting for her (in a preaching suit, which, it dawns on me, must be waterproof) and as we watch, he places his right hand across her back for support.

With his left hand he slips a white men's hanky over her nose. Then he lays her down backward in the water and quickly swings her up, using the handkerchief to mop her dripping hair and face. Afterward, the preacher closes the baptistery doors. While we sing a hymn, he gets dressed in a dry suit and then emerges to say the final prayer. Why, I wonder, has everything been arranged to appear as if the candidate has been baptized in a river?

I turn from the baptistery frowning, drifting toward one of the deaconesses, who is collecting cups. "What's that picture in the baptistery?" I ask her.

The woman, who is my mother's friend, is tall and big-boned and she's wearing a flowery dress with a wide, red, patent leather belt and a big bow under her chin. She pauses, her arms hugging three racks of glasses to her ample chest, and stares at the baptistery as if to locate the answer. "Well, honey," she says with kindness, "that picture is important. It's the Jordan River, you know, where Jesus was baptized."

"Oh," I say stupidly. But wait, I'm thinking, that isn't the Jordan River. It's a *picture* of the Jordan River. I don't say that, though, for fear it will sound sarcastic. And anyway, I'm pretty sure I know what she means: the picture in the baptistery is a painting that is supposed to make us think of the Jordan River.

This the first time I've ever thought about the fact that a picture is an image and an image *means something other than itself.* Such a simple idea. Such a complicated idea. She walks off to wash the communion glasses. Her husband and kids are waiting for her in the parking lot and she needs to get home to make dinner.

I gawk at the picture for a long time. To me it looks like the Platte River in western Nebraska. Its chunky trees and naïve perspective makes it look like it was painted by a child. Not that

I know much about perspective. I just think if that's the Jordan River, it must be a bad painting.

My head tumbles with questions I can't sort out. They gather into a bulge in my throat. If I could think of the words, I would ask who painted the picture, whether the person had ever seen the Jordan River. What if it's not accurate? And what happens if you get baptized *without* a picture of the Jordan River? If the Jordan River is so crucial to baptism, why don't we go stand in the actual river the way some Indians make pilgrimages to the actual Ganges? After all, baptism is so important to us that we call ourselves *Baptists*.

For some reason, no one else in our church seems worried about any of this. That Sunday night, during the evening service, feeling my boyfriend's arm around me, I sit in the back of the church, relieved not to be thinking.

That year one question after another battered me. I brought some of them to Mother, but I might as well have been shouting down into the Grand Canyon. She didn't hear me, couldn't understand a word of what I was saying. I suppose she wondered what kind of a creature she was raising. She was busy, working and keeping three children in food and clothes. She had no patience with anything but practical questions.

⸺

The unanswered grape juice and baptistery questions began working themselves up to a Mount Everest of trouble for both my mother and me. Like Mother, like everyone in her church, I believed Jesus might return any minute. I had believed this my whole life. I had a clear picture of what that would look like. I'd be outside, building a fort with my friends at recess, or walking to school. At the reveille of trumpets, I would look up to see Jesus' actual tanned feet slicing through the clouds like the prow of a ship through water. The light of the entire universe would rivet on his dazzling white robe. I don't know where I got this image. Probably from some Bible story book, or maybe our minister, Pastor Garland, described it in one of his sermons.

During the fall when I was sixteen, sitting in bed, doing math, listening to the rollicking lyrics, "It was a one-eyed, one-horned, flyin' purple people eater" on the radio, it dawned on me that Jesus might not be coming back in exactly those terms. I was astonished, first, then horrified. I lunged out of bed, flung our front door open, ran into the Nebraska night, and padded around our dark neighborhood, watching lightning strike and play just beyond the horizon. Thunder growled. The locust trees along the boulevard tossed ominously in a rising wind.

If lightning had reached out to strike me dead, I would not have been surprised. I had been taught that we're responsible for what we feel: that we believe what we choose to believe. So I figured that I must have decided not to believe in the Second Coming. I couldn't recall making any such choice. But one moment I knew exactly what Jesus' return would look like and the next I couldn't imagine it happening. The Second Coming had lent tension to my life and significance. Suddenly my whole understanding of human history crashed to pieces around me.

I thought I had lost my faith.

Not that I told my mother. I didn't tell anyone. Of course, I couldn't have explained it. I was just terrified. If the Second Coming wasn't going to happen exactly the way I had conceived it, it wouldn't happen at all, because I certainly couldn't imagine it happening any other way. After this, I felt different, marked, like the ugly duckling, no longer part of the flock. I wasn't any more inside-outside-upside-downside happy all the time, that's for sure. I had been schooled in silence. I carried this fact around as a sad secret.

In truth I also felt angry at my parents. I felt like a child who believes in Santa Claus, then discovers that her parents have been lying, that Santa is only the Spirit of Christmas. To say *there is no Santa Claus* doesn't mean pictures of Santa Claus have vanished or that Christmas presents stop coming. You might worry they'll stop, but the main point is that you feel tricked. Or at least you've misunderstood things. Granted, I could turn in my mind to the image I'd lost, as if it were a page in a book. I just couldn't believe it anymore. I thought petulantly, *Sure there'll be a Second Coming! Like snow on the Fourth of July!*

That extra level of knowledge—that an image might or might not be accurate—pitched me into a vast, world-weary, adolescent irony. If I could see the strings behind the puppet-image, I wondered, how could I believe it? I wanted to reserve my belief for what was *real*. Lying on our couch when I was seventeen, reading about Holden Caulfield in *Catcher in the Rye*, I began to view adult society, including especially my mother, as fraudulent. I wasn't the only one. When I got to college, I found friends (mostly men, since it was the 1960s) who had perfected the tossed-off mock. I never learned to do that myself. These issues of truth and the representation of the truth were life-defining for me. About them I remained halting and inarticulate for years.

A few years after that, I picked up and moved with my new husband to what I had heard all my life described as the liberal, intellectual, highbrow East Coast. It had been calling to me for years like a whistle that was pitched so high no one else in my family could hear it. After my husband finished law school, at the beginning of the summer, we took a road trip to pinpoint a town where we wanted to live. We chose Wilmington,

Delaware. Three months later, we packed everything we owned into a U-Haul trailer and moved there. It is odd that at the time I had zero awareness that I was repeating precisely the kind of move my parents made when they moved to Lincoln.

A couple of years later, when I announced to Mother that I had enrolled in a Ph.D. program at the University of Pennsylvania, she said, "A *what* program?"

When I explained what a Ph.D. program was, she demanded, "Why on earth would you want to do that?"

"I got a fellowship," I told her, knowing enough to stick to practical facts.

"Darling, that's *wonderful*." She smiled. "You take after your daddy. You don't act a bit like it, but you're smart as a whip!" This was the dubious compliment I heard from my mother many times in my life.

I went to graduate school to find an alternative to my mother's way of reading. Though I was in my late twenties, I was still the daughter sharpening herself against the mother, a knife honing itself against an immovable whetstone. I had learned from her that nothing was more important than reading the Bible. I understood the problem of reading as a religious question, too, but for me a profoundly complicated one. Like poetry, it was all about love and death and longing; that much I knew. I was already writing poetry. And I wanted to read poetry, the poetry of other writers and of other ages, all of it.

—

When I started working on my Ph.D. dissertation—which, not surprisingly, turned out to be about images—I found the rabbit/duck sketch in Ernst Gombrich's book, *Art and Illusion*. If you look at it one way, it's a rabbit. Squint, blink, and it's a duck. There are people who can't see the rabbit. They see only the duck. And vice versa. But the triumph of that sketch is that most people can see both. The rabbit both is and is not. The duck both is and is not.

Mornings when I was supposed to be scribbling my dissertation on a yellow legal pad, I stared at Gombrich's rabbit/duck until I got pretty good at seeing whichever I chose. It occurred to me that the Gombrich image is like a picture of metaphor. Metaphor, of course, is a figure of speech that poets use to fuse two images. It's written like an equation: X=Y. The rabbit *is* the duck. Like all metaphors, this equation is absurd. Of course, a rabbit is not a duck. But impossibly enough, in metaphor, two things that are very different can coexist in one image. For a brief moment the two terms strike against one another and a third meaning arises.

As Steven Pinker, the linguist-philosopher, has argued, we use metaphor because we can't help ourselves. We think in metaphor and have to be carefully taught how to translate those metaphors into logical sequences. My mother, who was gifted at simile and metaphor, often corkscrewed logical sequences. Her one experience with logic, a course she took at Nebraska Wesleyan University, nearly shredded her.

Around the time I finished my Ph.D., I said to myself: *The rabbit/duck sketch is just a sketch. It isn't true or false. And a picture of the Second Coming can't be either true or false, either. It's just a representation of a truth that lies in some other realm.* What followed was a new stage of belief.

Or perhaps I should say a second kind of belief.

But Mother was never bothered by any of this, even after she started painting. I doubt that she saw the images she painted as metaphors. At first she just copied other paintings, stroke for stroke. At a later stage, she bought fresh fruit, arranged it into a still life, and painted away. Sometimes she copied photographs.

But to her I believe the images just plain were what they were. They never became a language to talk about the world.

—

It would have been helpful if someone had explained when I was a teenager wandering the streets that night in Lincoln, that I wasn't losing my faith; I was just losing faith in an image. But who? Should I blame my distracted mother, who had been shunted out into the world to support the family after my father died? Could frail old Mrs. Duacheck, bundled in her black seal coat, have turned to me as we were waiting to shake hands with the minister, and explained the nature of imagery? Or, for that matter, was it the minister's job? How could they have even known that's what I needed? It's not that I had made my eccentric questions clear.

It would be one thing if the people in my mother's church had been punitive or cruel, but they were loving. They swapped recipes for green bean hot dishes and lemon meringue pie. They complimented one another's cooking. They would clean one another's houses, if there was a need, and take care of one another's children. One of the elderly church ladies spent weeks cross-stitching a cover for one of my mother's antique chairs. True, the people at Temple Baptist wrangled over the size of the new parking lot. And if you listened at Wednesday night prayer meeting, you could hear fabulous gossip. But we were devoted to one another. We were a besieged town that had closed its gates, rationed its water, and shared out its candles. I was held in the arms of that church. I wanted to belong and I had understood their warnings. If I strayed, they would disown me. If I fell out of the nest, I would return to them smelling unfamiliar, and the mother robin would no longer touch me.

I fell out of the nest.

My mother never missed a beat. She hung on to her beliefs and her people with one hand and onto me with the other. It was around that time she began to joke that she would stick with me no matter what I did, even if they sent me to jail. It might have been easier for her to understand jail than the kind of reading I was intent on doing.

Ironically, my obsession with reading, which took me away from my mother and from her church, allowed me to understand Mother during her last decade. I got much of what she said then because I began to understand it as metaphor.

# FIELD NOTE 7

## REMEMBERING PAST SELVES

*I am writing this on a Sunday afternoon, looking at
our backyard where the fall perennials are blooming
scarlet and yellow. Philadelphia is a place I could not
have imagined on that evening in Lincoln, Nebraska,
as I listened to "Purple People Eater" and did my algebra. As the sun
goes down, the azaleas and rhododendrons and lilacs create intimate
shapes against the bluish haze of dusk. I am older than my mother was
back then. Soon I will be old enough to be the grandmother of that
child—myself, a long time ago. If I could, I would put my hand on her
shoulder and tell her what I know about metaphor.*

*Out the window of my study, in the purple of sunset, I watch
a rabbit emerge from an azalea bush, stitch our backyard, and
disappear into the English ivy by the back fence. He's tiny, just
shedding his baby fluff for the speckled camouflage of adult fur. He
must have been born last spring. Frost on the grass, tender young
lettuce, a juicy carrot—the images he sees and remembers must be
brief, instinctual. I have a very different kind of memory than he does.
It includes poems I dashed in haste two decades ago when my child
was still so young I could lift him off the couch onto my lap. It includes
the recollection of myself as an earnest, believing child, and the story
of myself as a teenager, damned and trudging the streets of Lincoln,
after dark. These are stages in a journey—the child, the disillusioned
teenager, the mother, the poet, the grandmother—stations on the way
toward learning what it means to be human. They are not unlike the
many mothers who lived inside Mother.*

*Chapter 27*

# LAST KINHAVEN

The cardinals are making a racket in the trees outside our bedroom window. I roll over sleepily and threaten to buy a BB gun. Daniel reminds me that it's not fair to feed birds in the backyard and shoot them in the side yard. So I yawn, get up, and look out to see rose light streaking the eastern sky. A slight breeze is shaking the purple irises on their haughty stems.

"Shall we take Mother to Kinhaven in August?" I ask.

"But remember what happened last year."

"I thought she had fun."

"She got so tired."

"But it would give her a break."

"Okay, sure, let's take her."

He feels qualms and in my bones I do, too. But I have given up the possibility that Mother could come to live with us, and I'm on the lookout for other ways of including her. She's gone with us to Kinhaven for years. For decades it's been our role to take her on vacation. Neither of us can bear to leave her out. I dial American Airlines, mindful that this is the first time she isn't booking herself.

Pulling into the soggy meadow, which is Kinhaven's weekend parking lot, we spot Jack throwing a Frisbee. Whooping and laughing, he and his friends close in on our car. They look tan and strong as young gods. In the rosy air of sunset, and the smell of newly mown grass, I detect romance. How remarkable to be sixteen and healthy and blessed with nearly inexhaustible potential.

I hope it's catching.

I glance at Mother. Her dark eyes stare absentmindedly at the horizon. Her fuchsia button-up blouse looks several sizes too big for her. I wonder whether she's lost weight since I last saw her. Is she shrinking? I go to her, put my arm around her, and ask whether she'd like me to take her to the inn.

"I thought we were going to hear music," she protests.

"We are, if you're okay," I tell her.

"Is there something wrong with me?"

"Just checking."

In the concert hall Daniel finds seats for three in the second row, ensuring that Mother won't need to climb far on the risers. She takes Daniel's hand and he helps her up. Since Vermont evenings can be chilly, she's wearing her teal mohair coat.

In the warm hall, she stands in front of her seat trying to shed the coat, but she can't free her arthritic right arm. Daniel gently untangles her and hands me the coat. I drape it over her chair.

Mother sits down.

"Who's going to preach?" she asks in a holiday voice. I begin to laugh, thinking she's launched into her cut-up mode. But she isn't laughing.

"It's Kinhaven, Mom. The kids play music."

In the car on the way up she was subdued, but at least she ate a good lunch and she made sense.

I hand her a program. "Look! Mozart!"

"I know him," she tells me gleefully. "He visited me in Dallas once."

⁓

The first piece is Shostakovich's Tenth Symphony. The Shasty Ten, as Jack has lovingly called it all summer, was composed when Stalin ruled the Soviet Union. The piece has a big reputation for intimidating players and harrowing audiences. Although Jack is only a sophomore in high school, Jerry, the conductor of the orchestra and director of the camp, has appointed him to be concertmaster for this piece. Jack is psyched about the honor, and we're insanely proud of him. Daniel and I have looked forward to this concert all summer.

Jack comes out to applause, nods at the oboe for an A, and starts tuning his violin. All the instruments, section by section, swarm in a transcendent cacophony. I love to hear an orchestra tune up. It is the sound of community, a melody in and of itself, each voice speaking with a purpose that serves the whole.

Mother tugs on my shirt. "Do they pay people to turn the music?"

"What music, Mom?"

"You know, that thingamajig they put on the … The *music!*"

"Oh no. The kids turn their own pages. You remember how it is."

"No sireeee! I don't remember," she announces cheerfully.

As the kids finish tuning, the hall falls silent. They sit with their instruments in rest position, waiting for the conductor to step to the podium. They are racehorses before the gates open at the Kentucky Derby. No one talks. No one coughs.

Mother abruptly catapults into the air. She turns around and fusses with her coat. Maybe she was sitting on a lump. I smile at her reassuringly. She plunks down briefly, wiggles, then pops up again to adjust the coat a different way.

Daniel tries to pat it into place for her, but it slithers off the chair.

"Are you okay, Mom?" I whisper.

"It's being naughty," Mother bellows into the silent hall.

Daniel stands to help her, but the lining of the coat is slippery and it keeps sliding down. Mother grabs and shakes it as if she were a golden retriever with a rat.

"Why don't I just hold it in my lap?" I whisper. I confiscate the coat.

She snatches it away from me. "I'm cold. I need that!" she bawls, brandishing the bright garment in the air. I am aware that we're becoming a spectacle.

Just then Jerry sweeps in from the wings. He leaps to the podium, shakes his hair from his eyes, raises his baton, and holds it quivering in the air. The kids lift their instruments. Mother is still standing in the middle of the second row, turned toward the back of the hall, gazing at her coat, which is now, again, on the floor. For a minute Jerry seems to be waiting to give the downbeat until she seats herself. Time slows down and warps forward. I gently try to pull Mother down. She glances at my right hand, which is tugging at her, and shouts, "What are you doing?"

Every eye in the hall is on us.

Jerry's hand plunges into the downbeat. This calls forth a mighty jangle of clashing chords. The violinists' bows bite into their strings. The clarinets wail as if breaking loose from the orchestra. Then the brass marches in like an army of demons.

Mother stands openmouthed, transfixed by the terrifying music.

Out of the corner of my eye I see a blur of people to our right and behind us, staring at us, apparently waiting to see what we will do.

Mother is standing with her face toward the rows in back of us, doggedly trying to fold her coat. I tug at her, hoping against hope that she will not bellow again. I wonder whether Jerry, who does not tolerate fools, will stop the orchestra and pivot to look at us. But Jerry is too classy to be distracted. His hands gouge the air and his hair flies as he pounds out the terrifying dissonance.

Suddenly Mother is shuffling away from me, down the row, past peoples' knees, toward the aisle. I thought she was being contrary, but she must be disoriented.

I get up and follow her. As I step over people, all the way down the row, I whisper "Excuse me, excuse me, excuse me."

Mother wanders down the right aisle toward the orchestra in front. She's a small, stooped figure in a bright fuchsia blouse and dark skirt. Veering to the right, she disappears into a roughed-out space that serves as the green room for the stage. She shambles past the distinguished brass teachers who stand listening in the doorway. As I push past them, apologizing, following her, the percussion player onstage begins banging on the timpani. The vibrations travel from my feet up to my sinuses.

The room smells of rosin. It's cluttered with scores and instrument cases and music stands. Moving to the open music storage, Mother picks up a score, examines it, and puts it down again. I go to her, drape my arm around her, and say in a low voice, "Are you okay, Mom?" She smiles at me blankly. I realize she can't hear me. I ask again, but the clarinets are screeching.

She shambles off.

During the entire hour-long piece, she travels. I pursue her, trying to convince her to rest. She stares at me in puzzlement. When I lay a hand on her, she shrieks. She doesn't seem to remember who I am or what this place is or why she's here. Her aimless wandering rips the heart right out of the music for me. This is the very woman who taught me most of what I know about decorum and common sense. But the body that looks like my mother's seems to house someone else. The drive to Vermont, coupled with the flight from Dallas, has utterly unhinged her. Or maybe it's the wild clashing of the Shostakovich. I should have known better than to bring her here.

All night she keeps opening the door of our cabin and wandering into the Vermont woods. Hearing her, I stumble into the clearing, head for the trees, round her up, and herd her back to her bed. In ten minutes she's up again, shuffling out the door. I rouse myself and find her. All night I listen for her. She rambles and I pursue her. Under the moon the gentle, forested Vermont hills look ghoulish. Longing for sleep, repeating the same pointless journey over and over, I feel despair.

## Chapter 28

# A CHANGE OF HEART

The night we get back to Philadelphia, Mother eats vast quantities of dinner and sleeps for fourteen hours. The next morning, I crack the door to check on her. She looks defenseless in our guest room, huddled under three or four quilts, breathing regularly. I tiptoe into the darkened room, over to the dresser, where her medications flock together. I know she's supposed to be taking Zoloft. But Zoloft isn't among the medications on the dresser. I glance over my shoulder at her. The bedspread moves up and down. I feel comforted. I used to check on my children this way.

Alone in our kitchen, I page through the family phone book and try to make an appointment for Mother with our family doctor, but in the next two days he has no openings. This is probably for the best, I think. She needs her doctor in Dallas, who knows her history.

When Mother gets up around ten, she apologizes for missing breakfast. I make her toast with crunchy peanut butter and jam. Sitting on a stool in the kitchen she eats it while I wash the dishes. "This is just wonderful," she says with amazement. She holds the toast out and gazes lovingly at it.

I know how she feels, the astonishment a person can feel at

some very simple pleasure. I smile. Then I ask, "Mom, have you been taking your Zoloft?"

"Dr. Karp took me off it after six weeks."

"I don't think so. It takes an antidepressant six weeks even to kick in."

"What do you know about it, darling?" she asks, munching contentedly. "I'm the nurse."

I learned with my children that you have to pick your fights. This isn't worth fighting over. She's flying back to Dallas in two days.

"When are we going to Kinhaven?" she wonders.

"We already went," I say. "We're back."

"Oh, that's right."

"Remember the Shasty Ten?"

Maybe I shouldn't have asked her that. I don't know why I did. It was a test, I suppose, a question posed in hope. I wondered whether she would remember anything about the concert, anything about the awful night she kept trying to escape from her bed and I became her jailer.

"Wasn't Jack good?" she exclaims.

"He was," I agree.

"He just stood right up there in front of all those people and played all by himself. It goes to show, you can do anything you put your mind to!" she crows.

She is learning to dissemble, and I am trying to get used to her lapses. I glance at her and then away. I am quiet because I don't know what to say.

"What's wrong, darling?"

"Nothing," I say.

She cocks her head and frowns. "Are you upset?"

"Maybe a little."

She's alert suddenly, a fawn who's heard a sound in the forest. "Tell me what I did."

"It's not your fault, Mom."

Should I tell her what happened during the concert at Kin-haven? I should, maybe, because she's asking me. But she doesn't know what she's asking. Or does she?

How can I tell her without destroying her? Would telling her do any good at all?

Maybe it would scare her into taking her pills regularly.

"Why are you so quiet?" she asks.

"I'm thinking."

She gets very quiet herself, perched there on the kitchen stool with her legs twisted around the rungs, watching me carefully, as if the weather and everything else in the world depended on my mood.

A moment passes without either of us talking. I don't know what to say, where to go from here. So I tell her, "I'm a little sad. Maybe I need a change of heart."

Saying this out loud makes me laugh.

"What's so funny?" she demands.

I tell her I remember teaching a poetry workshop in Colorado a couple of summers before. "I had a student who was in her mid-forties, who told me that she'd had heart replacement surgery. A change of heart, she called it."

The worry lines between my mother's eyebrows deepen. "Is she okay?"

I tell her the story. In a couple of weeks she returned home, good as new. She'd been a lifelong vegetarian. But after surgery she found herself sneaking to McDonald's for a Big Mac. She went to the drive-through window because she didn't want to be recognized. She felt ravaged by guilt. She knew the misery of cattle and the brutality of slaughterhouses.

But she couldn't get over how good the Big Mac tasted. Later that week she slipped into her car and drove back. She found herself returning to McDonald's over and over. She disposed of the telltale wrappings in a public trash can and gargled with strong mouthwash. After weeks of this she got tired of creeping around like a crook. She made an appointment with her heart surgeon and told him.

My mother sits listening to me with dark, worried eyes. "And what did he say?"

"The surgeon explained that her donor was a twenty-five-year-old motorcyclist, and that he'd probably eaten a lot of Big Macs."

My mother, who is kind to animals, but doesn't see the point of vegetarianism, thinks for a moment and then starts laughing. Ha ha ha ha ha ha!

Watching her, I begin to giggle.

She laughs harder, which in turn makes me laugh harder.

One thing leads to another and before long I am quivering with the kind of helpless laughter that sometimes shook me when I was a teenager. It's the kind of hysterical gut-wrenching shoulder-quaking laughter that, to my horror, occasionally would strike me during a graduation or funeral.

Watching me, my mother laughs so hard she almost falls off the stool. She stands up, catching herself, holding on to the counter. This in turn increases my hysterics. We stand beside one another, both of us hooting and snorting, shaking soundlessly. Tears roll down our faces. We bend over, weak from laughing. We don't make any sound. We wheeze with mirth. I think I'll just close the door and leave the two of us together in our kitchen, laughing. It's the last time that ever happened.

# FIELD NOTE 8

## MEMORIZING A SCRIPT

*We're sitting in a theater in London, watching Shakespeare's* Henry IV, Part I. *I haven't memorized the play, but I can tell when the actor playing Falstaff walks onstage too early. He is a large man with a commanding bass voice. He delves right into his speech. His presence cannot be ignored. The other actors don't know what to do with him. Going with his lead would mean skipping ahead to the third act. I dig the nails of my right hand into my left palm.*

*Meanwhile, the other actors invent Shakespearian dialogue about the color and style of his doublet until it dawns on Falstaff that he's blundered into the wrong scene. When the penny drops, they can see it in his blue eyes. Between them they improvise several more lines to get him offstage.*

*Actors are threatened every night by the possibility of forgetting. I wonder how an actor's memory works, whether it is similar to my mother's memory, or my memory, which is always on shaky ground.*

*I write for the theater and I love actors. I want to write lines they can remember, dialogue with hooks they can hang on to. So I ask them sometimes, "What's a memorable line? How do you memorize?"*

*One tells me he memorizes lines as part of a conversation. He thinks of it as call and response. How terrifying! I tell him. How hairy, standing in front of four thousand people, trusting that the lines you hear—that slender little trickle of a momentary thread—will make you remember what to answer.*

*Another actor tells me she remembers her lines as part of blocking. The location where she's standing when she delivers them reminds her of what to say.*

217

Think of it. Standing on the red carpet where Agamemnon once vowed to kill their daughter, his wife, Clytemnestra, holds up the bloody heart of her husband. She's just hacked it out. You are the other daughter, the daughter who has escaped. You walk on and stand on the red carpet. Everyone in the house is looking at you and you try to recall what you're supposed to say.

## Chapter 29

# THE DIVIDE

Two days after the nightmare at Kinhaven, I deliver Mother to
a starched and professional American Airlines flight attendant.
She assures me that Mother *will be conveyed* safely to my sister.

I abhor the passive voice, which sneaks under the wire of civ-
ilization with creepy sentences in which no one takes responsibility. *Will be conveyed!* Two decades earlier, by contrast, when
I handed Molly to a Philadelphia stewardess (as they used to be
called) the young woman promised me that she herself would
place Molly in my mother's arms in Dallas. But now, who knows
whether Mother will get to the place she belongs?

*This is what things have come to!* I storm as I drive home. A
world gone mad with terrorism leads to draconian protocols at
the airport, and they, in turn, lead to passive sentences.

———

At home, I call my sister to report on our catastrophic trip to
Vermont. I stumble all over myself, trying to convey my apolo-
gies. My mother is, after all, Julie's mother, too. I am sending
her back in worse condition than she was in when Julie sent her
to me.

"It isn't your fault," Julie replies graciously.

"God help us, Julie, most of the time she was here she made no sense."

"Now you know what I mean when I tell you some of the stuff that goes on here."

I'm concerned that Julie is not absorbing the extent of the emergency. She'll be picking Mother up at the airport in an hour. I feel a pressing need to warn her. "I don't mean a few little slips of the tongue," I tell Julie. "It's been all day, every day."

"I know."

"We need to find out what's wrong. We need to get Mother to another doctor for a second opinion."

"I canceled her appointment with the neurologist because you didn't want her to go."

"How about a gerontologist?"

"Sure." But her voice lacks urgency. Julie sees Mother in her own familiar places. Julie has not witnessed the mother I've just seen.

"I'll find some doctors," I volunteer.

"Dr. Karp is one of the best internists in Dallas," Julie retorts.

"I'm not crazy about him," I tell Julie.

"Why?"

"He's condescending."

"He used to teach at Baylor."

"He's the one who told us to take Mother to a gerontologist!" I snap. "I'll get you some names of doctors," I volunteer again.

Julie raises her voice. "No! That makes no sense! Rich and I know reams of medical people."

"You and Rich have so much to do. Let me set up this appointment." This is one way I can be sure it will happen very soon.

"No!" Julie barks. "I'll still have to get involved with scheduling."

"I'll fly to Dallas and take Mother for the second opinion," I offer. But the truth is, I don't know how soon I could do that, since I have several business trips coming up.

"Before this is over, you'll need to fly here more often than you want." Julie's warning sounds ominous.

"We need a conference call," I say, hoping Daniel can help me reason with Julie.

"What for?" she asks.

"Mother can't live alone anymore." Given Mother's wandering at Kinhaven, I am now terrified for her most basic safety.

"I've already requested information about the next level of care," Julie tells me.

"You mean assisted living?" I ask.

"Yes."

Christian Care, where Mother lives, now offers two levels of care beyond her neighborhood of independent bungalows: assisted living and an Alzheimer's unit.

Anger unfurls its red flags in my chest. I wonder why Julie didn't tell me earlier that she was looking into assisted living for mother. "I'll call them and have them send me information," I say, trying to keep my voice steady. "After we all read it, we'll have a conference call."

"I realize you feel helpless," Julie says. This strikes me as patronizing.

"I thought we agreed to confer about everything," I counter.

"I wouldn't move Mother without telling you."

I feel so enraged that I can barely talk. Dimly I see myself standing way off, on the horizon, a tiny, critical dot of a self, listening to the real me here, arguing with my sister. I understand that I am much more irate than the situation calls for, but I don't know how to stop. I can't. "Maybe you could e-mail me with some dates and times for a conference call," I say, ending the conversation with as much civility as I can muster.

*Now you've done it,* I think after I hang up. I know that if we fight, Mother will get caught in the middle.

I go to bed. *Oh Lord, support us all the day long,* I think. But I'm too angry to pray. I pitch from side to side, too angry to fall asleep.

I turn on the light. I run a finger along the books on my bedside table and pick one called *Spiritual Classics,* edited by my friend Emilie Griffin. I leaf through it, reading a sentence here, a sentence there. It all sounds insipid. It all feels stupid. In the past I've found wisdom and consolation in this book. But fury has put me into a world no book can enter.

So, like Catholics who I believed as a child were misguided, I decide to pretend to pray, which might lead to real prayer, if I'm lucky. And that, in turn might lead to sleep. I open the prayer book and read. *O God of peace, who has taught us that in returning and rest we shall be saved, in quietness and in confidence shall be our strength: By the might of thy Spirit lift us, we pray thee to thy presence, where we may be still and know that thou art God.*

*Chapter 30*

# SEARCH FOR A SEMINARY WIFE

I wake up the next morning feeling like a hostage. At nine on the dot, I call Christian Care and ask for information about their assisted living facility, which is called Bentley.

Then I do what I've always done. I decide to read.

I e-mail Julie that I want to read Mother's medical records. I can either write directly to the doctors, or I can send Julie a letter and she can present it to them. I don't want to preempt her standing with Mother's doctors and I don't want them to become defensive about a lawsuit. But I need to know what's going on.

Julie responds that she has no idea why I want Mother's records, but if I send the letters to her, she'll forward them. In three weeks or so we receive thick packets with Mother's medical history.

Meanwhile, Julie drives Mother to Dr. Karp. He discovers that she hasn't been taking her Zoloft. Otherwise she behaves so normally during the appointment that he doesn't see what the big deal is. I scathingly mention to my sister that's because he's not very sensitive to his patients. But that's not Julie's view and

Julie has now taken charge. Of course, Mother is back at home in Dallas now. She's no longer so disoriented.

Wild for information, Daniel and I ask Mother questions on the phone every night and every night she equivocates. Or possibly she can't remember enough facts to offer them up. I can get no reliable intelligence from her and neither can Daniel.

Daily I pummel Julie with questions and suggestions: How soon can we get Mother into assisted living? Have you taken her to the new gerontologist? Give her Ensure. I'll fly to Dallas and hire someone to make sure she's taking her pills. While I'm there, I'll check on the assisted living facility. Do you need the name of another gerontologist?

Julie writes back: Stop! This is making me crazy.

I feel steady and unaccountable fury. I read books and articles about dementia. Many of them say that people who care for Alzheimer's patients experience anger. Knowing this does not help me become less angry.

When Mother's medical records arrive, I take the bulky folder to a gig in Boston and read them on the plane. Every minute I'm not at a podium speaking or having dinner with people, I pore over them. There's no narrative thread. It's a thicket of codes and medical jargon designed, apparently, to make it impossible for the patient and her family to decipher them.

When I get home I call doctor friends to ask for referrals in Dallas. Then I tell Julie that one of them can get Mother a speedy appointment with a woman gerontologist at South Western Medical. In our regular evening phone call to Mother that night, I propose this doctor, but she puts her foot down. She's not going to any woman doctor.

Period.

Julie e-mails me that she can't force Mother to go.

I keep working on Mother during daily phone calls. I send Julie an e-mail: "Time is of the essence."

Julie tells me she'll read my e-mail when she has more time.

I ask Daniel to draft an e-mail, which I send over my name, informing Julie that Daniel and I need to be involved in the actual decision-making process about Mother's health, rather than merely being informed by Julie about what she's doing.

Julie fires back: "Let me share with you how I spent my day." She lists a number of meetings with city officials and corporation executives. She is raising millions of dollars for a new Volunteer Center building.

I am both impressed and increasingly infuriated. I call the Dallas gerontologist and talk with her at length, giving her Mother's background. I schedule a trip to Dallas to intervene. Nearly every day I urge Julie either to move Mother to assisted living or to find someone to help her take her pills.

Julie tells me she is filling out the application to move Mother to assisted living. By now Mother is taking fifteen different pills every day. Or rather, that's how many have been prescribed. God only knows whether she's actually taking them. Julie assures me that she is, but given what I saw in August, I doubt it.

I write Julie an e-mail suggesting for the tenth or eleventh time that we need to hire someone to help Mother take her pills. Mother can afford to have someone come in, I point out. I offer to do the interviews to find someone while I'm in Dallas. I schedule a flight to Dallas and let Julie know I'll be arriving in a couple of weeks.

Julie ignores the issue of hiring a helper for Mother, but her e-mail is all hospitality. I am always welcome in Dallas, she says. If I want, I can stay with her and Rich. I understand that this is a generous offer, considering our feud, but I am too angry to appreciate it much.

I write back telling her that I need to stay with Mother.

We always sign our e-mails "Love."

⁓

Around this time I'm reshelving a book in the guest room, I notice a black-and-white photo of Julie and me. Julie was three, I was six. We are sitting shoulder to shoulder, outfitted in twin dresses. We're facing the camera and the photographer Mother hired to take pictures of the family. This is my mother's original copy, the one I asked for several years ago. It's hacked in half. At some point, Mother took scissors and sliced the two of us apart. When I inherited the picture, I taped the two of us back together and put us into one frame.

⁓

It is ancient, tribal wisdom that a mother can only flourish if her children cooperate while caring for her in her old age. So far neither Julie nor I have had the audacity to make unilateral choices about our mother's health or money, though Julie is usually quicker to make decisions than I am. Before long in this story, Julie will fire one doctor without consulting me and then another, though to be fair, if I'd I been consulted about the last one, I'd have concurred, and she knew that before she fired him.

Most important, though, the two of us have tried to be kind and to not get irritated with one another, to decide together what's best for Mother. We have written hundreds of e-mails to one another, most of them sisterly, only a few of them angry, some of them placating, about Mother's doctor's appointments, her weight, her eating, her sleeping, her frame of mind, the pea soup she had for dinner, the way she's stopped painting. Each of us has argued for what we think is right for her. We love each other and we both know that to act unilaterally would involve the risk of blame from the other for the rest of our lives.

The trouble is, we see two different Mothers. How could we not? All my life Mother has blissfully informed me, "You kids are different as night and day." This is what she meant: I'm the brilliant but helpless, hapless, oblivious artist. And I live in exotic Philadelphia, which she conceives of as her getaway spot. Julie is the practical genius. She knows how to flip the circuit breakers. When Julie was ten Mother consulted her before she bought a new car. Julie knows Mother's Dallas friends and shares Mother's no-nonsense, everyday landscape: She's lost a button, she's crashed into an oncoming car, she needs a roofer to fix a leak.

But hold on. I'm pretty good with insurance and roofers and buttons and circuit breakers. I know how to climb into our dark basement. I've shingled a roof and taken auto mechanics courses. And Julie adores opera. Neither of us relishes our confining roles. But for better or for worse, my mother's way of defining the two of us has shaped our differing views of what she herself needs. It's no surprise that we sometimes disagree. How could it be otherwise?

And that's not the only factor that seems to conspire against harmony. There are also the differences in our geographical perspectives, our old childhood rivalries, the anxiety and rage and heartbreak we separately feel as we watch our mother fall apart, and our ardently held, conflicting political views, amplified by a foul-spirited decade of American politics. How easy it would be for us to turn on one another. There are endless opportunities to second guess one another's decisions.

It terrifies me that the bond between my sister and me could shatter under the weight of this shared caregiving. That would leave us, maybe for the rest of our lives, without one another. And if Mother knew, it would destroy her.

———

It's only after Mother sees the female gerontologist and then Dr. Karp gets wind of it, that he at last orders lab tests for Mother.

"Good work!" I tell Julie. I am overjoyed and relieved.

Meanwhile, the gerontologist prescribes a different set of medications and also orders lab tests. She emphasizes the need to get Mother to a safe place, where someone can help her take her pills regularly. She argues that we should move Mother to the assisted living facility close to her own office.

Julie argues vociferously against the move, informing me that if we move Mother there, Julie won't be able to see her nearly as often. This makes sense, of course, but to me it sounds like intimidation. It would be so much better for Mother to have a woman doctor, a gerontologist, someone who is not Dr. Karp.

A week later, Julie calls me to say the gerontologist still hasn't gotten back to her with Mother's lab results. The woman doesn't return Julie's calls.

Julie points out that this is the doctor I recommended.

Meanwhile, Dr. Karp calls Julie to deliver the good news that the tests he ordered for Mother have come back and now he thinks her short-term memory loss must be caused by a galloping thyroid. He announces his new plan, prescribing tablets to lower her thyroid level. Eventually, Julie tells me, he will zap her thyroid gland and then give her pills to bring her thyroid level up to normal.

"What does that mean?" I ask Julie. "Zap?"

"Take out her thyroid."

"Surgery?" I yelp. "She's eighty-six!"

"It's okay. Dr. Karp says it will work."

"No!" I fire back. "She's too old for surgery."

This is a hill I will die on.

I politely request that Julie ask Dr. Karp whether he means surgery.

Julie asks him.

No, he says. It's not a surgical procedure.

But I am not placated. Well then, what is it? Why would a doctor shut down a working organ if he didn't need to? Why not just give Mother medication to reduce her thyroid output? I get second opinions from doctors here. They tell me that to turn off her thyroid would be unusual. Instead her doctor could give her pills to lower her thyroid level.

Julie checks with Dr. Karp and then explains to me at complicated length why he prefers to zap her thyroid. It comes down to this: the thyroid medication might become less and less effective over years.

Does that usually happen? I ask.

Julie calls Dr. Karp to inquire.

Now that both her children are engaged at a high pitch in this skirmish about Mother's thyroid, she becomes chipper and begins to eat again. She sits up perkily at the table, chatters with the family, roars how good the food is, and asks for seconds. She begins to gain weight. Either this is proof that she needs us both hovering close, or else it's evidence that Dr. Karp's thyroid medication is working. Maybe both.

In the following weeks, Julie becomes increasingly irritated that the new gerontologist has not checked in about lab results. She repeatedly phones the woman to find out whether her lab results confirm those of Dr. Karp. But the woman has gone AWOL and she stays AWOL for weeks. When Julie finally reaches her, Julie reams her out but good. She makes oblique threats about a lawsuit, and announces that Mother is never coming back.

This Julie calls me to explain in painstaking detail.

I am annoyed that I wasn't consulted before Julie fired the female gerontologist. But I do not mention this to Julie, because Julie is already madder than hell. Instead I reply tartly that at least this second-opinion strategy brought us to a diagnosis that seems to be working. It has taken two doctors to get there, I point out. Dr. Karp didn't order lab tests for Mother until he knew that his rival, this second opinion doctor, was ordering them.

Julie's reply is short and cold.

I don't continue this line of reasoning because, really, in the end, it doesn't matter who's right. I don't want to fight with my sister, because I see darker, more threatening storm clouds gathering on the horizon. No matter which doctor prescribes them or how right they are for her, Mother either can't or won't take her pills regularly.

For weeks I nag Julie to hire someone to visit Mother every morning to make sure she takes them. Although Rich has plainly said that Mother can afford it, I think Julie doubts that. I doggedly press the case. Since Mother is so often lonely, now that she doesn't drive at all, maybe we could find someone who would spend several hours with her in the morning, someone who could talk and joke with her, who might read to her, who would unabashedly *like* her.

"Who?" Julie asks.

"We could place an ad."

"You mean in a paper?" Julie is thinking about the predators who will call, the feeble, the insane, the criminal.

"Well, maybe in the neighborhood paper."

"No. Mother needs someone who speaks her language."

I understand this is code. "I can call your church office," I suggest.

"Why do that? I see the church staff every Sunday morning."

"Will you talk to them?"

"All right."

"And if that doesn't work, how about finding a seminary wife?" I ask. Mother's minister teaches at the Dallas Theological Seminary. Over the years Mother has befriended many seminarians and their wives, inviting them to dinner, slipping them money, buying them clothes, taking care of their children.

But Julie points out that she'll be the one who will have to ride herd on whomever we hire. It's true. She lives there.

"Then what can we do to make sure Mother takes her medication?" I ask.

Julie, undaunted, announces that she will call Mother every morning and stay on the phone until she hears Mother swallow her pills.

I think Julie is losing her mind. "How will you know whether she's taken all of them?" I ask.

"I dole out her pills into those pill dispensers," she assures me.

"But sometimes Mother forgets she's taken them and takes two doses in one day."

"I know." Julie sighs.

"And remember the time she got mixed up? She took all the blue ones on Monday and the pink ones on Tuesday and the—"

"I know," Julie laments.

"And besides, who could keep calling her every morning? We need to hire someone like a seminary wife."

"Then *you* write an ad for a seminary wife."

"Good," I say. "I'll do it right away. I can interview the applicants when I'm there." I have a trip to Dallas scheduled in two weeks.

The next morning I compose an ad and e-mail it to the seminary. I do not spell out my mother's name or exact circumstances, but I list my name, phone number, and e-mail address, where people can apply for the job.

A day or so later, Julie calls to say that the office at the seminary intercepted my ad, which they cleverly figured out must refer to our mother. Some of the office workers at the seminary attend my mother's church. They're street smart and they're suspicious. They refused to post the copy before Julie read and approved it. So Julie is drawn in against her will.

And as for me, I am defined as the danger against whom the seminary is protecting my mother. Although these people greet me lovingly when I sit with her at the eleven o'clock service, although they know that I am her daughter, these people who have provided my mother sanctuary have plainly locked the church's door against me. I feel profoundly foiled. Angry as a nest of riled up hornets, I swarm without a place to land.

Julie tells me that she will take over the search for a seminary wife. But after I return from Dallas, weeks pass, months pass, and nothing happens. Mother is in danger of wandering like a nomad off the Christian Care campus and getting lost, or hit in traffic. She is almost certain to suffer a stroke or complications of her Crohn's disease from not taking her pills.

*Chapter 31*

# SIBLINGS AT WAR

More than twenty million adult children in America take care of a parent who is drifting into dementia. Many of these caretakers are siblings and they are torn by conflicts. One child lives in her parent's town, for instance, while the others don't. They occupy different places in the birth order, so growing up they absorbed different lessons. Each sibling has such a different relationship with the parent that her view of what her parent needs differs sharply from that of her siblings. Many suffer from rivalries that have never been worked out. Under the pressure of caring for a parent, that smoldering competition can explode into fires that burn the family tree right up. There's also the fact that the earning power of siblings varies, so they have unequal amounts of time and money to travel. And who judges what's fair between these presumably equal siblings? Not the parents, who are aging and besieged by their own problems.

Now imagine that the parents don't have enough money to live on. Then God help everyone.

—

One Saturday that fall I could not stop thinking about my tangled relationship with my sister. The following week I would be flying to Dallas again. I felt remorse. I had no idea when I was in my twenties, the trouble it would cause to live so far from my mother.

Maybe I should have known.

Should I?

I took a walk. I kicked the leaves.

The wind blew them back.

I kicked them harder.

When I was twenty-two, Mother moved to Dallas from Chicago, where we were all living. I did not follow her to Texas. In fact, later, in my late twenties, I took off with my husband for the East Coast. My sister moved to Dallas. But good grief, is a grown child obligated to follow her parents wherever they move?

The truth was I didn't want to live in Dallas.

Sometimes, just hearing my sister cast aspersions on Darwin's theory of evolution, listening to her diss Bill Clinton, I felt woozy. Gay people, I thought, should be allowed to make unions guaranteeing the same civil rights as I had in my own marriage. But she believed that would threaten the institution of holy matrimony. Unregulated corporations, I argued, had a bad track record, and I was furious when George Bush rolled back taxes on the wealthy. Julie, I guessed, spoke for a majority of the people in Texas, favoring business.

I was always an absurdity in Dallas. Without knowing a thing about that city, my mother had moved to a place I did not belong. I felt tongue-tied there. Not that I discussed politics or religion with my mother anymore. But the language my sister and I used to talk about these issues seemed retro-fitted to get us into endlessly entangling arguments.

Even as children, not surprisingly, the two of us had differences. They were small. It was a hairline crack in a sturdy bowl. I was the middle child, blond, serious, the reader, the empathetic, no-trouble kid. Julie was the caboose of the family. With her dark hair and quick, impulsive decisions, she skewed off into exciting projects that often worked, but sometimes ended in catastrophe.

When I chose to move to the East Coast and Julie chose Texas, the divide between us widened. We moved when we were in our twenties, joyfully following our hearts. We were so young that neither of us understood how deeply those moves would affect us. Our differences were enflamed by the hostility between factions in the two regions: the Bible Belt South and the liberal, secularized Northeast. By the time we were in our fifties, the divide between us had widened to a Grand Canyon. I chose a hundred-year-old fieldstone house while she chose a single-floor contemporary in a housing development with great light. She sent her kids to Baptist school while we sent ours to secular private schools. She worshipped at a Bible church while I am part of an Episcopal community. She rarely ever came here. I, who ardently love the verdant, rolling Pennsylvania countryside, found myself standing in lines at airports and spending almost a month a year in the parched and terribly mushrooming suburbs of Dallas.

I approach our front door, having resolved nothing. The wind is picking up and the brittle leaves click against one another as they scuttle down the front walk. A neighbor who is out jogging stops by and we chat about an upcoming block party. Then I close a couple of windows and steel myself to fly to Dallas after school the next afternoon. The trip to Dallas turns out to be horrific.

———

After a day of teaching and meetings at my university on the East Coast, my flight finally arrives at the Dallas–Fort Worth airport at midnight. I step into brutal heat. When I turn the key to start the red Ford Fiesta rental car, the voice of a preacher leaps into the air. "Brothers and sisters, get right with *Jee*-sus. Will you live to see tomorrow morn—?" I snap off the quivering sweet Southern tenor. At any time of the day or night about a quarter of the radio stations in the Dallas area feature radio preachers. Stopping to buy a Coke at a convenience store, I park beside two Ford trucks with rifles hanging in their back windows and DON'T MESS WITH TEXAS bumper stickers. Outside the store the drivers are loudly joking and swilling beer in T-shirts with torn-off sleeves and cowboy boots and ten-gallon hats, slapping their thighs and pounding one another's backs. They get threateningly quiet as I pass.

It's the turn of the millennium and Texas is basking in its most glorious hour. The whole country is listening to George Bush tell it like it is. Political pundits and talk show hosts like Bill O'Reilly and Glenn Beck and Rush Limbaugh rule the airwaves, not only in Texas, but all over the nation, which has become an echo chamber, reverberating with hate speech. At home and in their offices Julie and Rich display pictures of themselves arm in arm with George Bush. And in a year Julie will be invited to join Bush's national council on volunteerism, which meets several times a year in Washington, D.C.

I am remembering the last time I came to Dallas. While Julie and Rich and I sipped wine after dinner one night, I failed to notice that we are heading toward a debate about the Middle East. Suddenly we found ourselves in the thick of it. We wrangled over whether the Jews are God's chosen people. More chosen, that is, than the Palestinians. We fought over who has a right to the Holy Land. I was just launching into a diatribe about the way some Israelis in Jerusalem and the occupied West Bank brutalize Palestinian men in front of their children. Then

I came to. I looked around and tabulated where I was and what I was doing. I stopped. I knew the conversation would come to a bad end.

~

As I hurtle through the night toward Mother's house, I have a vision. Come November, I will fly here and take Mother to vote. I know she'll ask me who I'm voting for and I'll tell her the guy's name is Gore. G-O-R-E. I'll spell it for her. If Julie takes Mother to the polls, Mother will vote for Bush. This is part of the problem, I think. I jumped ship and became a Democrat during the Vietnam War. I'm the only Democrat in our family. For years I have been outnumbered and outvoted.

But of course I'm not flying to Dallas to help Mother vote. That's an infantile fantasy. It would involve nakedly using Mother. Still, I feel outraged that someone who stumbles around in the English language might be representing me as president, since the ability to speak English clearly indicates an ability to think clearly. My wrath about the election blends into the smoldering rage I feel as I watch our mother unravel. And my rage is mirrored in the incivility I see all around me. On the radio, on television, in newspapers, and online, everywhere people are insulting one another. And I am just as foul-tempered as everyone else. I can't see how to stop it, and I am miserably aware that it might ruin any chance my sister and I have of taking care of our mother peacefully together.

~

This rage about politics feels familiar and personal. No wonder. It's the child of the split between me and my mother when I was in college. My sister, unlike me, stuck with my mother's politics. I was the daughter turncoat who protested the Vietnam

War. Though I haven't thought about it for decades, I begin to remember my first trips to Dallas to visit my mother, who had just moved there. I remember lethal, boiling fights over that war, made the more exasperating by the fact that I needed to be polite to the man my mother had recently married, the one whose house I was sleeping in, the one who insulted Eleanor Roosevelt every time he got a chance.

During the years before my stepfather died, when I visited them in Dallas, my mother and I haunted museums and stores, never even thinking about politics. But one night at dinner, my stepfather, who was usually mild-mannered and openhanded, began ranting against what he characterized as the spoiled, presumptuous, out-of-control youth who were taking over buildings on campuses.

That would be me, I thought.

I got up from their dining room table, clearing plates, and then paced their kitchen, fuming. I stuffed a red plaid dish towel into my mouth. In truth, at the time, my mind wasn't made up about the war. I sometimes lamented the inexperience, the entitlement, the self-centeredness of our generation. But my mother and Jim's staunch, unflinching refusal to think or to investigate or to consider alternatives drove me nuts.

After a while, I came back, sat down, and explained to Mother that Josh and Mike and Larry—young men from Wheaton she had frequently fed, quick-witted and decent young men, kids like me, looking forward with pleasure and hope to their lives—should not have to die because *old men* like Lyndon Johnson had the power to order them to war. The implication was that my mother and stepfather were equally as selfish and twisted as the old men.

"I'm sorry," my mother said sweetly, "that your generation

isn't willing to sacrifice." She meant the way her own generation had sacrificed in World War II, for the sake of the country.

"It isn't the same kind of war!" I snarled.

"Daddy Jim served in the army," my mother said, beaming at her new husband.

"Not on the front line, sweets," he rumbled modestly in his South Georgian accent.

"We're not exactly fighting Hitler!" I snapped.

"We're fighting Communism," my stepfather drawled.

"We shouldn't be there. Vietnam has nothing to do with this country's self interest."

"Do you want America to go Commie?" he asked me pleasantly.

My mother, smelling conflict, turned anxiously to me. "Paula called. She wants to take us to lunch." I felt like a trophy my mother wanted to show off to her new friends in Dallas.

"I have to grade freshmen themes," I said.

"Lunch at Neiman Marcus!" Mother sang, trying to tempt me.

"Maybe some other day."

A cold, hard wall grew up between us.

For years we stood on opposite sides and glowered at one another. We spoke to each other about the war in prefabricated, ready-made language codes that we had probably picked up from radio or television. After that, the subject of the war flared up only occasionally, but it lay beneath the surface of our visits, the implacable conflict that defied resolution or even civil discussion.

The differences between Julie and me, as we struggled to care for mother, I begin to realize, had their roots in that day at my Mother and Jim's house.

# FIELD NOTE 9

## MAKING A LIST

*I sit in church, thinking about that most famous of Mother's own personal memory devices, the list. Maybe it's genetically coded in her offspring, because it certainly lives on. Molly's oldest, Sophia, began writing lists at the age of five. As the crucifer carries the gold cross to the back of the sanctuary, my mind snaps back to what I'm doing here. We are standing, singing "Be Thou My Vision." Then we shuffle down the aisles, chatting, pulling on our mittens and hats.*

*When I get home, I find my three-page list of what to pack. It's a memory device I've been compiling for months. Tonight at six p.m. I will meet twelve students at Philadelphia International Airport and fly with them on British Airways to Heathrow. We will stay in London for five weeks. My job is to teach theater and to help the students discover and explore the city. I pull out two suitcases, toss them on the floor, and stand at the mouth of my closet.*

*I own too many clothes. Advertising, or maybe the forced asceticism of my youth, makes me buy too much. I've just taken in our DustBuster to be repaired (again). Yesterday we retrieved from Ernie my black Toyota with its tuned engine and new fan belts. I keep a running list of what needs to be repaired, cleaned, and bought. I am a contemporary woman. I am the servant of objects.*

*I decide to take as little as possible to London. I wad up my memory device and throw it into the trash. What's the least I can live with for five weeks? I begin to think of this excursion as a spiritual retreat. I don't know what that means, exactly, but all afternoon, lyrics I never memorized echo in the sanctuary of my memory:*

    Be Thou my vision, O Lord of my heart
    Naught be all else to me, save that Thou art
    Heart of my own heart whatever befall
    Still be my vision O Ruler of all

## Chapter 32

# NAILING THE WALLS TO THE FOUNDATION OF THE UNIVERSE

My mother craved certainty. She was driven by anxiety about change. I realize now, as I could not have at the age of twenty-three, that my mother had her own history, which predisposed her to see the world as she did. She was a teenager during the Depression, when her parents lost a good bit of their farmland. I can see her staring out the kitchen window of the farmhouse at the hailstorm moving across their property, listening to her mother and father discussing in muffled voices whether they would have to sell a section of land and which section it would be. In 1933, at the age of sixteen, for $60 a month she taught twenty-two kids in a one-room schoolhouse in rural Minnesota. My father dropped out of college. After they married, they wanted something they could count on at any cost, something that would not change. They experienced a conversion.

Shortly after they were married, they spent a blowout weekend at the cabin of some friends on Lake Miltona, a resort community close to Parkers Prairie, where my father served as postmaster before he took over the general store from his father.

Apparently during that weekend, which later became notorious in our family stories, a number of couples my parents' age had celebrated the mild June weather by drinking and dancing and playing cards on the shore of the lake. My father had grown up with these people in Parkers, and his with-it childhood friends now socialized as couples. He had brought his farm wife home to the town and she had, apparently, passed the test. They'd been swimming, the women in their flowered World War II bathing suits with pleated skirts, the men daring one another to take off their shorts and skinny dip. For Saturday night dinner they splurged on butter and eggs and meat and they told ribald jokes and bet a small amount on card games. The next day they skipped church, lingering at the beach until late in the afternoon.

That Sunday night, as my mother and father drove back to town, they talked about the money they had lost, which was not much, but which they needed to pay the rent, and about the drinking, and the way they had reveled in the loose lifestyle of my father's friends. Later that night, in a solemn ritual that my mother could still describe when she was eighty, together they carefully descended the precarious stairs to the furnace. My father lit it and my mother tossed their playing cards into its yellow jaws and they watched as flames lunged to devour the pack. After that, my parents did not allow cards in their house. They renounced alcohol of all kinds.

My parents' love of stability and permanence may have been what made my father design and build three houses for us with his own hands. He knew the plumbing was reliable because he had put it in himself. He could depend on the electrical system, because he had wired the place. The first house he built was in Parkers Prairie. Then he bought and hauled a garage from Parkers to Lake Miltona and renovated it. The third house he built in

Lincoln, where my parents moved us so my mother could find a job, where after my father died, we kids could save money by living at home while we attended the University of Nebraska. None of us went to school there. But we could have. What my parents wanted was insurance. If we needed a university, it would be close.

Every day after school I watched my father build our third house. On a spring afternoon when fledgling leaves were budding on the dogwoods, I stood beside him at the edge of our new lot line on the outskirts of Lincoln and watched an earth-moving machine slowly roll onto our land. The din of the machine made us plug our ears with our fingers. I could feel vibrations in my feet. As its jaws bit cleanly through the grass, I felt as if something inside me was flying together. The way to start building a house, I understood, is simply to subtract earth.

For months afterward, whenever I wasn't in school or doing my homework, I was helping to raise the walls of our house. My father let me pound nails until every time I whammed the head three times, the shaft flew straight in. The hammer hit home and I thought, *there*. That's in there, done, eternal. I still hear the clang of my handsome father's pounding, and I can feel the rhythmic swing of his freckled right arm as he nailed the raw studs in place. He was *going to die, going to die, going to die*. For himself, he wasn't afraid. He wanted to finish this house before he left us. I suspect he wanted to anchor the studs of that house to the foundation of the universe.

My father was not afraid to die, and my mother was not afraid to lose him, because they both felt convinced of the one most essential and final thing. With absolute certainty they believed that to be absent from us was to be present with the Lord. There we would all be reunited. My parents repeated that often as a fact. As a result they faced my father's death with bravery that— especially since I've been a parent—seems inconceivable to me.

My father, who was terminally ill, never became an invalid. He was still looking for adventure until the week before he died.

The certainty that buoyed my mother until her death fifty years later was esteemed among my fundamentalist people, many of whom later joined the "political right." It was strengthened by hymns. We sang about blessed assurance. We harmonized, *"I'm a child of the King,"* and *"When the roll is called up yonder, I'll be there."* Our private dialect and pot lucks and prayer chains and Christian school reinforced the certainty my parents so prized. We lived in a feedback loop like a recording studio with a reverb that never quieted down. But that kind of absolute, unambiguous, dead certainty is a value I don't favor anymore. True enough, that kind of assurance feels comforting. But people who are certain they're right won't compromise, and without compromise human relationships and democracy might as well be dead.

My odd and secret love for the green fluorescent cross at Bible camp was my earliest inkling that some life force might be stronger than the need for certainty. Following it, I discovered the shining ambiguity of this world, the endless unfolding of it, the mystery of how a tree can be both a tree and a symbol, standing for something besides itself. I found the possibility of paradox, and also the ongoing chance that I might be wrong. I didn't know at ten that I was defying my mother's literal way of reading when I bought that cross—well, not when I bought it, exactly, but when I loved it—because it wasn't the buying but the loving that started the acts of attention that taught me to honor ambiguity.

～

So after my Thursday classes I've flown to Dallas, and it's now after midnight. I rent a car and head for Mother's house. I'm deeply preoccupied. I'm pondering how I will convince my sister to hire someone to help mother take her pills. I'm wondering what to say to Mother's minister and her friends at Lake Ridge Bible Church, who have blocked me from posting a request at the Seminary that might help us find someone to help her.

Then I understand that I've overshot 635. Suddenly I know I've taken the wrong exit at the spaghetti bowl. It's one in the morning, and I've taught all day, and I'm stupid with fatigue. I exit again, hoping to retrace my steps, but the new express-way shoots off in a direction I don't recognize. I exit several more times, trying to get back on 635, but each time I'm further entangled until I have no idea where I am.

I doubt that I can make it to Mother's house. The lights above the expressway have been turned off. The lights of stores and fast food restaurants have been turned off. The landscape is a forbidding witches' brew of unknowns. I can barely make out the malignant new subdivisions that have been hastily tossed up on both sides, brand-new today, destined to age badly tomor-row. The landscape I'm passing might as well be Saudi Arabia, because I recognize no landmarks. I'm driving at seventy miles per hour farther and farther from anything I know.

I contemplate pulling off, locking the doors, and sleep-ing, but that wouldn't be safe. Sixteen wheelers drive this thing at seventy-five miles an hour and who knows what rov-ing opportunistic criminals might spot prey and pull over. Some automatic pilot inside me keeps driving, scanning anxiously for a place to exit where I can ask for directions. For thirty miles, forty miles, fifty miles I barrel away from Mother with no idea where I am.

Then I spot a Wendy's with lights on. I exit and speak to a pimply high school kid at the takeout window, the only part of the restaurant that's open. From memory he reels off the five

turns and one U-turn I need to make. I jot notes on my toll
ticket. I thank him. I waft up thanks.

—

I'm still pondering, as I kiss Mother hello and get ready for
bed in her small second bedroom, how inflammatory this visit
might be. Given my differences from my sister, our potential
for anger and hatred scare me. The Other Side for me is not
Mother now. The Vietnam War is over. Vietnam, thank God,
has become green and prosperous, and Mother has long since
forgotten about politics. Now the arguments have shifted to Iraq
and Afghanistan and the national budget and the Middle East
and health care and gay rights and the national debt and taxing
millionaires. For a moment my nerve fails. I fear that Julie and I
will have nothing to say to one another. Or we will say hideous
things that we can never take back.

What happens next in our family now depends not upon
Mother, but on my sister and me.

I am angry at my sister and I don't know how to stop.

—

Then I remember. Just days before flying to Dallas, I'd run a
poetry writing workshop in a nursing home in a particularly
depressed suburb of Philadelphia. The wiry, energetic director
of the nursing home informed me that she had invited a special
needs class from the local high school to join us. This freaked
me out slightly because I knew the age differences in the audience would be huge. I wondered how I'd ever find something
that would work for both groups.

Soon the students arrived. The young women were sporting
a lot of low-cut black and purple lingerie. Many of their orifices
were beringed with metal, and the entire bodies of several of

the men were smothered in tattoos. The white-haired nursing home residents, who were wearing carpet slippers and flowered cotton dresses with zippers up the front, glared stonily as the students trooped in. Each group sat in its own little enclave with a no-man's-land of empty chairs between them.

I asked them to close their eyes and picture the house where they had lived when they were ten. Obediently they squeezed their eyes shut. Suppose they were walking up the front side-walk, I suggested. What did they smell? The greenness of grass as a father mowed? A mother cooking spaghetti sauce in the kitchen? What did they hear? Quarreling? Someone practicing scales? A dog yipping? What did they see? The assignment was to write for twenty minutes as fast as they could—everything they felt and sensed.

They didn't want to stop writing, but eventually I asked for volunteers to read the images aloud. Every single one of them read. They didn't weep. Not openly. Well, not the high school students, at least. But a surprising number of them ended the session with smudged mascara. And they all lingered afterward to talk to one another. The muscular little director, who knew what she was doing, as it turned out, served us all cookies and coffee.

All the preconceived notions we had in our heads about one another got short-circuited by sharing our stories. Ironically, I, who was being paid to run the workshop, also got out of my own story for a while. And I realized that it was our stories—our own images and emotions—that gave us a way of talking to one another.

Remembering that changed something inside me.

Maybe it was because the kid at the Wendy's window had given me directions so cheerfully. As I followed his map, I was surprised to find myself wiping my eyes. At twenty minutes after two on Friday morning, after despair, I found myself once again speeding down the expressway that took me toward my mother.

The name for what the kid had given me, I understood, was hospitality. I needed to pass it on. It was that simple. I saw that, for all our differences, Julie and I were not enemies. We were sisters on the same journey. For the first time, I understood that journey as a pilgrimage. As a teenager, I had read *Pilgrim's Progress*. I saw my sister and me in the landscape of Bunyan's allegory, walking a rock-strewn path through dangerous mountain passes where the air was thin and we carried only a little food and water. We had no map. We didn't know the terrain. Either of us could slip and fall on jagged rocks to her death. I saw that there would never be a way to figure the long and complicated math of who was right and who was wrong. I simply needed to forgive myself and my mother and my sister for whatever choices we had made in the past.

And I did. There must be a hundred ways to forgive. But what I'd like to say is how happy it made me, how surprised. It felt like learning my trip through Texas would be safer than I thought, like learning death is a window we can look out of.

That night I didn't know where my mother's last years would take us, but I knew that Julie and I—speaking different languages, forged by different regions and politics and personal choices—were on a spiritual journey and that we needed to work out the way together. To do that would require patience and hospitality and forgiveness and I didn't know what all else.

*Chapter 33*

# THE CHOICE

$F$inally, a year after the last concert my mother went to at Kin-haven, Christian Care calls to inform Julie that an apartment has just opened at Bentley Assisted Living. To me this vacancy seems swift and unprovoked. Julie explains that there is a wait-ing list, but Mother has been moved to the head of the line, presumably because for years she has allowed them to show her two-bedroom to prospective residents. She has. I know that. She has loved those fortuitous meetings with strangers.

Although this explanation sounds slightly implausible, I don't care. I can see daylight, a place where Mother might live safely, where someone will help her take her pills, where she won't have to light her gas burners in order to eat nutritious meals.

Hallelujah.

Then we find out that the Bentley unit is Mother's only if she takes it immediately.

She's been telling us she wants to move, but suddenly the idea panics her. Now it's maybe *yes*, maybe *no*. She informs me in a supercilious voice that she needs time to think.

She dithers.

I should be ashamed to write that: she dithers. *Dithers* is a mean-spirited verb, generally reserved for old people. But I've done it myself and I know why a person dithers. Your imagination rings the doorbell at two a.m., wearing a lurid devil suit, scaring you half to death. You see yourself wandering unfamiliar, dark halls without friends. You believe that for the rest of your life you'll sit in your tiny apartment, staring into the murky silence. The hours pass, each more bitter than the last, and sleep scatters like milkweed feathers to the wind. Your heart pounds. You circle and circle your diminishing possibilities. I am making Mother's anxiety look like a cartoon so I won't imagine it accurately. If I do, I'll be too daunted to help her.

Mother has to move; that much, I know. I request an emergency phone conference with Julie and Rich and Daniel. Julie and Rich have toured the unit. It's spacious, Julie gushes, with a ton of light, a kitchen, living room, separate bedroom, and walk-in closet. The cost is just under $3,000 a month. Rich assures us that Mother can afford it. She'll be getting communal meals, a home health care team, staff to dispense her medications, and a calendar of social events. Three times a day an aide will administer her pills.

I argue like a regular cheerleader that we should push for this move, that we will surely be able to convince Mother to do it. Later, if she hates it, if she's sorry, if she wants to move back, we'll all four face the dirge music together and find another solution. I will come, I promise, to move her. We bond. We agree. We hang up. The next day all four of us counsel Mother to take the offer at Bentley. She concludes, yes, that's probably best for her.

Within twenty-four hours Julie hires movers who haul Mother's bed, couch, cedar chest, table, china closet, and a few other pieces to her new apartment. I hastily arrange for someone to take my classes and tell both our kids that I'm flying to Dallas again. Molly insists on helping. She'll drive up to Philadelphia and we will fly together to DFW. We'll stop by supermarkets, pick up boxes, drive directly to Mother's house, and get to work sorting and packing her small items.

Tomorrow is Thursday. I have promised that I will have her place empty and clean by Monday, when Julie and Rich and Mother and I will sign contracts and other papers to admit her to assisted living. I have asked Christian Care to send the documents, but they haven't arrived, so I won't have time to read them before I fly out.

⁓

As I toss my hair dryer into the suitcase, I'm thinking about how familiar our family has become with emergencies. So familiar that we almost crave them. Mother taught us to lean into them. Weather.com predicts that it will be raining in Dallas as we're moving Mother's things tomorrow. It figures. I pull my navy slicker from under our cat, Tiger Lily, and fold it into the suitcase. Tiger gives me a long, hard, reproachful glance, during which she seems to be reviewing my moral deficiencies. She gets up, as if getting up were her idea all along. She begins licking one paw. She pulls it over her head and down her face several times. Then she steps gracefully over the side of the suitcase and settles herself on my slicker again. I run downstairs to find a roll of green fifty-gallon garbage bags, pitch it into the suitcase, and call it good enough.

*Chapter 34*

# CRISIS

$M$y mother's children shift into crisis mode instinctively, the way a trucker shifts into a lower gear to get traction on an uphill climb. No wonder. We spent every Sunday hearing hellfire and brimstone sermons, followed by repeated altar calls. On Sunday afternoons, we listened to Billy Graham's "Hour of Decision." And every summer we went to revival services where gifted young evangelists suspended us over flames. We learned to survive in a spirit of religious emergency, which was a good rehearsal for our crisis-prone family life.

Among our family emergencies I count the death of our father. That was preceded and followed by our ongoing financial peril. Then there were the endless asthma attacks and the abrupt death of our brother, Michael.

But our family also elevated everyday events to the pitch of catastrophe. I'm thinking of Saturday nights when I stayed out with a boy ten minutes beyond my curfew. Belatedly checking my watch, hurrying back from the parked car, I'd find Mother supine on the couch, her eyelids fluttering over her rolled-up eyes. Julie, who'd be fanning her, would look panicked. And I would feel stung by deep remorse, knowing that if our only remaining parent died, the two of us would be utterly adrift in

the world. I'd swear never again to be drawn into the pure sensual swooning that could render me briefly oblivious to time
and disaster.

The next weekend, I would run over the deadline, again, by a
few minutes, quadrupling my penitence.

Increasingly I felt infuriated by our mother's unreason-
able panic. No one else I knew had to come in at ten o'clock
on weekends. No one else's parents got hysterical over a five-
minute curfew violation. I started setting my watch back, then
sputtering when I got home that I was only four minutes late. I
would bring Mother a glass of water, my hand tremulous with
fury. Then I'd head for my bedroom so my mother would have
a dwindling audience for what I thought of as her theatrics. I
knew she was terrified of losing another child. I didn't care.

After so much real life experience with calamity as children,
after getting hooked on the continual electric buzz of worry,
Julie and I enjoyed the relative nirvana of early marriage and
happy child-rearing years. But we moved back into a zone of
crisis when we began taking care of our mother. In fact, we were
just getting used to the long Alzheimer's crisis—if a person can
get used to it—when the Uncle Lloyd Emergency loomed.

Every week during Mother's Alzheimer's years, Daniel and I
phoned Uncle Lloyd. We did it because once Mother could no
longer make the trip to Pipestone to work like a galley slave
to keep his house from skidding slum-ward, she asked me to at
least phone him. She kept remembering the promise she made
to her own mother. On her mother's deathbed, she said. So
Daniel and I kept the holy promise on her behalf. We called
Uncle Lloyd on Saturday afternoons. From one end of the week
to the other, the two of us were the only people he talked to. We

chatted with him about his soybean crop, their weather, and the baseball standings, which I researched on the Web before we dialed. He was courteous and formal and so deeply reserved that he sounded like he was reading from a script.

In the winter Uncle Lloyd would let the phone ring twenty-five times before getting up from his Naugahyde chair in the breezeway where he sat most of the day, being covered with drifting snow until only his brown leather hat with the ear flaps was visible. Sometimes for days Daniel and I would take turns calling him, with mounting alarm, because who could tell what had befallen him? Maybe he kept his money in our grandfather's safe and someone entered his house and murdered him. Maybe he'd had a heart attack. Was he lying in a pool of blood? How could we find out? He knew no one anymore but the minister at St. Paul's Lutheran. He never went out. Finally we hired Darlene, a benevolent middle-aged woman in town who had known my grandparents and my mother, to do some cleaning for him every week. She would call me every month or so with a report and I, in turn, would report to Mother.

The day after the terrorists struck the towers in New York City, when the entire nation was staggering in disbelief, our phone rang. It was Darlene calling from Pipestone with the news that when she had unlocked Uncle Lloyd's door that morning and yoo-hooed, he hadn't answered. So she pushed the back door open and entered the kitchen. She stalked through the dark rooms, hearing the TV blaring, and discovered Uncle Lloyd, still leaning back in his recliner chair, dead, with his gray eyes open, staring at the black-and-white screen. The vertical hold was slipping wildly and the picture kept dissolving and reuniting.

With a pounding heart, Darlene prowled through the rest of the shadowy house, fearing she might find an intruder. But if there had been one, she told me, he had left. She didn't know, she said, what had happened. Maybe Uncle Lloyd had a heart attack, watching the endless reruns that we were all watching, the heart-stopping footage of the planes hitting the towers. On grandmother's perfectly made bed, Darlene had found three of his suits. She figured Uncle Lloyd had taken them out as potential funeral clothes for himself. She wondered whether she should call an ambulance and have his body taken to the mortuary.

Yes, I said, and thanked her.

After Darlene called, with the nation already on terrorist alert, our family took action. Daniel and I called Julie and Rich to tell them about Uncle Lloyd and we made plans to fly to Minnesota. But the FAA had grounded every airplane in the country and closed airports and we had no idea when we could get there. Julie phoned the mortician in Pipestone, with whom she said she shared many subsequent talks and not a few jokes as they figured out what to do with Uncle Lloyd until we could get there for the funeral. I conferred with Darlene and our cousins and our children about who could come and what we would do when we got there. None of them wanted to go through Uncle Lloyd's things, though some loyally agreed to fly in for the funeral. Daniel found a lawyer in Pipestone who said he could probate the will and sell the house and eventually put Uncle Lloyd's farm on the market if we could find the deed and if the title was good.

Meanwhile Uncle Lloyd lay in a freezer and I dreamed grisly dreams at night, though on the phone I told Mother everything would be just fine, really, everything would be just fine. By day Julie and I anxiously conferred about what to do with his farm, with his house. What if we couldn't find the documents we needed to prove ownership? We phoned banks around town to find out whether he had a lock box. We wondered what he kept in the safe, what was stashed in his cluttered 1920s mission-style desk, whether there were secret compartments in the basement.

Finally, in early October, the airports reopened. We bought plane tickets, meandered through the cavernous, dimly lit, deserted Philadelphia airport, and took off for Sioux Falls, South Dakota, the major airport closest to Pipestone. It was just us on the plane and a few other passengers. Everyone looked like a terrorist to us. We were tended by a nervous flight crew. In Pipestone, we picked up the keys to Uncle Lloyd's house from Darlene, hoping to enter before dark, but she needed to talk. Finally, as the last chilly northern fall light was dying, we approached his side door, struggled to unlock it, and then heaved it open. We stepped into the shadow-webbed kitchen and tiptoed over the familiar, ghostly speckled gray linoleum into the dining room, where we knew Uncle Lloyd had died, to discover his greasy Chrysler engine jutting up from my grandmother's tatted lace tablecloth. On his desk in my grandmother's sunroom lay a small spiral notepad where Uncle Lloyd had scribbled in pencil the date and time of every phone conversation he'd had with Daniel and me, along with a list of subjects to talk about.

The next day we sang, buried Uncle Lloyd, and then sat through the luncheon of marshmallow-lime Jell-O, creamed chicken over biscuits, fresh corn, home baked coconut cookies, Rice Krispies Treats, and Kool-Aid with relatives and a couple of friends in the St. Paul's Lutheran Church basement. Then we drove back to his house, changed our clothes, and began ransacking the rooms for papers. For days, Julie and I and our husbands and children swilled coffee and sorted every single object in the house into boxes to keep, to give away, to take to the dump. We cut ourselves no slack; we hardly slept. Mother sat in a chair in her purple suit, looking like a tiny, catatonic heap, mumbling, "I can't believe he's gone. I can't believe he's gone. I can't believe . . ." He was the last of her siblings. She had the dubious honor of being the lone survivor from her generation.

Scattered at random among fusty, mouse-chewed cardboard boxes, we found Uncle Lloyd's bonds, and in our grandparents' cluttered oak desks we found life insurance papers. Finally we tracked down the deeds for the house and farm and Uncle Lloyd's will, which divulged that he had left Mother several hundred thousand dollars. Wearing an elegant printed suit, she sat in her chair in the lawyer's office, flanked by the four of us, listening to the final will and testament of her last sibling. Uncle Lloyd's bequest guaranteed that she would have enough to pay her bills until she was a hundred.

*Chapter 35*

# CHANGING PLACES

It's already dark when Molly and I arrive at Christian Care to finish moving Mother to Bentley, the assisted living facility, her new home. Molly waits in the parking lot with Rich and Julie's daughter, Eve, while I walk up the path toward Mother's old apartment door, past the tough, bristly Dallas lawn and the magnolia trees in flagrant bloom. I knock. No one answers. Of course. No wonder. Mother isn't living there anymore. We'll need to get the key from Julie. But when I push the door, it swings open.

I step into her shadowy, haunted entryway and stand in the spot where, two years ago, I watched my mother dish out presents to three children. Now I feel assaulted. Piled up against the walls is a staggering amount of rubble. It looks like it's been dumped out of drawers, pulled down from the shelves of closets, tossed in from the windows. The vast detritus of junk is humped against the edges and drifting toward the middle of each room. There's hardly space to stand. Since Mother is compulsively neat, I can't fathom what happened. The anarchy feels like a hideous violation, a mockery. The white walls are scarred and the wall-to-wall carpeting is smudged with footprints. Mother's heavy white drapes still hang at the windows. All her pictures and oversize gilt mirrors are still mounted on the walls.

Who did this? Not Julie and Rich. The movers, maybe? Perhaps they were given orders to empty the drawers and cabinets, to take only the large items. And they're trying to make a living, hired for the day, or if they're lucky, for the week, paid by the hour. They can't afford to worry about an old lady's mementos.

I hear the melodic voices of Molly and Eve, laughing and exchanging news in the parking lot. I step closer to one of the chaotic mounds in the bedroom and wait for my eyes to adjust. Along the bedroom wall, a tangle of Mother's wind chimes, a crimson heart-shaped box of chocolates, emergency flares for her car, potting soil, folded bedsheets, skewers for shish kabobs, the Hummel figurine I brought back from a triumphant violin concert thirty years ago, the cut-glass butter dish she revered, which we were never allowed to touch. It's as if a tornado picked up and trickily redeposited things to see whether we could organize them again. Since I don't want to think about who might have scattered Mother's things this way, my imagination helpfully reverts to a natural disaster.

But I haven't said hello to Mother yet, so I quickly cross the campus to Bentley, where I press the buzzer and a woman wandering by in a paisley housedress lets me in. I find Mother on the second floor, where her door is unlocked. She's hunkered down on her couch in the dark. I kiss her.

"Let's throw a little light on the subject," I say, sounding just like her. I switch the lights on and look around. Her beige couch and chairs have been arranged attractively around her new living room, probably the handiwork of Julie and Rich. But the place feels like a movie set. There's the smell of fresh paint and a slight breeze from the ceiling fan. I know all the drawers are empty.

Mother blinks as if she's just waking up. Then shyly, apprehensively, she shows me around. "What a terrific apartment," I enthuse, hoping she'll catch the spirit. "Look at the huge windows! This will be so light!" I hate the bravado in my voice.

Once we've toured her new place, Mother is keen on clearing out. She believes I've come to take her to a restaurant for dinner. "Come on, let's go," she calls, setting out for the door.

I remind her that she's already eaten her dinner in the dining room.

"Are you sure?" she challenges me.

"That's what the lady at the desk told me."

"Will wonders never cease!" She sits down suddenly, the wind taken out of her sails.

I sit across from her and we try to chat, but I'm eager to get back to work, and she's not rooted in the conversation, either. She gazes around the room, trying to take it in. Soon I explain that I need to get back to the girls, who are packing her things.

"Well, that's the way it goes," she says.

"I mean is that okay with you?"

"That you're running off to Peru?" This makes no sense, but I know what she means because I am getting better at reading her metaphors. She means that she feels deserted and bereft the way she did the summer I flew to Peru.

"Not Peru!" I protest. "I'm just going to your old apartment to clean."

Absentmindedly, she gets up to prowl, lurching from room to room and back again like a wild animal that's been moved from its natural habitat. I follow her.

"Do you know where I'm going, Mom?"

"Where?" Her back is turned to me and she's poking restlessly at something on the floor.

"To your old apartment. To pack your stuff and bring it over here."

"That's fine, honey."

But she's skittish, not focusing. I put my arm around her to anchor her in the here and now. "Will you be okay?"

"I'm always okay. When can I go home?"

"This is home."

She spins around. "Oh no sir-eee! This isn't where I live."

"You do now."

"You're teasing me," she says in a refrigerated voice.

"No, you moved yesterday. Remember? We talked about it and you said you wanted to change places. I'm here to help."

"I should have my head examined! I said I would move?"

"Once you're here for a while, you'll love it."

"Oh, I will, will I?" She sits down, looking defiant.

I'm worried that Molly and Eve will feel deserted. "Mom, there's a lot to do over there," I tell her, "so I need to go. I won't be back till late. The kids and I will sort your things and bring stuff here."

"Alllllllll right, then," she sings. She means, okay, if you want to behave that way to your mother.

—

On top of the debris in her old apartment lies a new man's wallet, still in its box. I wonder whether Mother bought it for one of the children for Christmas: Jack or Andrew, Julie's son, maybe. Or maybe she didn't realize it was a man's wallet and purchased it for herself. Peculiar, because she isn't dealing with her own money anymore. I hold it up so Molly and Eve and I can thrash out alternatives. Does she need it? If she were here, would she keep it or let it go? At first each decision feels earth-shaking. These are my mother's hallowed objects, some of them things I've been friends with since I was born, others I was forbidden to touch. All the stuff, even the clap trap, feels like talismans, amulets.

I know at the time that I'm making way too big a deal out of it, that I am allowing things to get out of proportion. Some sane self inside my head stands up and shakes a finger and tells me to cool it. But I'm horrified by the responsibility of making these choices. It's being chased by a bull in a dream and not being able to run.

I'm reminded of something that happened years earlier. I'm pushing a grocery cart out of the supermarket across the parking lot at dusk. Huge drops of rain are splattering around us. The kids are little. I have Molly by the hand. The baby is sitting in the cart, heaped with purchases. A strong wind picks up. It whips my coat violently around my legs and lashes my hair against my face. I can barely push the loaded cart against the mounting gusts. The baby whimpers and begins to cry. The older one puts her head down, determined to get to the shelter of our car, and sets out, running, directly into the path of a red, oncoming Ford. Still pushing the cart, I shout and sprint after her. The cart catches on a rough patch of concrete and ricochets out of my hands. With the baby in it, it careens downhill in the opposite direction toward the entrance of the parking lot.

Maybe I can rescue one child but not both. I stand still, my brain whirling stupidly. I don't know which child to save. I can't move. I feel as if I'll be rooted to this spot forever. I feel certain that both children will perish.

That's over, thank God. The children are safe. But deciding among Mother's objects feels like that. How will we ever get rid of over half of what's here? The used ribbons and unidentified hardware and eyelash curler are easy. I toss them. But what about a pair of glasses, her stretched blank canvasses, her gardening trowels, her beloved second set of dishes, the legendary sandstone from Israel that she's labeled with Magic Marker? Together Molly and Eve and I consider one item at a time. We are overexcited and scrupulous.

Around midnight our nervous systems move on to another
stage. We split to different corners of the room. We work separately, hectically. Soon I begin to feel slaphappy, too light-
headed to linger over a figurine or a bracelet, recipes, documents,
Christmas letters from her friends. It's hot. I'm dripping and
itchy. My scalp prickles. I throw clothes into a box with a huge
girth. When I try to pick it up, I feel it slipping and let it go.
What is this, again? Clothes? Bedding? I reach down to pick it
up once more, but it slips out of my arms. Oh well. I blithely
shove it toward the trash corner. This feels like driving down a
highway with the window open, tossing out hundred-dollar bills.

Molly suggests we'll have more space and more boxes if we
take out the trash, but I haven't asked anyone where to put
trash. I find a flashlight and the three of us venture forth into
the night. Following the beam, we discover hulking Dumpsters
in the parking lot. They bear a sign: NO DUMPING! Clandes-
tinely I lift one heavy cover. It's smelly, but there's room. So I
hold the lid up while Molly and Eve heave in one heavy box
after another. Thud. Thud. Then the tinkle of breaking pottery.

"What if someone hears us?" Eve whispers, freezing. We
know we are exaggerating the danger. Nerves make us begin to
giggle. In my hysterical gaiety, I lose my grip on the lid. It slams
down, echoing through the night. We halt like statues, waiting
for retribution, but none comes.

When we finish, we're falling-down tired, and still Eve suggests one last job: hauling Mother's bookshelf over to Bentley. It
will give her so much more storage space. But the shelf is seven
feet tall and four feet wide, sturdily built of heavy oak. We tilt it
experimentally and manage it through the bedroom door to the
hall, through the empty hall to the kitchen, and out the front
door, onto the bed of the truck. Eve drives us over to Bentley
and we unload it. Calling directions to one another, we haul it

off the truck bed and walk it precariously toward the building. Everything is dark and calm at Bentley. The old folks are all asleep, watched over by the night aides.

"Shhhh!" We hiss at one another melodramatically. Since the building is guarded and the aides don't know us, we worry that we'll be shot, or at least ordered out. We get the bookcase inside, miraculously, and then we try backing it into the elevator, but it won't fit, so I find the fire exit and we furtively inch the massive piece up the concrete stairs.

"Farther left, Aunt Jeanne."

"Okay, you got it? I'll open the door."

As we clear the railing around the landing and hoist the shelf toward the second floor, we are giggling, laughing, and hiccoughing. In the concrete stairwell, our voices boomerang and ricochet.

Barbara, the night aide on the second floor, swings the door open and stands in a halo of light above us, her face a sculpture of sharp wrinkles. She demands to know who we are, what we're doing. I sober up and take control of the situation. I'm the mother, the aunt, I explain, helping my mother to move. I tell her Mother's name and introduce us all. Worn out as I am, I can manage only a very thin veneer of civil behavior. Nevertheless, she lets us carry the bookcase up.

When we arrive in Mother's apartment, Mother is dressed to the nines, sequins, four necklaces, a whole zany circus of colors, but she is rampant with anxiety, shredding paper towels. Tatters flutter around her apartment. She begins shouting and sobbing that Eve and Molly and I have been out enjoying one another's company, that since she's old and not useful to us anymore, we've abandoned her. *I had no idea where you were! This dumb phone doesn't work! I can't even call out!*

We comfort her. We put our arms around her and tell her

that we love her. We point out for proof that we're sweaty because we've been sorting stuff in her other apartment. That makes her cry harder. *That's exactly why I'm worried sick! What on earth is happening to all my things? I'll never see them again!* We don't tell her that we have already tossed some of them into the Dumpster. All trails circle back to the same central fact. Mother is paring down, losing what she thought of as hers.

I feel exhausted, suddenly, buckling at my mother's compounding health problems, at the geographical distance between us, at the sheer uncompromising weight of physical objects, at the awful truth that the body breaks down, at my mother's gross misunderstanding of our motives. Although Molly and I have flown across a continent to take care of her, she believes we've betrayed her.

It's almost three in the morning.

There are times when the human condition can get a person down.

A charismatic sixty-year-old preacher at a megachurch, a student of mine in a writing workshop a decade ago, told me about visiting one of his parishioners in a nursing home. The man had been the CEO of a major corporation, though I don't remember which one. He'd lived in a twelve-bedroom mansion. By then he was over ninety. Everything he owned fit into the top drawer of one small cabinet in his room. Naked we come into the world, the preacher told me, and naked we go out. He sounded like he was trying to grasp this fact himself. Who can hang on to it for long?

I had given up a great deal by that time to fly to Dallas and take care of my mother whenever I could. That night I wondered why. I wasn't sure. I just knew that I needed to. Years earlier I remembered watching my mother take care of her own mother. Perhaps a woman becomes the kind of daughter to her mother that her mother was to her grandmother. It's common to say that we parent the way we were parented. Not that a person can't change the family pattern, but that the pattern serves as a kind of default. Maybe in the same way, we "daughter" our Mothers the way we saw them "daughter" theirs. My mother took care of her own mother the way she took care of her children, tirelessly, thoughtfully, with a firm grip, and a great deal of love.

~

Molly and Eve and I got up early on Saturday and Sunday to sort again. The motion became a satisfaction, an end in itself. We survived by scooping and hauling. The truck bed was so high that to pack it we needed to lift boxes above our waists. We leveraged them onto the metal floor with our wrists, then scrambled up onto the hard deck and shoved them back toward the cab, blowing our sweaty hair out of our eyes. Motion is most of what I recall from the weekend, bending, sorting, hauling, pulling.

We unhooked Mother's heavy ivory curtains, folded them into boxes, and vacuumed the carpet. We unplugged her vacuum, loaded it into Eve's truck, and locked the door behind us. We hauled the last boxes of Mother's things to her new place and stacked them. Then we fell into bed.

~

The formal signing is scheduled for a conference room at Bentley on Monday. I've showered and put on a dress and hose and heels in an attempt to look like a responsible adult. While Molly and Eve go for a well-deserved brunch, I meet Rich and Julie in the hall outside the conference room. I can't remember who brings Mother or whether she arrives under her own steam. She's dolled up in a swishy flowered blue dress and her dark curls shine. The Powers That Be converge, introduce themselves, and unlock the door. There are about five of them, each with a different role. We pull up at the massive, shiny Queen Anne table, surrounded by florid wallpaper and silvery bowls filled with plastic fruit. They introduce themselves and give us their titles. The air feels zipped with significance.

I don't remember exactly what follows, but I'm pretty sure it included long, funereal explanations of contracts. One contract is for Mother's apartment at Bentley. Another is for a living will. A third is an advance directive. Then there is the do not resuscitate order. Mother signs each document, but Julie and I are required to sign on her behalf as well. In the large, formidable silence we pass the papers around the table for the solemn ritual of signing.

Julie signs everything. I sign everything except the do not resuscitate order. The woman in a navy suit asks me whether I understand what that means. If I don't sign, our mother could be hovering for years between life and death on a ventilator.

I glance over at Mother. What does she want? But she's gazing around the room. She hasn't been following the discussion.

"How can you be sure," I ask the woman, "if your mother is unconscious and the ambulance comes, that she is actually beyond hope?"

"You can't be sure," she concedes. "But chances are, at her age, she's not going to recover. The whole family may be stuck in this heartbreaking catch-22 for years."

I tell her I'd rather err on the side of keeping Mother alive. I do not sign.

$\sim$

Hours later, Molly and I are backing our rental car away from Bentley, waving good-bye to Julie and Rich, who watch us, each with a supporting arm around Mother. She looks like their baby bird.

After we merge onto the expressway to the airport, I tell Molly how grateful I am that she came. She and Eve scattered pleasure, even comedy, into what might have been a dark weekend.

In return, Molly thanks me, looking radiant in her blond, blue-eyed Scandinavian way, maybe because she's performed this act of generosity for her grandmother and me. It strikes me that she's safely launched into adulthood. Improbably enough, this thoughtful, feisty adult is my daughter.

"I wish we didn't have to leave Grammy," Molly says.

"That's how I feel every time I come here."

"Do you think she'll be okay?"

"I don't know. But there are people helping us take care of her."

"Who besides Rich and Julie?"

"The people at her church," I say. "And the women she counsels." We laugh. "And grocery clerks and mailmen and friends from her old neighborhood."

"Maybe new friends at Bentley."

"I hope she finds friends. They've assigned her to a table with the same people at every meal."

—

You can't tell a story just any way you want to, because finally things happen one way and not another. I'm thinking about the fact that Molly might have been killed in a supermarket parking lot twenty years ago. As we drive to the airport, I explain to her how the episode ended, when, desperate to get out of that historic rainstorm, she ran directly into the path of an oncoming car. I stood transfixed, unable to choose between her and her brother, who was hurtling downhill in a shopping cart. Because I couldn't move, I imagined they would both die.

But the woman who was driving the car saw Molly and stopped to let her pass.

And out of nowhere another middle-aged woman darted to grab the lurching shopping cart that carried Jack. Consoling him, she pushed him back to me. I thanked both women effusively. It was fine, they said, goodness, no problem. We were all cold and wet. We parted quickly. What these women accomplished seemed trivial to them, a small blip in a busy day.

But I was astonished to get my children back whole. I was surprised by the breathtaking generosity of the two women who had kept them safe. And I learned something. I'd thought that no one but me could save the people I loved, but that isn't true.

# FIELD NOTE 10

## ACROSTICS

*If today is the thirtieth of April—quick, then, what's the date tomorrow?*

Thirty days hath September,
April, June, and November;
All the rest have thirty-one
Excepting February alone.

*Tomorrow is May first.*

*My mind has a tendency to circle around, to check whether it's right, like a cocker spaniel preparing to lie down. But some things one doesn't have to ponder. They're cut and dried. I learned to pin them in place with rhymes or acrostics and mnemonic jingles like "Thirty Days."*

*I also used an acrostic to remember the order of the planets: My Very Educated Mother Just Served Us Nine Pizza Pies. When Jack recites that, I am the mother. When I say it, my mother is the mother. For nearly my mother's whole life, Pluto was a planet. Now, suddenly, the facts have changed. Pluto has been demoted. A little over a year later, Mother died.*

271

## Chapter 36

# FINDING COMPANY

I tell Daniel about moving my mother's things to Bentley, about laughing with Molly and Eve, about the hideous signing ceremony earlier that morning. We stand in the kitchen, slicing paper-thin pieces of cheddar with a cheese knife and wolfing them down with crackers. Outside, rain falls. When my plane took off from Dallas five hours ago, it was drizzling and the runway was one massive gray sheen. Now as we talk, the heavens open and turn loose bins of water. Through the screen door I can see big drops drumming into the puddles on our parking apron. The black water roils and churns. It is vengeance falling for moving Mother. Our house lights blink and go out, then waver on again.

"How's she doing?" he yells. The racket from water falling on the air conditioner is so loud I can hardly hear him.

"I don't know," I shout. At this moment modernity seems to be giving way before the dark barbaric onslaught of thunder and rain. Worry rides a roller coaster in my stomach. This is Mother's third night at Bentley.

Daniel grabs the phone and dials her. It rings and rings.

He hangs up, then dials again.

I prowl the house restlessly. If Mother is not in her apartment, where could she be? She doesn't know a soul at Bentley. Before she moved there, she had probably never stepped a foot in the building. The different levels at Christian Care are like separate solar systems. Yes, they're connected by walkways, but nobody from one campus visits any of the others.

Back when Mother still lived in her bungalow, I mean in the olden days—before yesterday—the two of us watched Bentley residents strolling one afternoon. We joked about how slow and ancient they seemed.

Now I repent of that slander.

Now Mother lives among them.

I get out the Christian Care folder and search for information about Mother's new life. Here's the picture of Bentley, shot from the most attractive angle a photographer could find, with blooming magnolias and curved walks. A gray-haired couple strolls by the fountain, which glitters in the sun. The photographer evidently wanted to make old age appear idyllic.

But right now mother is alone in that building and I worry that she's afraid. The folder offers no clue to the residents' meal schedule or events calendar, or when they'll be free to take phone calls. It doesn't even disclose prices.

Later that evening the rain lets up and I finally get hold of Mother, who sounds so crestfallen that my heart stumbles. She doesn't like any of the three people who sit at her table and she's decided the food is mediocre. She can't find her things. Most especially, she doesn't have any idea where her drapes are. I make my voice cheerful to boost her spirits. I stick to the truth, that I like her apartment, that the people seem friendly. But her voice sounds oily. I don't give a tinker's damn about her, that's clear, she says. Advising her to move to Bentley, this dungeon, abandoning her here!

After we say good-bye, I phone Julie.

I don't sleep.

I imagine that Julie doesn't either.

The next day she locates Mother's drapes. During the next night's phone call, Mother tells me she can't get the maintenance men to put them up. Julie calls Kathy, who manages Christian Care, and Kathy sees that Mother's drapes get hung immediately. Then Mother can't find the laundry room. On the phone that night, I explain where it is.

One night when Mother again reports that she's been sitting on her couch, watching TV with her curtains pulled all day, I suggest, "Why don't you go hear the pianist tomorrow?"

"How do *you* know there's a pianist?"

"I've got a Bentley events calendar."

"Where did you get that?"

"I called the desk and asked for it. The concert's at eleven. You love the piano, Mom."

"I don't even know what happened to my piano."

"Eve's keeping it for you."

"Well, there you go!"

"Do you want me to call and remind you?"

"Of what?"

"Of the concert."

"They'll call me."

"Who?"

"The desk. They call everyone."

The next night, I discover that she didn't attend the concert.

I make a Friday appointment at the Bentley hair parlor, asking them to call Mother to remind her. The night after her appointment I phone her to see how it went.

"Just wonderful." Her voice is dripping with irony. "Now I look like everyone else in the building."

"You didn't like it?"

"They don't have any imagination!"

"What do you mean?"

"Oh, don't ask me." She sighs with frustration. "If you want to know, it's zorky in there."

"What do you mean, Mom?"

"It's a zorky... business in here."

"Oh no, I think they're just thrilled to have you at Bentley."

"Have you checked the mailbox?" she demands.

"What mailbox?"

"To see whether my piano lesson has come."

"I'll check tomorrow."

"I need to practice."

"Your piano is at Eve's house, Mom."

"I wouldn't pay one red cent for that place."

"Mom, listen, there's another concert at Bentley two weeks from now. Will you put that on your calendar?"

"They're having music? Here!? You know me. Of course I will." But I know she won't. She doesn't even remember where she put her calendar, a fact I keep forgetting.

I go to sleep worrying about Mother, who is, in my dreams, sitting friendless in her strange, dark apartment.

For the next weeks, Julie and I go to the barricades together, telling Mother that if she attends exercise classes and stops into birthday parties and concerts and exercise class and lectures at Bentley, we're pretty sure she'll meet people she likes. But she's bored to tears by shuffleboard and she believes that playing cards is both shallow and immoral. She's not interested in knitting or embroidering, she informs us.

When Mary Frances, who plans social events at Bentley, turns the dining room into a pretend veranda and throws a Hawaiian luau complete with hula hoops, grass skirts, a ukulele-strumming band, fruit drinks bedecked with tiny umbrellas, and door prizes,

Mother perches just inside the exit and gazes on coldly. That night on the phone she describes going for a walk by herself, leaving by a door she doesn't recognize on the first floor, walking around the golf course. Her voice sounds weepy. Julie and I beg her to go to one group event every day. Julie lines up lunches for her with her church friends. We worry that she's depressed. Again I am haunted by the idea of moving her to Philadelphia.

After six weeks of misery, Mother finds Marian. Marian is a warm, handsome woman with gorgeous skin and a distinguished thatch of white hair. She lives just down the hall from Mother. The two of them begin exchanging visits to one another's apartments and then they branch out to stroll around campus, arm in arm, because, as Mother explains, she needs to support Marian. Marian is slightly older than Mother and I realize the next time I visit that she may be verging into Alzheimer's. Mother, the therapist, is thrilled that she has a new patient, but I notice it is usually Marian who does the listening while Mother peppers her friend with hot opinions and jokes and stories.

The happiness Mother feels around her new friend becomes a key to other pleasures. Mother begins to report that a few nice people are turning up at Bentley. She begins to work at making them her friends.

One day after Mother settled into Bentley, Julie announces that she's fired Dr. Karp, and switched our mother to the kind, troll-like Dr. Wright, who took care of most of the residents there. This is not joint decision-making, but Julie has known for a long time that I don't like Dr. Karp. We are finally both happy with Mother's doctor. Maybe he wasn't listed as a top ten physician by *D* Magazine, but he adjusts Mother's medications so they work, and he laughs when she tells a joke. He gets a kick out of listening to her stories and craftily employs the information he gleans to diagnose and treat her.

—

As I write this, I am pondering the clichéd Alzheimer's narrative, that relentless downhill slide. When the main character in a story is an old person, we readers think we know the plot, the steady edging toward ruin. But our mother's story was not so predictable. Once she got through the bad patch at the beginning of Bentley and tucked into her apartment, she grew clearer, saner, happier. It was five years before she needed to transfer to the Alzheimer's unit, and one more after that before her death.

Her gift for holding people in thrall is what made that move work for her. Like a healthy body slashed by a surgeon's knife, she began repairing herself soon after she moved. She forged a fresh social network, which, as Julie and I both knew, was every bit as crucial for her as food and sleep. Doing research in an effort to help my mother, I read studies of older adults that claimed the more social activities they pursued, the less likely they were to experience cognitive impairment. Adults who live alone are twice as likely to develop dementia as their peers.

Mother probably inherited her quicksilver connection with people from her father. This was the man who, at the age of seventy-eight, hung by his toes from our homemade jungle gym. Who dug horseradish roots from our backyard and, to amuse us, ground them with his old farm meat grinder, releasing such a fiery bouquet that we had to vacate our house for an hour. So he took us to get ice cream and as we sat at the table and slurped our cones, he explained that the roots of the horseradish plants snaked through our backyard and reached down to emerge on the other side of the earth, in China. Once he offered me twenty-five cents if I could run barefoot in the 115 degree heat on the sidewalk from our back door to our garage. When I accomplished this feat, he handed me a quarter and mused, "You're tougher than you look." I basked in his approval and concluded that I should set up ordeals periodically to test my own spunk. This lithe, dark-haired grandfather was just as pleased to chew the fat with a filling station attendant as to converse with a senator. Like him, Mother talked to any and everybody.

Once I saw her chatting up a man in her hall and when we got back to her apartment, I asked who he was. "Oh *that* old geezer!" She laughed.

"Who is he?"

"I don't know his name. But you know what he's thinking."

"No, what?"

"Oh, come on, darling! Don't pretend you don't know," she shot back.

"I really don't know."

"You can't be such a pushover, honey."

Is she talking about sex? I wondered. I was becoming aware of how often I served as my mother's straight man.

Once, after an impromptu visit from a friend, my mother announced, "That woman is too easily led."

Then there was the time she spotted an obese woman walking down the sidewalk and mumbled under her breath, "Honey, you're too big to wear orange." To be fair, it was a flaming-orange net tutulike skirt with orange tights.

Mother might have been full of devilish verdicts about people, but when she actually found herself in their presence, it was another thing altogether. She allowed herself to be charmed. She chuckled and nodded and told stories and concurred with them. When I was a child, that kind of inconsistency confused me. As a teenager, I accused her of hypocrisy. But now I believe her verdicts on people probably occurred to her later. In some odd way they were flotsam and jetsam, not really attached to the people they described. Maybe they were born out of her need to fashion yet another community with whoever she was confiding in. Maybe they swam into her head while she and I talked, for example, and then swam out again.

———

Imagine Mother sitting in the Bentley dining room across from Bill, who is the other regular at her lunch and dinner table. Together with several other lucky women, who have been promoted to Mother and Bill's prestigious table, they wait to be served tonight's chicken fried steak and mashed potatoes and beets and corn cut off the cob. I'm hurrying in, having just driven from the airport. The dining room smells tantalizingly of red chiles. I approach Mother and stand quietly until she spots me. Her whole face leaps with joy. She pushes out her chair, hauls herself to her feet, and throws her arms around me.

Bill hollers a greeting to me from his wheelchair. He suffered a stroke when he was in his late forties, so he's younger than everyone else in Bentley. He is the resident intellectual. He reads copiously and does research on the Web and he composes books about Texas Hill Country in Microsoft Word. From time to time he prints out his manuscripts and asks Mother to proofread them. She passes them on to me, thrilled to avoid reading, delighted to knit me into her social network. When I visit mother, I bring Bill books I've been sent as desk copies from publishing companies. When I stop by his apartment bearing Dante, Jane Austen, Thomas Churchyard, and a couple of anthologies, he frowns with pleasure, opens them, scans the title pages, and tells me this will keep him going for months. We are making harmonious music together.

Mother conducts not only the duet between Bill and me, but a chamber-size orchestra, seeing to it that we all stay on the beat. She tells each of us a slightly different story. "Bill needs you, darling," she confides in me. "Read this and mark the mistakes for him." Typos she means, God bless her. To Bill she undoubtedly says, "Jeanne adores reading your books about Texas."

One of those summers Jack flew with me to Dallas to play a concert at Bentley. He was now a free-wheeling, ironic undergraduate at Oberlin, much occupied with the beautiful girl, Bobbie, who later became his wife. Jack was no longer putting his feet under our table. That winter I suggested the concert to Mother and she snapped up the offer enthusiastically, like the social maven she had always been. Then I had second thoughts, not sure Jack would agree to play. But he did. He agreed so quickly that I was ashamed of having wondered. When I called Kathy and offered Jack's performance, she asked me whether he would be willing to play all their units.

Yes, he said, yes. He would.

On the day of the concert Mother took Jack and me on a tour of the posters Kathy had taped up in the halls, on the elevator, in the dining room. The performer: ERNA KELLEY'S GRANDSON. Holding Jack's arm, Mother steered Jack into Marian's apartment, where she introduced her grandson to her best friend with airborne, flamboyant rhetoric. All afternoon she shuttled him in and out of her friends' digs. He stood patiently as a dray horse while she trumpeted his accomplishments. Their eyes glistened, though none of them had the faintest idea what she was talking about.

Jack's debut Bentley performance was scheduled for the dining room. The residents dressed up, women in their Sunday dresses, men sporting string ties with their Texas plaid shirts. They parked their walkers off to the side and sat around the tables, chattering softly until Jack stepped to the stage that Mary Frances had cleared for him at one end of the room. She introduced him. Then he was standing there, perfectly at home, chatting with the old people, describing what he would play. There was a Bach Partita, I believe, and a movement of the Tchaikovsky violin concerto, and several other short classical works.

After each, the folks clapped, nodded to one another, and murmured.

When the concert was over, one of the women boldly raised her hand and asked whether Jack took requests. She wanted hymns, for instance, "Let the Lower Lights Be Burning," which Jack didn't know. One of the aides plunked a hymn book on his music stand. He sight-read the hymn. Then he tried it again. Better. The third time, one old man in back began singing the words in a quavering, thin tenor.

After that someone requested the "Navy Hymn." Jack apologized. Alas, he didn't know the melody. The man looked incredulous and then so crestfallen that Jack asked him to hum it. Jack tried playing it by ear. Mother sat there beaming at him. He played it again, swelling some phrases loud, diminishing others to pianissimo. Mother kept grinning herself silly, sitting right there in her blue flowered dress beside her amazing grandson.

At the end, Mary Frances thanked Mother for loaning Jack to the Bentley community. Everyone clapped for her. Then Mary Frances passed around butter crunch cupcakes and lemonade, while Jack and I went off to another concert in the Alzheimer's unit.

Mother was eighty-six when she managed that move between communities at Christian Care. One minute I see her curled on her couch in her gloomy apartment. The next I see her sweeping dramatically down a sidewalk in the sunshine, arm in arm with

Marian. Between those two frames, a seismic shift occurred. Geological ages passed and tectonic plates moved. With heroic courage she picked herself up by the scruff of the neck and tried. I mean, in spite of her painting with the dark storm clouds descending on the small farmhouse, in spite of the trouble she must have seen coming, she made an effort. I was teaching and traveling and, oh yes, I wanted her to be happy, but at the time I didn't comprehend what an uprooting that must have been for her. Imagine: to lose your only means of transportation—and therefore, many of your friends—your house, your neighbors, your garden, your painting, and two thirds of your worldly goods—all within a couple of years. If Mother had pitched a tantrum for the rest of her life, if she'd decided to turn bitter or to curl up and die, Julie and I couldn't have pulled her back from the brink. Thinking about that brings me smack up against the mystery of the human will.

So here's my mother, ambling down the hall at Bentley after lunch. She's wearing a peacock blue shirt with an open boy collar and a mauve, spangled suede vest. Her back is slightly crooked, but she's not using a walker. Because her head is up, you can catch her charismatic smile. As she travels by the open doors of her friend's apartment, she calls, "Hi, Mable." Mable steps out to chew the fat briefly. Then Mother shuffles on. "Flossie, how are you?" Flossie stands in her living room, beckoning to Mother, holding up a box of Godiva chocolates. "You want to get rid of those?" Mother asks. "You asked the right woman!" Mother veers into Flossie's apartment. Mother is collecting these old souls like charms on a bracelet, and, meanwhile, distributing her own invention, which is new every day. Call it pleasure.

She casts a flirtatious look at the woman who is standing a little way off, studying her. Who is that? Call that me, still amazed at how she did it.

## Chapter 37

# FRIENDSHIP

As Mother began to flourish at Bentley, I started to remember the fall I switched from Lincoln Christian School to a public junior high school. Memories arrived the way my father's black-and-white pictures bloomed when he developed them in the basement of our house in Lincoln, Nebraska. Odd patches of the picture would appear on the white paper under the red light in the developing room. At first nothing linked the patches. Gradually they swam together to make sense.

As more and more memories surfaced, I began to see connections between them.

It seems idiotic that I didn't ask my gregarious mother for advice that fall when I switched schools. My move to a new school was not unlike her move to Bentley. But that is to think like a lunatic, of course, because when I changed schools, my mother wasn't yet fifty. How could I have asked her to give me advice about the strategies she used to make friends in her mid-eighties?

These are the odd juxtapositions of time that I live with now that I'm in my sixties and selves of all ages live inside my skin, insisting on their memories. Often they seem funny and sometimes they are revealing. But at other times the bizarre intervals of memory bear down on me and make me feel downright addled.

What I mean to say is that if I had paid attention to my mother when I was thirteen, I might have noticed how skilled she was with people, even then. I might have guessed that she could tell me a thing or two about how to make friends. She might have informed me, for instance, that I should not just sit like a dope and wait for someone to talk to me. She might have suggested that I smile at people. But back then I thought she was merely my mother, a piece of furniture I'd lived with since I was born. How could she give me useful advice? Besides, we were into a mother-daughter struggle of such proportions that I wouldn't be caught dead giving her the satisfaction of counseling me.

Our eighth grade class at Lincoln Southeast was fifty times as big as my class the previous year, which consisted of three girls and one boy. My friends and I had run out of grades at Lincoln Christian School. We lived all over the city and we had scattered to different public schools. None of us could drive, so we almost never saw one another. Southeast was so vast that on the first day I got lost and wandered for forty-five minutes before I found an exit. Every hour we changed classes. The first day I was late to all of them because I couldn't locate the room numbers, which I later discovered were just to the right of the doors.

I had arrived in junior high a year after social groups formed. I knew no one. When the bell rang, students would crowd out of the classroom in tight little clusters, joking about weekend parties, or arguing in shrill, flirty voices. I had no one to walk with.

When I got home from school that afternoon, I ambled through the living room, into my bedroom, pretending to be normal. I shut my door, sank onto my bed, and sobbed. I was utterly bewildered by the strange universe of the big public school.

But if I had noticed, I was also feeling something else. The school was large enough to offer possibilities I had never before glimpsed. A small ray of hope flashed on the horizon of my mind, the smallest sparks of possibility, even as my shoulders shook and the hot tears fell onto the bedspread.

———

Mrs. Trimble clutched the bottom of her white Ban-Lon sweater and tugged it toward the floor. In her high, piping child's voice, she began to recite the minimum requirements to run for president of the United States: *"A person must be a natural born citizen, must be at least thirty-five years old, must have resided in the United States for . . ."*

Out the window, the maples were firing their colors in the sun. By now, the third week of junior high school, I was floating on the dark undercurrent of boredom that carried students from one class to another at Southeast. Here the zip was homogenized out of civics and history and English. Those subjects now seemed so boring, I couldn't remember why I'd been interested in them. So on this October afternoon, the fall after I left the Lincoln Christian School, I blocked civics out of my mind and turned to the problem of how to make a friend. One friend, I thought, would be a reasonable number to go for.

Barb was a candidate. She sat ahead and to the left of me in civics, a girl with a perfectly oval, shiny face, short, thick, light-brown hair, and eyelashes so abundant that they cast a shadow on her cheek. In the lunch room I had seen her fold and save her brown lunch bags for reuse, and several of her knife-pleated skirts must have been homemade, since the pleats wouldn't stay in. Mine didn't, either. Barb avoided extreme colors like red and orange. Like me, she chose clothes a person could wear for a long time without getting sick of them.

"People!" Mrs. Trimble cheeped in her tiny voice. "Did you read the chapter?"

Barb was the only one in the classroom paying attention. Her head was tilted slightly upward, and her face glowed. Of course that could have been from running to class, but it made her look like a cherub. I wondered why she was so interested in the requirements for becoming senator. Maybe she wasn't. Maybe she just liked Mrs. Trimble.

As I did.

I considered exiting the classroom with Barb after the bell rang, pretending I needed to go whichever direction she took, then asking her what she thought about civics. As I write this, I'd like to tell my younger self, *Do it, do it!* But to pick out Barb as a target felt manipulative to me back then. I figured that people were either likable or they weren't, that I probably wasn't, which explained why I had not yet attracted a friend.

———

For months before I started public school, my mother had beseeched me not to join a gang of bad kids. Kids who drank and slept around is how she defined *bad*. My parents sketched swift, powerful tales of apparently decent kids who would lead me down an evil road. In our kitchen, frying liver, which was a cheap dinner, yelling over the hiss, my mother informed me that students in her public school used drugs and drank. They got addicted. She should know. She was a public school nurse. Girls came into her office complaining of headaches, wilting onto her cot, and after twenty minutes of her kindness, they confessed that they were pregnant.

I wasn't very sophisticated, but I knew it was physically possible for me to have a baby, and I was haywire with terror at the prospect. It happens fast, my parents told me. One thing leads to another and before you know it, you own a squalling red-faced infant. *And don't bring your illegitimate child home to me*, my mother warned. I would have to quit school to take care of it. Privately I worried that my own baby would be no more lovable than the children I babysat for.

Mother's warnings led me to believe that the landscape of Lincoln Southeast, from which I needed to pluck a friend, was strewn with the kind of explosive devices terrorists hide under trees and in trash cans. Like IEDs, the teenagers at Southeast might appear innocent, but were actually lethal. As Southeast became my daily routine, my past comrades faded from my memory. I called them less often and when I did, we didn't have much to talk about. I couldn't remember exactly what they looked like, or why we had liked each other so much.

One night I had a nightmare. Barb had invited me to her house and I was sitting beside her at her aqua Formica kitchen table. She had found plastic glasses in one of the cupboards and poured us lime Kool-Aid. A bag of store-bought chocolate chip cookies sat in the middle of the table. Her mother tripped into the room wearing a low-cut red dress and red velvet heels. She swung a small heart-shaped purse. She appeared to be going out.

"Oh, hi kids," she chirped, drifting over to us at the table. She was clutching a bulky bottle in one manicured hand. "You should try this," she urged me. She dashed a little of the transparent liquid into my glass of Kool-Aid, then stepped backward to watch my reaction.

Manners dictated that I try some. My parents were teetotalers so I'd never tasted alcohol. Within minutes of the first sip I slumped to the floor, drunk and senseless.

I woke up from this nightmare in my dark bedroom. Prickles of alarm were exploding like Roman candles in my hands and chest. My heart was thumping like a tom-tom. I lay listening to the shade banging softly in the breeze against my window. I didn't know how the dream ended. I lay there trying to imagine where you end up if you befriend the wrong person. The breeze from my window was getting downright cold, but I was too sleepy to get out of bed and shut it. I drifted into a reverie.

I saw myself slumped on the tile in Barb's kitchen. She and her mother picked me up by the arms and legs, and stuffed my body into a large black rubber bag. A man in dark glasses got out of a sleek, black limousine parked beside their back door. He opened the trunk and together they crammed me in. Then he drove away. His car merged onto a highway and sped toward the horizon. I tried to envision where he was taking me, but my imagination had shut down. I might as well have been inside the bag. Everything was black.

A mosquito hummed beside my ear. I had just been bitten on one knuckle.

This woke me up.

I bounded out of bed and slammed my window shut.

I needed more firsthand knowledge to test reality. I needed to experiment. But down the short hall outside my bedroom I could hear Mother, who had apparently heard me slam my window. She was up, prowling around. It was spooky. She had a sixth sense. She was weirdly hypervigilant. I needed to get away from her.

⁓

One morning before school I locked myself in our bathroom and with a Q-tip I dabbed a red food coloring on my lips. I'd cut the intensity of the scarlet with water. I planned every morning before I went to school to closet myself this way and stain my lips a bit darker, accustoming my mother to the change slowly so she wouldn't notice. At school I watched girls suavely drawing on crimson lips without even glancing in a mirror. At the Lincoln Christian School no one, even the teacher, wore lipstick. Lipstick was forbidden.

At seven thirty, when my mother called "All aboard," gathered her height-and-weight charts, and grabbed her purse to drive me to school, I flushed the toilet and exited our bathroom, looking, I hoped, innocent. As Mother walked by me to the front door, she glanced at me, but didn't say a word.

———

Shortly after that, I began bargaining with my mother to wear my skirts shorter.

She was sitting on the floor beside a box of straight pins, her legs sticking straight out like a child's. She plunked the end of a yardstick on the floor and held it against my pink skirt. The daughter of a dressmaker, she believed that a perfectly even skirt hem speaks volumes about a woman's character. I had learned, at such fittings, to stand patiently, just trying to get the job over with.

"Thirteen inches," my mother intoned, taking a pin out of her mouth, marking my skirt with it.

"Fifteen," I negotiated.

"Thirteen and a half," my mother countered, smiling.

"Everybody at school wears their skirts shorter than me," I argued.

"Well, you're not everybody!"

We settled on fourteen inches. That is, my mother settled on it. In our house the children did not do the settling.

———

One Sunday a year before my father died, after our family had devoured our ritual evening meal of cheeseburgers and potato salad, I returned to my bedroom to finish my homework for the next day. Or rather, I returned to my bedroom because I wasn't crazy about spending time with my watchful, wired mother anymore. Very soon both my parents trooped into my room. Mother sat on my bed. My father leaned in the doorway. I don't remember exactly what they said, but they addressed me about my accumulating mutinies. I could tell they had discussed me earlier. They were united and affectionate, and pleading.

"You're changing," my father said. "Do you realize that?"

Because I had lived in my family for more than a dozen years, I understood that changing was a bad thing.

"You don't want to do what everyone else does," my father said. "You're not a sheep."

I didn't answer. I couldn't find words to explain the truth— that I didn't have any friends at my new school, that I was lonely, that I had begun to suspect the bright line we had drawn between our church and "the world" was in some way wrong.

"Darling, what's going on?" my mother entreated gently.

Silence.

"Do you really think you know more than we do?" she asked.

This set a forest fire of anger blazing inside me. I could feel the flames leap to my skin and travel across my face.

⁓

After dinner one night while I was drying dishes, my parents again asked me what was going on. I stared at the ceiling and envisioned the advice session they'd subject me to if I told them. So I said in a matter-of-fact voice, "What do you mean?"

My father stood in our kitchen doorway gazing out the window silently, as if his cornflower blue eyes were glimpsing his teenage self. He had dropped out of the university and begun carousing, as he put it, and running around with loose girls.

Now he couldn't work. He believed our family was suffering because he had thrown away the values his parents had taught him. He didn't want me to repeat what he had done.

The next afternoon I missed the bus on purpose. I was tired of being disgraced by having no one to sit by. Setting out for home, I walked by a house whose bushes were clipped to look like a sideshow of performing animals.

"Hello," I said to the animals, testing whether my voice still worked. The eccentric noise rising from my throat disappeared into the air like fog.

I remembered how slackly my father's shirt hung on him. When did that start? Was he losing weight? A shadow of fear for my big strong father passed over me and clipped my breath off. I stopped walking and stood still, holding my side. The trees were blazing against a sky that was growing gray and scaly with clouds like a fish. The wind was picking up. It whipped the red and yellow leaves into eddies. I smelled a leaf pile burning on someone's lawn.

I realized I was threatening my father. I might be worsening his heart condition. Four and a half years ago, the doctors at the clinic in Temple, Texas, had given him three years to live. Didn't I care enough about my own father to do what he asked me to do? He was surely right that I was drifting away from my former friends. And what would I do without them—my family, the church, our friends?

—

But hold it. Who did my parents think they were, appealing to me out of pity for my father and fear of the future? They were utterly self-interested. And they were limited to their own little group. What did they know about Lincoln Southeast High School or the kids there? They didn't have such hot taste themselves when it came to friends. Some of the people my parents ran around with were definitely nutty. I needed to find a way out of their pathetic little group! And my mother was still making me take cod-liver oil, still threatening me with the collywobbles, still enforcing a bedtime. *I'm not a child*, I thought. *I'm thirteen*. Thirteen sounded to me like a mythically large number.

I began running, the houses blurring, the wind tearing at my hair. After blocks and blocks, I stopped with a stitch in my side. My civics and algebra books were growing heavy. I trudged along the sidewalk again, less than halfway home. It was almost dark and getting cold fast. My hands were already numb as rocks. I had no coat to put on. How could I have predicted that morning that I would have to avoid taking the bus home because of my embarrassment at having no one to talk to? In my misery I blamed my loneliness on my parents.

I got home around the time dark fell. My mother had been driving the streets looking for me. When she pulled into our driveway, she rolled her window down and asked me what I had been doing.

"Thinking," I told her.

"Thinking? You mean you can't think and walk home at the same time?"

"Well, I was tired."

"What were you thinking about?"

"I don't know."

"You don't know what you were thinking?"

"No, I guess not."

"Are you in trouble?" I thought she meant with the authorities, at school, for instance.

"No."

"Really?"

"Really."

"Are you okay?"

"Yeah."

"Then change your clothes. It's time for supper."

I simply could not grasp what was so rapidly happening to me. It felt like I was becoming transparent, nonexistent, a blown-out candle. I wanted to become real again. I needed a friend, someone smart and funny, someone I could give the key to my diary, someone with whom I could fight and make up with on a daily basis. The way to find her was to seize a moment at school and open my mouth and say something. If I sounded idiotic because I didn't know the slang, or stupid because I hadn't heard the latest gossip, so be it. Then I would have to try again with someone else. And I would have to keep trying until I found someone who would accept me for myself—whatever kind of creature that was. I could feel steam rising, fuming, boiling, apt to erupt through any fissure it could.

Not long afterward, I noticed a short girl with a blond pixie cut—white blond, a shade you can't get out of a bottle. She wore tidy, plain, understated skirts and blouses. Her gray-blue eyes were kind. But I recognized irony when I saw it, even though I didn't yet have a name for it. I had begun to experience irony myself. Like me, she knew more than she said. I think I knew that I'd seen her walking from the school bus to her house. It slowly dawned on me that she lived on our block, but I'd never talked to her because I was so utterly taken up with my friends at Christian School.

I don't remember exactly how it happened. Maybe in the hall I fell into step beside her. "Hi," I said. "Don't we live in the same neighborhood?"

"Do we?" she asked.

"I live in the turquoise and stone house on the corner."

I told her my name. She told me hers. She had algebra next and I had science.

One of us walked the other to class, where we stood talking outside the room until the bell rang. Maybe I was late to science. Maybe I scooted down to the office for a hall pass. A student was only given a small number of free hall passes a semester, and then the boom was lowered. I didn't care. I didn't even care when I gave my science teacher the pass and he cast me a harried, disappointed look, meaning that he had not pegged me for a troublemaker. But I'd have been late to class every day, I'd have welcomed any lowering of any boom as the price for a friend. My heart sang with possibility.

What I remember for sure is that the two of us began to eat lunch together in the school cafeteria, which reeked of starchy food, where frisky students hurled vittles and bellowed, where teachers patrolled to keep bedlam to a minimum. Neither of us liked the unidentifiable meat or the limp vegetables the school served, so we brought our lunches in brown bags. I sat with her group, geeky girls who had banded together before I started Southeast, back in seventh grade, against the popular weekend party in-group.

Within weeks this new friend and I were taking turns sitting on her bed or mine, our bedroom doors shut against our parents and siblings. We mimicked Vanda Kaye, the star of eighth grade, a squawky-voiced, put-it-out-there girl we both loved and hated. We were both enrolled in college prep, it turned out, but we both took typing, in case we needed something to fall back on to make money. Between what the two of us were thinking at any given moment there wasn't space enough to slip a piece of typing paper. Except that she studied less than I did, and got better grades.

My mother unreservedly welcomed this new friend into our family. When we wanted to cook, she turned her kitchen over to us. When we needed a ride to football games, she ferried us. She never complained about our loud music. She made it clear that I'd made a brilliant choice.

—

Two months later, in mid-December 1957, my father died.

—

Three years after that, after my brother died, my best friend's father rang our doorbell. I happened to be out at the time. The handsome blond professor of zoology at the university stood on our concrete porch, awkwardly asking my mother what he could do to help. "This shouldn't have happened to you," he told my mother. I had spent a lot of time in his house by then and I knew him to be a brilliant and gentle man. "What can Margaret and I do to help?" he asked in a husky voice.

—

Thirty years later, my mother told me about that. She told me that she explained to my friend's father there wasn't much he could do to help. But just knowing they were there, two houses down, made her feel stronger.

—

The winter of my father's death, or maybe that next winter, my best friend's mother was diagnosed with multiple sclerosis. As the two of us tried to comprehend what was happening to our families, we listened to the Kingston Trio sing, "Hang down your head, Tom Dooley, hang down your head and cryeeeeeee." We couldn't get enough of the melancholy, unearthly, close blending folk harmonies. We joined the Pep Club. Every so often we baked chocolate cakes, frosted them with fudge, and binged. We listened to her records of the Smothers Brothers and laughed ourselves silly.

Three years ago, more than fifty years after I met this friend, she flew across the continent to Texas for my mother's memorial service.

# FIELD NOTE 11

## CULTURAL MEMORY

*It occurs to me that history is really cultural memory.*
*I must have stolen my world history book from*
*tenth grade, because several years ago I found it on my*
*bookshelf, and I can't remember how I got away with*
it. *Threads trail from the cloth cover of the beat-up old navy blue*
*thing and the pages are so slick that pencil marks bounce off them.*
*We weren't supposed to write in our books anyway, which is part of*
*the reason I never felt like textbooks were mine. There's not a shred*
*of evidence either in this book or in my memory that I ever read or*
*thought about it. It seemed to me the closer I got to history, the more*
*of it there was, dates, places, people, battles, laws. It was like focusing*
*a Google map of the planet down to blades of grass in the backyard of*
*a single house in, say, Toledo, Ohio.*

*But there was also a mystifying amount missing. The voice of*
*the book sounded detached and far away, like the voice that made*
*announcements over the PA system at school. It talked about wars,*
*kings, plagues, and the discovery of the New World. What it left*
*out was losing a tooth, school cafeterias, fights between best friends,*
*chocolate, and many other secrets.*

*The history book also left a big black hole between the end of the*
*Roman Empire and the beginning of the Early Modern Period. I had*
*to memorize the fact that this dark space existed before the Italian*
*Renaissance. I had to explain that fact on a world history test.*

*In graduate school I discovered that after the Dark Ages were over,*
*Petrarch went around telling people that they were lucky to be living*
*at the beginning of a renaissance. He's the one who named the long*

*forgetting that preceded the 1300s "the Dark Ages," thereby making it real and significant.*

*It's no longer politically correct to call any historical period "the Dark Ages," because the metaphor of darkness implies that nothing went on. Plenty went on, as anyone who thinks about it will realize. People were born and they died. Rulers rose and fell. The crop either fed the children or it didn't. It's just that during the Dark Ages, fewer scribes and historians wrote down the details of what was happening.*

*History has everything to do with memory. If we don't write down what we've witnessed, we will forget it and then lose it entirely. We will be encouraging a new Dark Ages.*

*I am trying to record in these pages what I witnessed.*

## Chapter 38

# DOWNHILL SLIDE

When Dr. Wright ordered Mother to get a walker, Julie bought her one sweet, sexy, cherry-red baby walker. It had black grips on the handles, a platform for her heavy purse, and a row of hooks where she could hang a bag of groceries if she wanted.

Right off the bat, Mother loathed her walker with a deep and personal hatred. She stashed it like an offensive aunt in her closet, where it wouldn't remind her of her unsteadiness. When I coaxed her to try the machine, telling her how chic and zippy it looked, she said, "I don't come from people who use walkers." She reminded me of how nimble her father was, jumping over fences instead of opening gates.

"When he was young," I guessed.

"Until he left the farm!" she countered.

"I never saw him jump over a fence."

"You think my father would have ever used a walker?" Her voice dripped with scorn.

"Mom, what about your balance problems?" I asked.

"What balance problems?"

"And your arthritis."

"Some peoples' children build them up and make them feel better." Whereas, by contrast, she was implying, I didn't.

So I let it go. Even when she was sitting down, sometimes energy still shot out of Mother like sparks from a bonfire. She hadn't yet slowed down to the tempo of a walker. Although Julie kept trying to persuade her to use the thing, Mother navigated without it for another three years. Then one morning she pulled the dreaded machine out of the closet and took it to her heart.

As she became more forgetful, Julie and I set out to repair whatever we could. Maybe there was a rivalry involved in this, but mostly I remember that like a good defensive front four, together we tried to hold the line. We picked up mail from her box, which she forgot to check. We fought chaos in her drawers and closets. We sewed on buttons and snaps and hooks. We weeded out socks with holes and hose with runs. We washed her clothes and hauled them to the cleaner. We took her shopping for new dresses and shoes. We phoned or e-mailed her friends, thanking them for visiting her, encouraging them to visit her again.

She needed the whole month of December to address her Christmas cards that first year. The following year she pretended to work on them, but never sent them. She told me she was sick of the same old routine every year. So my sister and I began sending Christmas cards to her vast list, enclosing a letter we had ghostwritten for her. We aimed to get them out in late November so she would still receive cards at Christmas from everyone on the list. Or at least the ones who hadn't died.

I don't remember when Mother began pairing red skirts with orange blouses and matching polka dots with plaids. After a couple of years, she flung rules for harmonious design entirely out the window. She might wear long exercise pants under her dress, or layer herself in two blouses and a sweater. In the hope that the desk wouldn't read her helter-skelter fashion as a sign of dementia, my sister and I began to coordinate Mother's wardrobe. We left her notes about what to wear with what. Just before I flew out one March, I tied the hanger of each skirt with a twisty to its companion blouse. Two weeks later Julie told me that Mother had ignored my outfits, snatching a blouse from one outfit to wear with a skirt from another.

During that visit, I noticed Mother had begun to drop food when she ate. She had always been so modest and clean. When I got home, I bought and mailed her eight white blouses. But the next time I flew there, I saw that she didn't remember to switch her stained blouse for a clean one. The problem wasn't that she didn't have enough blouses; it was that she didn't notice the stains. They might have embarrassed me, but she didn't even know they were there. And a heap of unopened mail lay on her dining room table and her vacuum cleaner wasn't working and three lightbulbs were out and her bathroom was so cluttered with cosmetics and over-the-counter drugs that she couldn't use the sink.

That spring, after several accidents, I grasped that I needed to buy Mother adult diapers. I hunted for them under the fluorescent lights of a grocery store, circling the aisle with a faint heart several times before I turned in and stood there with other children of the elderly. Unlike some of them, I wasn't yet hardened to the fact that we had to take care of my mother that way. I picked up one unwieldy white plastic package after another, trying to read their labels, but I couldn't focus and in the end I just grabbed a giant package of Depends. When I got back to Mother's apartment, I could not bring myself to have a frank talk with her about wearing them, so I tactfully left the package in her bathroom. Weeks passed and Julie said Mother didn't touch the Depends. So while Julie and Mother were doing her wash, Julie explained to her that we had found ingenious new underpants that would prevent accidents. She showed them to Mother.

"Why, I never heard of such a thing!" Mother retorted. "They're diapers! Babies wear diapers!"

"Lots of people your age wear them."

"Thank you for thinking of me, but I'll pass."

"Just give them a try, Mom," Julie coaxed.

After Mother tried them, she informed Julie that they made her skirt bunch up, and she certainly didn't plan on wearing them again.

Once a week during that period, my sister sneaked up the back way to Mother's apartment to scour her rugs, and set dozens of deodorizers behind the curtains and under the furniture. We didn't want the desk at Bentley to know that Mother was having a problem. We didn't want them to make her move out. Over time, the situation became dire. Knowing that all Julie's arguments had failed, I told Mother straightforwardly one night on the phone that if she didn't wear her Depends, she might have to move to another apartment. This shocked her. She didn't want to move. But what really stunned her was the idea that Julie and I were ganging up on her. She thought that the diapers were Julie's idea.

"I never in a million years thought you girls would take sides against me!" She sniffled.

"We're not, Mom. We're both concerned about you." I was leaving for a two-week teaching stint in Vancouver early the next morning, and I still needed to pack and to round up books to bring along, but I sat down on the kitchen floor, heartbroken for her. "Mom, listen, everyone wears Depends."

"Who?" she demanded.

"Every single person in your building, for starters."

"Annie doesn't."

"Trust me. Everyone who's over sixty has a little dribbling problem."

"Well, I don't do what everyone else does. I'm not a sheep."

The more Julie and I insisted that Mother wear Depends, the more slyly she subverted our rules. Face-to-face with the blunt processes of the body, as we had not been since our childhood—or since our own children were infants—my sister and I talked by phone and e-mailed and buoyed one another up.

—

The next time I visited Mother, I bought a couple of good maps of Dallas. Those maps signaled a new era. All the Dallas I needed to know had been in my mother's head. Now I needed to spread Dallas out on the table and study its streets so I could ferry Mother around her own town. When we got into my rental car and headed for her bank, she insisted on telling me where to turn, but we didn't find the bank where she predicted it would be.

"Well lo and behold, it's moved!" she announced. After that, I checked the maps and drew diagrams of the routes before we started out.

For a couple of days during that period she wore a button reading: I DON'T RECALL.

Until she lost it.

Then there was the afternoon Mother took me on a tour of her apartment, lifting pictures off the wall and turning over vases and dishes to reveal names she had scrawled on the bottom in Magic Marker. She'd been thinking, she told me, about who should inherit what. There we all were: Andrew. Julie. Eve. Jeanne. Molly. Jack. Rich. Daniel. As Mother and I moved around the house, she changed her mind, gaily crossing out names and scrawling in different ones. And I knew, because I had read her will, that the names she scribbled were different from those she'd given her lawyer. *Ai yai yai*! I thought, this is going to cause unbelievable chaos. But at least that chaos would be down the road a ways. By this time I was learning to let the chaos of the day be sufficient thereunto, as Mother had advised me to do all my life. After all, I thought, she was having fun, and the stuff was hers to do with as she pleased.

The last day I was there, we climbed into my rental car and I drove Mother to her back doctor. Her disks were disintegrating from osteoporosis. The nurse ensconced us in an examining room and when the towering Dr. Hills swept in, he hugged Mother and proclaimed in a jubilant voice that she had always been his pet. He marveled at how beautiful she looked, and let her talk for forty-five minutes.

Then he asked if she was ready. He left the room while I helped her don a paper gown with the opening in the back. He knocked then, and burst in, bearing a syringe with a foot-long needle, which he kept as much out of sight as possible. I asked Mother if she wanted to squeeze my hand. She grinned and grabbed it. Then, as she winced and whimpered and wrung my hand, Dr. Hills inserted that long needle and shot steroids right into Mother's spine.

That afternoon I drove her to Dr. Wright, her internist, for her regular monthly checkup. In his waiting room one elderly woman with crossed eyes and long, flowing gray-brown hair gripped a cane. As Mother eased herself into a chair, the woman asked, "Are you seeing Dr. Wright?"

"I hope so," Mother said.

"I think Dr. Wright is fun," the woman said, fixing Mother with one of her eyes. "He's so nice."

"I'm seeing every doctor in Dallas today!" Mother bragged.

They both laughed.

"This getting-old business is dangerous!" Mother addressed this comment to me.

"I don't like it one bit," the other woman agreed.

"It's scary that they call a doctor's work *practice*!" Mother muttered, wiggle-waggling her right foot in the air.

The woman grinned. "What's your ailment?" she asked.

"I don't have a thing wrong with me," Mother told her, gazing around the waiting room with its laminated fake wood wainscoting and the end tables piled with fishing magazines and *Popular Mechanics*. "It's all in my head."

But in the examining room, Mother stopped quipping. She arranged herself on her chair to look alert and adorable and I sat beside her, feeling her anxiety rising. "Are you okay, Mom?" I asked.

She nodded. She was too nervous to chatter. She had such a love-hate relationship with doctors that it was impossible for them to get an accurate blood pressure reading because her pressure zoomed up every time she walked into one of their offices.

Dr. Wright strode through the door, a wiry, fifty-something elf in his white coat and white running shoes. Flicking a shock of hair out of his eyes, he shook my hand, then rested his hand on Mother, as if in a quick blessing. "Come on, Mrs. Kelley," he said. "Jump up here. Let's take a look." He helped her climb a stepping stool so she could sit on his brown upholstered patient table.

He took her pulse, counting intently, then studied her and asked, "How are you feeling?"

"How do you think an old lady like me is feeling?" she demanded. Then she grinned triumphantly. She was not about to list her aches and pains for any doctor, even her darling Dr. Wright. After thirty years of nursing, she knew no mere doctor could fix what was wrong with her. Besides, to list her troubles would be to trivialize them. It would be to move them out of the permanent, immutable, Platonic realm, where they rightfully belonged, onto a medical chart.

## Chapter 39

# THE GENTLEMAN CALLER

One night when Mother was almost ninety, she announced to me on the phone that she had regretfully decided not to marry again. She just plain wasn't going to take care of any more men.

"Good for you," I said.

She confided that a man had phoned and asked to visit her. He was nice enough, but she had explained to him that she wasn't taking "social calls." She hoped she hadn't hurt his feelings.

Later that week, she mentioned that the same man had knocked at her door and introduced himself.

Several days later he knocked again. He would not relent. He couldn't live without her, he pled. It was getting embarrassing, she said. She wondered how she could say no without wrecking his life.

I thought of phoning the desk at Bentley to find out what was going on, but I didn't want them to focus on her. By now she was on the border between assisted living and the Alzheimer's unit, which had just been finished and christened the Courtyard. Several of my mother's friends had just been sent there. Cards we addressed to them came back with *Addressee Unknown*: a country never heard from.

So I didn't ask the desk for help. Instead I worried that a stranger might be preying on my elderly mother. But I didn't worry too much; I thought it would be hard for anyone to get into her locked and well-staffed facility.

I wondered whether Mother was lying about her gentleman caller, but I couldn't think of anything she'd gain from telling this lie. Maybe she had only imagined encounters with a man. But if so, her imagination was remarkably vibrant and persistent over several months. Almost every day she reported on another visit. Her descriptions were detailed and consistent.

I had heard about Mother's suitors all her life. Several years after Jim died, when she was off-loading three quarters of what she owned so she could move to her bungalow at Christian Care, she unhooked all the pictures from her walls, separating the mats from the artwork, flattening the art she wanted to keep, and storing it in large envelopes. In the process, she found, between a picture and its backing, a letter from the boyfriend she had rejected to marry my father. This boyfriend had given her the framed picture just before he shipped out to World War II. Sixty years and two husbands later, she discovered his letter and read it. He told her how desperately he loved her. He would still love her, he wrote, no matter when she found his letter. It was typed on an old typewriter with all the *e*'s filled in and he had signed it. It was the first time Mother had ever seen it.

I was flabbergasted. "You mean you didn't know it was there?"

"Nope."

"You just found it."

"Yep."

"That's mind-blowing."

"You like that?" she chortled.

"Mom, what if the poor guy meant it?"

"He doesn't mean it anymore."

"Where is he?"

"Who on earth knows?"

"Maybe you could find him."

"Oh, come on, honey. That was sixty years ago. He'd be in his late seventies. Anyway, he owned a furniture store. He probably never got out of Alexandria, Minnesota." She was proud that she didn't stay put. She was proud of moving all around the country.

Although finding that letter tickled Mother, I think it pitched her into another briar patch of self-examination about whether she'd been kind enough to the suitors she had disappointed. All her life she lived and relived those choices. In that way our mother was like Amanda in *The Glass Menagerie*, only our mother was nicer.

———

Thinking about all this, I began to believe that my mother's gentleman caller might have been real, at least in a way, even though he probably didn't knock on Mother's door. Her report might have been puzzling, but it wasn't exactly crazy. She was doing something brave. She must have been imagining her own past so clearly that it felt to her as if it were happening again.

It must have been like dreaming. When you dream, you see characters, including yourself, opening a door, say, and walking through it, eating, getting into a car, driving, fighting with people. In your dream you can touch them.

Even recalling what happened to you in the past, you can smell it sometimes, you can taste it. It is, in a way, *going on*.

When I was an adolescent, Mother described her boyfriends to me so colorfully and repeated their arguments so powerfully and elaborated so enticingly on the gifts they brought her, that I could see them in my mind's eye. There were the teenage sons of farmers who fell headlong in love with her, the callow, arrogant doctors who had pled for her hand in marriage, the most eligible bachelors in Alexandria, Minnesota, where she worked as a night nurse. I could hear their footfalls as they walked toward the door of her farmhouse, or approached her when she was on night duty at the hospital. She explained where they stood, how they gestured. Men showed up again after my father died, and briefly after my stepfather died. So when Mother told me about the man who knocked on her door, maybe she was reliving a whole lifetime of conflict over suitors. I reasoned that she was not just losing control of the various selves inside her, she was actually reimagining excerpts from her past. She was reliving conflicts she had experienced. I suppose it was the equivalent of chewing a cud.

That explained the persistent gentleman caller.

I believed that then, and I still believe it now, as I write this.

Believing that, I began paying closer attention to what Mother said. I started accepting, as a matter of faith, that what she said could be made sense of as references not to the present but to the past. I believed that might be happening not just once in a while, but a lot of the time, even when she sounded really unhinged. It mattered enormously to me that even her seemingly random gibberish might connect to and be explained by our history. I didn't "get" some of her comments. But demented hallucinations are one thing; mystery is another.

And what a relief, not to have to set Mother straight! If she said that she had been to London that day, or that Bertha had visited her with a pet alligator, or that she had to get dressed for work at the store, I didn't feel obligated to correct her anymore. I told myself, all right, think of this as metaphor. I had been fascinated by metaphor all my life, had studied it in graduate school and published six books of poetry. In fact, my life could be described as one long education in how to read and write metaphor. If the metaphors Mother used were drawn from her past, I thought, bring them on. At least I had a chance of understanding her.

At the time, I was feeling my way toward this conclusion.

Later I found out I wasn't the only one. I wish I had read Tom

Kitwood's ground-breaking *Dementia Reconsidered* while Mother was alive. He argued that what demented people say often refers to their history and experiences, which they often use as metaphor. The language of demented people is a feeling language, he argued, and is closer to poetry than to any other kind of speech. I take him to mean that their language reenacts the past in order to communicate their present emotions. I had just been reading Neruda, the Nobel prize-winning Chilean poet, that morning and, I thought, yes, Neruda and my mother sound alike. Surrealistic poets stuff their poems so full of metaphor that it's next to impossible to find a literal meaning. Here's an example:

> *Every day is an empty pail*
> *I fill and carry*
> *to the kitchen*
> *where I can sometimes*
> *unlock her*
> *handcuffs*
> *with a stem of grass*
> *and then, look!*
> *She's standing on the verandah*
> *of Mozart's Third Concerto.*

My friend, Virginia Stem Owens, in her book, *Caring for Mother*, which was published a year before my mother's death, but which I didn't read until afterward, also argues that her mother was fathoms deep in metaphor. She reasoned by analogy and referred to the analogy without explaining how she got there, the way she might have explained earlier in her life. "As time went by," Virginia writes, "I grew increasingly convinced of one thing, at least: [Mother] had an underlying signification system, even in the midst of her dementia. Her intelligence was now entirely emotional. One understood it only by attending to metaphor, not logic." And then there's Elinor Fuchs's book, *Making an Exit*, which lays out and celebrates some of the zany and poetic exchanges she carried on with her own demented mother.

As Mother verged into Alzheimer's, she grew quieter. On the phone with her at night, Daniel took over more and more of the conversation. He is a great monologuist, but I am not. I tried to refrain from asking questions, which my mother had trouble answering. But I wanted to persuade her to talk somehow, because hearing her, I'd remember the woman I grew up with, the one whose voice I recognized in the womb, who chattered as she washed the clothes, and drove me to orchestra rehearsals, full of advice about babies and men.

By Easter of 2007, Mother had fallen several times, even while using her walker. She mislaid her glasses and we never found them. In her refrigerator she amassed a towering collection of small plastic jam containers from breakfast. One morning when I was visiting she hooked her underpants on in place of a bra. She took her pills, then spat them out when she thought the aides weren't watching. She decided that one of the women on the desk hated her, that that woman harbored dark recriminatory vendettas against her. And her osteoporosis had progressed so far that her spine looked like a modified S.

Julie and I hired aides to help Mother bathe and dress five mornings a week. The first week this strategy seemed promising. On Monday of the second week, Mother angrily met the aides at the door and sent them away. Every morning they came and every morning Mother threw them out. We didn't discover this for more than a month, during which time they kept submitting bills and we blissfully paid them, happy the arrangement was working. When we discovered what was going on, we

interviewed and employed a new set of aides from an agency—
women who were bonded and insured, who'd had experience
with dementia patients. Mother ordered them out of her apartment, too, and, of course, they left.

Trying to get to the bottom of this, I asked Mother whether
anyone had knocked on her door that morning to help her
bathe and dress.

"A girl with a bandanna?" she asked.

"Maybe. I don't know. Is that what she was wearing?"

"How would I know?" Mother sounded puzzled.

"Mom, are you saying someone with a bandanna knocked on
your door?"

"I haven't seen anyone wearing a bandanna."

"Did you get a bath this morning, Mom?"

"A person can do anything she puts her mind to!" Mother
breathed fervently.

"I know. But did you get a bath this morning?"

"Oh," she said. "Probably."

When the Powers That Be at Christian Care first talked about
moving Mother to the Courtyard, Julie and I resisted. We fought
the move valiantly for several years. But in the spring of 2007
Mother's weight had fallen to under a hundred pounds and she
needed an aide to help her eat. Bentley didn't have enough staff
to care for her.

Julie gave the administrators at Christian Care the word.
They found Mother a room in the Courtyard so fast it made my
head swim. So during a week when I could least afford to go, I
bought a flight to Dallas. I hired a terrific graduate student to
teach my two classes, composed an e-mail to undergraduates,
answered messages from students, editors, and colleagues, and
ran off proofs for an essay I needed to correct before I got back.
A script deadline with a theater loomed. The title had already

been announced in the PR brochure for the upcoming fall, which meant I had to finish the play in the next two weeks so the cast could start rehearsal. Realizing this, I sat down in panic and started revising it. Around two a.m. that morning I ran off pages and stuffed them into my computer case to bring to Dallas. In the kitchen I jotted a list of the fruit and vegetables I'd bought for Jack and Daniel. I left several cookbooks and cans of cat food on the counter.

Will you believe me when I tell you it's exhausting to fight aging? Like a slow-moving glacier, it levels hills and valleys, mows down redwoods, and kills animals. Flying to Dallas five or six times a year, coordinating Mother's outfits, buying and sending clothes, taking her to doctors, filling prescriptions, battling her about Depends, arranging lunches, finding what she lost, cleaning and mending and organizing her apartment, reassuring her when, in fact, I was worried myself—I couldn't keep cheerfully fighting on so many fronts.

Eventually, even I started to relent. On the clothing front, for example, I thought, why shouldn't Mother wear what she wants? Timidly I begin to look forward to her seemingly random, garish combinations as if they were statements of extravagant taste or quirky jokes. It was nothing I could change. Even as they became wilder, more outlandish, I didn't try to stop her. I was right to let go of that. It became practice for more letting go later. I began to think of letting go as a discipline.

So Mother led her children further into the odd, metaphor-strewn terrain of dementia.

# FIELD NOTE 12

## THE ART OF MEMORY

*I go to my bookshelf and find the book that might answer
the question: How can we remember? It's Frances Yates's*
The Art of Memory. *It tells how Europe rediscovered
the system Greeks had invented to recall information.*
*I know it is too late for this book to help my mother. But it might
help me.*

*Cicero claims that Simonides, a Greek poet, first thought up the art
of memory. Simonides was hired by a rich man to chant a poem about
the twin gods, Castor and Pollux, at his dinner party. Simonides and
the host agreed on a price and the poet sang his poem brilliantly. But
when he tried to settle up with his employer afterward, he got only half
of what he was promised. For the rest, the rich man sneered, "Go ask
Castor and Pollux."*

*Soon after that, one of the servants told Simonides that two men
were asking for him outside. But when the poet stepped outside to find
them, he couldn't. While he was out there, the roof of the house fell in,
crushing everyone at the dinner.*

*The bodies of the dinner guests were so mangled they couldn't even
be identified. Their families were distraught. The poet, who had stood
in the banquet room delivering the poem, remembered the place each
guest had been sitting. From the position of their dead bodies, he was
able to identify them.*

*Slowly it dawned on the poet that Castor and Pollux had rewarded
him for the honor of his poem by sparing him from death. And Cicero
claims that this awful experience inspired Simonides to develop the art
of memory.*

*Memory, Simonides realized, must be tethered to* place.

*Say you want to remember a long speech. Stand in the room where you will deliver it. Starting on the right-hand side and moving around the room, place one paragraph on each architectural feature—for instance, a column or a chair or a window or a pedestal or a vase or a statue. Then when you stand up to talk, you can glance from right to left, picking up your ideas, one after another.*

*Cicero went on to argue that you don't even have to be in the room when you give the speech. You only need to see in your mind's eye the details of the room, and presto, you will remember what you wanted to say.*

*What a good plan, I think. But who can remember the details of a room in their exact order? And I put the book back on the shelf.*

## Chapter 40

# ALZHEIMER'S UNIT

Julie and Rich moved Mother's large furniture into the Courtyard and installed Mother in her new apartment the day before I arrived. When I walked in, I discovered Mother sitting on her couch, staring absentmindedly out the door. She smelled strongly of perfume, which she had begun to use to mask other smells. Hugging her, I felt alarmed at how tiny and bony she felt. After I released her, she looped her arm in mine for balance.

"Do you like it?" I asked, scanning the furniture Julie and Rich had chosen to bring over.

"Weeeeeell, yeeeessssssss." By this musical reply she meant no.

"Oh, Mom, look! Your pictures are already up!" I chirped.

She turned and studied them. "How nice. Are those my pictures?"

"They belong to you. And you painted that one." It was the picture of her childhood farm with the dark storm clouds moving against the tiny farmhouse.

"That's good, isn't it? If I do say so myself." She let my arm go and wandered over to stare at the picture.

"That's my favorite," I tell her.

"You can do whatever you put your mind to."

"That's right. You've done some wonderful paintings..."

"I'm a hardship case," she confessed sheepishly, touching the painting.

"So am I." I laughed.

She wrinkled her nose. "Who painted this?"

"You did."

"Who put it up?"

"I guess Julie."

"She did?" Her voice was full of wonder.

"Wasn't Julie here yesterday?"

Mother turned to me. "You girls would know."

"Julie and Rich were here helping you."

"Well, there you go. Is it time for dinner yet?"

"Are you hungry?"

"What do you think?" she asked coyly. "Let's shoot the raccoon!" Then, tuckered out from exertion, she sank onto her couch.

As I sallied forth to ask the aide with the tattoo about dinner, I was remembering the summer my mother had told me about her mother shooting the raccoon. In front of me, down the hall from Mother's apartment, three or four aides were gathering residents for dinner. I could smell the gravy and hear the plates being set out, the tick of ceramic on tables.

I sat with Mother while she ate, my mother, who had drilled into me the proper way to eat soup, scooping the spoon away from myself, who had made me practice how to set a table with eight pieces of silverware per place setting. This same mother pushed her mashed potatoes onto her fork with her left hand and dropped most of them on the way to her mouth. So I stabbed her potatoes onto my fork. She opened her mouth like a baby bird and I fed her.

Three bites and she was finished. I smiled, hoping to encourage her. "Would you like more?" She returned a dazzling smile, picked up a green bean with her fingers, and twirled it in the air.

Someday, I thought, maybe I'll write about this. At that

moment, I felt I might lose it, blow up or collapse, skid off the edge of the known world. I tried to remind myself of the place I belonged, reading and writing, teaching and cooking for a family. I desperately wanted to walk out of my mother's story. Maybe that was unforgivable, but I don't think Mother knew. And if she had known, I don't think she would have minded. She might have laughed and asked to come along. She loved me. And after all, I had flown there to help her, though I'm not sure she was aware of that. At the time, sitting there, I registered nothing but loss. Now as I look back, I also recognize and honor Mother's gumption and patience.

I helped her back to her apartment and then excused myself to schlep boxes from her old place. Getting into my rental car and driving the short way back to Bentley, I felt heady as a teenager. I loved it, I just loved it. Steering a car, a person has some control, or at least the illusion of some control. And then I thought about how Mother was now without a car, in fact, how she was without the skill to read a map or the coordination to drive, and I wondered whether she still missed it or whether she had forgotten she ever had it.

I returned to the Courtyard, hugging a massive cardboard box, and stepped off the elevator into the hall. An older woman dressed in white wool slacks, a white V-neck sweater, and a little silver belt accosted me. I was sweating, and my shirt was sticking to me. I was aware the woman must find me rather disgusting. But she strolled alongside me, past the front desk, by the immense fish tank. When I got to my mother's apartment, Mother was not there. So I awkwardly stuffed the gargantuan box through the door, and it landed with a thud on the beige carpet. My companion waited beside me, smiling. I turned to her, wondering what she had to tell me—about my mother, about her medications, about her visitors and her doctors.

"You won't find her," the woman said.

"Why not?" I asked.

"She hides."

"Who hides?"

"You don't know me, so I don't have to tell you."

The woman was not a health care worker but a resident.

I was tired. I couldn't imagine what lay ahead for Mother. I felt we were sliding into a nightmare. I wondered whether this world might be, indeed, governed by chance, by darkness, or by nothing at all.

I looked toward the desk, hoping to be rescued. There was not an aide in sight. I was on my own in the uncharted country of this woman's mind. I knew that whatever I said, in two minutes she would forget.

"I'm sorry. I don't understand you," I said, and I set off to find my mother.

The woman followed me. "Are you looking for her?"

"I think she's getting her pills," I replied.

Then I noticed my mother snoozing in one of the Queen Anne chairs by the desk. I stepped over, scrunched down, and put my arm around her. She woke up and looked at me without recognition. Then her eyes cleared. "Well, look who's here!" she shouted brightly. She never called me darling anymore. She couldn't afford to be that revealing. But she stood up and flung her arms around me as if she hadn't seen me for years.

The woman persisted. "I told her not to, and she went ahead anyway."

"Not to do what?"

I glanced at my mother. She shrugged, grinned at me, and drew a ding-a-ling with her finger in the air beside her ear, blissfully identifying herself with me and other sane, rational people of the world. I grabbed her bony hand and walked her slowly to the massive fish tank, where we stood watching angelfish swim in patterns around shells and pebbles.

"Sing, everybody, sing!" a woman behind us squawked. She was grasping a table knife, with which she was conducting. "Sing! Sing! Sing!" she burst forth in a warm contralto, "La la laaa la, la la laaaa la."

A dapper, white-haired man walked by us, then turned and explained to me, "I'm shirting the morph." He cupped one hand and held it out to me. "I needed to skole the warp," he went on, in the tone of a company president extolling his quarterly profits to his board.

I smiled and took what he offered, which was air.

Around us, old folks were slumbering in their wheelchairs. Affixed to one vacant chair was an oxygen tank. Its owner had climbed out and was kneeling on the carpet in her red velour robe, urgently searching for something.

For hours the woman we called the Pacer had been tromping up and down the hall in her jazzy matching purple sneakers and baseball cap, regalia that suggested that someone, one of her children, possibly, cared about her. Lean and athletic, she pumped her bent arms enthusiastically as she walked. One of the aides moved to divert her but she broke free and pushed on. Trailing her, the aide finally convinced her to rest, then led her by the hand to a chair as if she were a child, coaxed her to sit on her lap, and rocked her.

That night I returned to the guest room at Julie and Rich's house, where I had slept so often that it practically felt like my own home. I heard the bell-like voice of our priest, Claire, *Life is short and we do not have much time to gladden the hearts of those who travel with us. So be swift to love, make haste to be kind, live without fear. Your Creator has made you holy, has always protected you, and loves you as a mother. Go in peace to follow the good road*

*and may the blessing of God: Creator, Redeemer and Sanctifier, be*
*with you now and always.*

And I fell asleep.

—

Now, as I write this, I am holding one of the files I found when
I was cleaning out Mother's Bentley apartment. She stapled the
file at both ends so the papers couldn't fall out and scrawled
with Magic Marker on the tab: "Memorial Helps on Mom:
Requests and Wishes." She wrote the list on lined paper in her
even, Palmer-method hand:

> *Don't mourn: I'll be with Jesus!*
> *No jewelry on*
> *Have a bright colorful dress*
> *Wear glasses (good) for sure*
> *Small opened New Testament to cover my lumpy*
>   *fingers*
> *Whoever preaches, He's to use my old Scofield Bible*
>   *that is all written full, that I dearly loved.*

I found several other scrawled lists in this folder: who might
sing solos at her service, who might serve as her pallbearers. She
included programs from other funerals. I took the folder home,
as I suspect she wanted me to do.

Julie and I were told we could not bring Mother's valuables,
even her rings, to the Courtyard because too many things disappeared from the place. So the two of us drove Mother to the
local fire station in Mesquite, which, as a public service, saws
off rings that won't slip off with soaping. I sat in the car with
my mother while my sister went in to find a fireman. Because
mother was over ninety, he brought his equipment outside rather

than making her walk in. He was the age of her grandchildren, kneeling in the parking lot beside her like a Boy Scout. "Tell me if this hurts, ma'am," he said. "I don't want to hurt you." The way he held her veiny old hand was so courtly, my eyes misted over. We put her diamond rings in a lock box in her name and bought her two rings with very large glass stones. I don't think she ever knew the difference.

Without a backward glance, my mother shed the objects of a lifetime. She forgot her eighty-year-old china doll with the milk glass eyes named Marianne, and the mink collars she had scissored off her coats to save. She no longer remembered the genuine red wool blanket my father bought her on their honeymoon in Sault Ste. Marie. She gave up her Lenox and never mentioned it again. Once they slipped from her attention, all her alluring things grew lifeless. Her love was what electrified them.

I didn't understand that until I went through her cedar chest. After we moved Mother to the Alzheimer's unit, I sat cross-legged, alone in my sister's double garage in front of that chest. The key clicked metallically as it spun in the lock. In the shadowy light, I couldn't figure out why the lock wouldn't open. I half believed the chest was forbidding me to touch it. Mother had bought that trunk with her first paycheck as a nurse, and no one ever opened it but her. Occasionally she would summon us and we would lean forward as she pulled things out of the chest. She would permit us to touch them briefly.

She had the knack of limiting her possessions to the number she could really use, maybe because she was a teenager during the Depression. Even later, after she married my stepfather, when she could afford what she wanted, she would buy a dress and hoard it in her closet as it accumulated glamour for several months before she wore it. So in the chilly garage, when I finally got her cedar chest open and unfolded the ancient tissue paper,

I was looking for razzle-dazzle. What I found: the sweaters were peppered with woolly pills and her long, white leather gloves had stiffened with age. Her spell had departed from things after she no longer cared about them. Sitting on a shelf in my daughter's house, Marianne now looks like any other antique doll. The same goes for Mother's teacup collection, her tatted and linen tablecloths.

In one of Mother's steel boxes I found the letters I sent to her in 1968 when I was first married. After she moved to Dallas with her new husband, I wrote her a letter a week because she asked me to. I took my letters home; I couldn't bring myself to throw them out, but I don't know what to do with them. They were half-truths, concocted with bravado to make her happy, and they make no sense without her.

This litany of relics is a list of my own losses, not of my mother's. I'm quite sure as I write this, that my mother didn't mind losing her things. It often seemed to me that she experienced their leaving as a lightening, a lifting, a freeing.

## Chapter 41

# A PLAY WITH A HAPPY ENDING

It's Mother's second day in the Alzheimer's unit and the aides have gathered the residents for afternoon cookies and coffee. I see Albert, a white-haired gentleman in a snappy denim shirt, take Elsie's arm and no matter how hard Elsie pulls away from him, Albert hangs on. Elsie is his new love and he's thrilled. He's determined to court her. When coaxing her in his charming South Carolina accent doesn't convince her, he shyly slips her two unwrapped chocolate Hershey's kisses, which have been in his drawer so long they look chalky. She pushes his hand aside, but he croons a couple of lines of "You Are My Sunshine." He has a pretty good voice. She ducks her head and wheels her walker expertly away.

That afternoon when aides gather the residents for what the aides call "Bragging Time," Elsie casts Albert a flirtatious look and plops down in the midst of the women—that old junior high school girl trick—so Albert can't sit beside her. He turns his cobalt eyes on her and grins mischievously from across the room. She smiles back. Then he falls asleep.

Watching Albert and Elsie reminds me of watching my

students in the spring who, upon shedding their winter coats, see one another, and fall in love for the first time. There's tragedy in this, of course. Albert has lost his wife. Elsie has buried her husband. If friends visit Albert or Elsie, more than likely neither will remember the visit, though the pleasure they take in the attention will linger. Their lives are not entirely dismal. There is daring in their story, and flirting, and wit, and chocolate.

The people who understand this most clearly are the aides in the Alzheimer's unit. These women revel in love as it unfolds. They do not discriminate against Albert and Elsie for being old. They carve a place in the grief of Alzheimer's for the joy of the moment. After the terror of moving Mother to the Courtyard, I discover that these women are more talented and generous than I could have imagined.

⁓

Although most of the accounts I've read about Alzheimer's are characterized by horror, the truth is, even my mother's final months were not relentlessly grim. Although our mother was never diagnosed with Alzheimer's, she clearly suffered from dementia. Looking back, I see the progress of that dementia was uneven, surprising. Watching her was like watching a rowboat come loose and drift away from a dock. I was the one standing on the dock watching the boat glide away. It felt like my mother was getting lost, but maybe not. What if you're in another rowboat in the middle of the lake and the boat is drifting toward you?

I think of my mother's last years as a tragicomedy. I mean one of those tragic comedies where the characters can't remember who they are. In Shakespeare's *Twelfth Night,* Viola crawls out of the sea, half-drowned after a shipwreck she believes has killed her brother. She finds herself alone on an unfamiliar shore in a strange country. She worries that she might be murdered or raped, so she puts on men's clothes. After that, because the characters in the play think Viola is a man, they start making life-changing, potentially tragic mistakes. Except for Viola, all the characters in the play act like the Alzheimer's patients who lived on my mother's hall.

Still, *Twelfth Night* is a *comedy*, however dark. That doesn't mean it's filled with jokes. It means the play has a happy ending. Long before the end, though, a comic spirit guides the events of the play. Even in the first, troubled scenes of *Twelfth Night*, enough joy and love flash through the dialogue that only a tone-deaf writer would end the play in catastrophe. In the same way, I saw flashes of tenderness and humor even in my mother's Alzheimer's ward. I felt what I often feel when I am walking on the nature trail at Haverford College, where thirty species of trees shade the meadows, where a nimble resident heron stalks fish in the stream, and every May a snapping turtle creeps across the running path and stands, blinking for hours, patiently depositing her eggs. There's plenty of evidence that in spite of suffering, our universe is ordered by a force that is not chance, not brutality, not evil, but goodness.

———

Now the aides are gathering the old people in the lounge to see the Animal Lady, who stops by with a different pet every month. Mother sits in her chair, craning her neck to see. "Look," I say. "She's going to talk about ferrets."

The woman gives a talk about the habits of this long, skinny creature, his natural surroundings, how he responds. She bribes the quick little mammal with food to perform tricks and then lets the old folks ask questions.

"Who takes the ferret swimming?"

"Where are the ferret's children?"

"Who belongs to that ferret?"

They're such wonderful questions! the Animal Lady exclaims jubilantly. She answers them and then rewards us by bringing the ferret around so each of us can pet it.

Although Mother never even liked our own dogs, when the ferret comes close, crawling on the arm of his owner, Mother valiantly reaches out her trembling hand and pets him. When one of the aides gets up and dances with the Animal Lady, Mother giggles. When the Animal Lady gives a quiz at the end of the show Mother's hand shoots up. She answers two questions: What do we feed ferrets, and do you like this ferret?

"Yes," Mother shouts to the last question. She knows that's the right answer. "Yes!" She crows with happiness.

Whatever Mother has lost, and it is much, she is still in the game. She trusts the aides. It's true the creed means nothing to her now, since her language is almost gone. She sleeps through church. But she's hanging on to her faith. Sometimes when I hold her hand at night and recite the Twenty-third Psalm, she says every word with me perfectly, calling them up with some life force that seems deeper than memory. *Yea though I walk through the valley of the shadow of death, I will fear no evil. Thy rod and thy staff, they comfort me.* That fits her life, I think. She's always preferred perennials, the flowers that wither in the fall and come back in spring.

I watch as she smiles briefly and joins the procession of residents who line up their walkers. The aide leads them, wearing a yellow button: SMILE: GOD LOVES YOU! The residents look like slow, trained elephants whose knees are slipping down. From the line Mother waves to me.

I am thinking about how plucky she is. You don't get to practice for old age.

Or maybe your whole life is practice.

They take the elevator upstairs to their hall. I climb the steps to meet her.

*Chapter 42*

# A MILLION COUNTRIES
# TO SEE

As I walk upstairs to greet Mother at the elevator, I am remembering what happened that spring before I announced to Mother that I was leaving for Peru. I send my memory out on an errand. How on earth did I get up the courage to tell her I was leaving her? She held on to me so desperately, particularly after Michael died. When I finally left, it was a shattering that required courage from both of us.

By the time I was seventeen, I was sick of my mother's advice and rules, but I was also terrified of leaving home. I viewed going off to college as the event that would finally provide a showdown. Either I would survive or I wouldn't. I had no intention of living at home with Mother in Lincoln and attending the University of Nebraska.

After we had driven Michael to Wheaton, that place became a splendid and terrible magnet for me. I thought of it as an intellectual paradise, a holiday from our dull, repetitive life. I longed to join a flock of like-minded teenagers. Together we would soar into the future. But I also knew that Wheaton was a place where, if you weren't careful, you could die. A year after

we buried Michael, when I informed my mother that I intended
to go to Wheaton for college, she didn't reply.

Several days later, she requested a talk with me. She was
wearing her worn, often-washed, blue-turned-gray cotton
nighty and she was rubbing cream into her face, walking down
the hall toward my bedroom. I was passing her on my way to the
kitchen for a snack, peanut butter on a rusk.

"About Wheaton," she said.

I knew she was about to tell me I couldn't go. Where would
we get the money for tuition and travel? she would ask. Or
maybe she would inform me that she'd just lost a child and she
wasn't about to lose another so soon. I was sure there would be
some excuse for why she needed me to stay close to her.

"I refuse to send another kid there alone," Mother said. She
let that soak in.

"But I'll go with you."

It took me a moment to realize that she was bargaining
rather than dictating. She had economic power over me, and
she knew it. True, her power was complicated by the fact that
she had already promised to pay my tuition to the college of my
choice. However, she didn't need to ask me; she could have simply informed me that she was moving with me. But she didn't.

And I could have told her not to come, but I didn't.

Later, I regretted our bargain. I had wanted to measure my courage, to experience a new reality, to test my wings, to get away from
my mother. As the buyers traipsed through our house, as we packed
her Lenox in strips of newspaper, as I sweated, and squinted, and
watched movers carry our furniture to the van, my heart felt like
an empty shack. I believed I would never get away from Mother.

After the move, though, my astute mother loosened her grip
on me. To save board and room in the fall, I lived at home.
I discovered that other freshmen were required to be in their

dorms by ten on weeknights, but Mother announced that I was officially out of the house now and even though I was sleeping there, she would impose no curfew on me. After that, she never asked me where I had been, and she never met me in her nightgown at the door with heart palpitations. Occasionally I drove into Chicago with college guys who lived in town, who didn't have curfews either, and sometimes I sneaked back into the house at four a.m. I suspect Mother never slept until she heard the door lock behind me, but she didn't raise a murmur.

I was mindful that this required monumental self-control on her part, and yet I was restless. After damping down a lifetime of curiosity, after grieving my father's and brother's deaths, after working for academic glory to make my mother proud of what remained, I was crazy to get out. I didn't even know what that meant. If it had been the seventies, I might have tried drugs. Instead, I opted for travel. I fled the States because I so desperately needed to get away from Mother and to make it clear to myself that I had really gotten away.

I wanted to go somewhere radical. I had friends who flung their toothbrushes into rucksacks and traveled in Europe, but I wanted to migrate to a realm beyond any place I'd heard of. I wanted to tear the seams out of everything I had previously imagined. I think I wanted to go to a country my brother talked to on his ham radio. I knew nothing about Peru. Without realizing a revolution was in full swing there, I decided that's where I would go.

And how did Mother take it?

There she is, standing in the sun by the white siding of our house in Wheaton. She's been gossiping with our neighbor, Mary, about Mary's mother-in-law. Mary is telling Mother that the ferocious old woman still has her talons in Mary's husband, though he's pushing forty. Mary's beginning to read the tea leaves. Her husband will live the rest of his life in thrall to his mother.

I head out the screen door to announce to Mother that in a few weeks I'm leaving for Peru. I find her squatting in a bed of snapdragons, pulling a few weeds.

She shades her eyes and squints up at me. When I tell her, she blares, "Peru! Why Peru?" As if she were a jealous lover and Peru was the rival. "Do you have to go so far away?"

"Yes, I do."

"Why?"

Because I have to get out from under, yes, I do, or I will lose my mind. That's the truth, though I don't say it. I wonder whether Peru will be far enough, whether a summer will be long enough. I wonder whether she will figure out a way to follow me. But I don't want to hurt her, so I don't make that the center-piece of my explanation. I tell her the few colorful facts I know about the country. It boasts a coastal area, another region with high mountains, and a vast jungle zone, for instance. She looks at me as if I've got two holes in my head. What's so great about that?

"Save Peru for later," she urges. "Travel around here this summer."

"Mother, I'm going to Peru."

"You don't want to experience everything now, darling. What will you have left to enjoy later?" This was Mother's man-tra, her theme song, the dilapidated and eternal argument she had used since I could remember to prevent me from having new experiences.

"It scares you, doesn't it?" I say, watching her.

"It scares me that you'll use up everything and feel jaded and there won't be anything left for you to do."

I am infected with the yippee of travel, mad with anticipation. I tell her, "There are a million other countries to see. I'll go to all of them and when I've seen them all, I'll go to the moon!" I know that President Kennedy is bent on sending men to the moon. Of course, I fail to notice that it is *men* he's planning to send.

I scoot inside and phone a friend whose parents are missionaries in Quito, Ecuador, and soon I have a cheap ticket on a cargo plane to Lima. All that day and the next, I listen to Nat King Cole croon "Ramblin' Rose." I turn the song up as high as is possible and fling the windows open.

Mother, who has put on lipstick and combed her hair and descended into the basement to wash the clothes in our old ringer washing machine, pokes her head into the kitchen and yells, "TURN DOWN THAT AIR TRASH!"

When Mother finds out there's no phone service in the jungle and letters rarely get delivered, she asks around and discovers that friends of friends who lived several blocks away from us own a shortwave radio. She makes me promise to find a shortwave radio in the jungle so we can talk. I promise. This time it's Mother who's worried about getting homesick.

⁓

I flew to Lima with a high heart, and in Lima I hopped a rickety second-hand bus to ride over the Andes into the jungle. As our orange bus labored over the mountains, I felt free of the flat, two-dimensional calendar-illustration Midwestern world I had dwelled in. The steep, husky, endless, snowy mountains gave me vertigo. I felt thrilled by the smallness of my own body and by the way the road ahead dwindled to a gray thread. Peering thousands of feet down, I saw three dozen iron crosses, where some bus must have catapulted over the railing and fallen. The crosses were the size of the plusses in my childhood addition problems.

Forty hours later I stepped from the bus onto the dusty road that ran through the Amazon jungle. Everything in the small clearing was vivid and buzzing. The violently green, fecund trees exploded around me. The draping vines reach menacingly down for me through the force field of muggy, aggressive heat. Jungle insects vibrated with incessant racket. My eyes blurred and my head felt stuffed with rags.

Within two hours I was submerged up to my chin in a tepid oxbow lake with the children of missionaries. As I doggie-paddled, I noticed a shadow swarming around us, and asked what it was. "Just piranhas," they explained, relaxing on their backs against their inner tubes, paddling luxuriously in little circles. The piranhas were swarming to discover whether I had a wound, they told me. If they found one, they would strip me to the bone so fast it wouldn't hurt. Otherwise, I would be fine.

I remained in the water against my better judgment, because I was convinced that this was a test of my courage. I was aware that I had not even traveled to college by myself and I needed practice at passing such tests. Later that afternoon one of the girls, who took me in hand like a seasoned diplomat, introduced me to Max, her pet cheetah. She opened the cage and let Max out. The two-hundred-pound predator followed her around like a kitten, while I struggled against my compulsion to climb into the cage and lock the door.

To a girl who had been raised in the Midwest, Peru offered plenty of novelty. The trouble with travel is that you can get used to anything, and then, to make you swoon again, you need another jolt of novelty. For the first month, I encountered one startling novelty after another. But I became acclimated after several months to the blue, blue skies of early morning, to the brief, violent thunder and rain at three every afternoon, to the bottomless black night sky with no light pollution—nights speckled with stars so large and articulate that I felt I could pick them like fruit.

It was living with the missionaries I discovered in the Amazon jungle that changed me permanently, the way travel should. They were all translators, or at least most of them were. Those who weren't, the grocers and pilots and secretaries and accountants, acted as support staff for the translators. Each had left a home and a family and moved to the jungle to become enmeshed with a tribe.

Since none of the tribal languages had been written, a translator would learn the language of her tribe by listening, then creating an alphabet. Then she'd compose a dictionary and transcribe the tribe's folklore. After she organized a school and taught the people to read their own stories in their own language, she finally began translating the Bible, starting with the Gospels. This took thirty years, nearly a lifetime. I could not fathom such a long-term project. I had fairly short attention span. I liked novelty. The missionaries modeled a different lifestyle for me. They had taken vows. They understood what they wanted their lives to be about. Paradoxically, being with them, I felt more freedom than I'd ever felt in my life.

I was absurdly happy on my own in Peru. Nevertheless, every two weeks I walked down a dusty road under the green awning of trees, through the buzzing, hissing jungle, to the radio shack on the base and chatted with my mother on a shortwave radio. I don't remember exactly what she talked about: which of our neighbors and friends had a cold, which neighbors stopped by to visit, how much the tomato plants needed rain, who at church had found a new job.

As for me, I tried to explain to Mother the impossibly beautiful, savage jungle.

When I told her for the second time that I planned to bring home a monkey, she blew up.

"Why on earth do you want a monkey?" she fumed.

"They're great house pets." Almost every family on the base kept a monkey.

"They let monkeys run around in the house?"

"Sure."

"Do they pee all over?"

"I don't know. They're funny. They're cute. They sleep in cages at night."

"Darling, no. We aren't going to keep a monkey."

Then static overtook our conversation and we broke off. I wanted to bring home some talisman, some creature to remind me of this jungly, impromptu, free way of life. I wanted a memento to mark this portal I had passed through into my own life. In fact, I wanted to bring the whole jungle home. I had no concept of the hoops I'd need to jump through to get a monkey into the States.

—

Mother, it turned out, wanted to travel, too. Maybe she was learning from her children. When I came home from Peru tanned as a chestnut, with more than thirty mosquito bites on each leg, a burn on my arm from an exotic spider, and a revamped view of life's vast possibilities, my mother paid attention. With unaccustomed respect she listened to my stories, then confided in me that she had always wanted to travel.

The next fall, when my younger sister moved into a dorm at Wheaton, leaving Mother alone in the house, Mother began walking around her high school nurse's office like a zombie. She would drive straight home after work and fall into bed. One of Mother's friends diagnosed the problem as depression resulting from loneliness. By phone she introduced Mother to Jim, her cousin in Dallas, whose wife had died.

Punctually every night Jim called Mother. Occasionally I was home doing laundry, eavesdropping, amused that two elderly people—that is, adults in their late forties—could be infatuated with one another. Mother ordered a phone installed in the basement for privacy and every night she talked to Jim for hours down there.

In March, Jim flew to visit Mother. He pretended that he needed to come for business. For all the hours Mother had spent klatching with Jim on the basement phone, she had never laid eyes on him. Once she knew the date he was coming, she jittered-jabbered about it like an excited teenager. She decided that she would pick Jim up at O'Hare by herself. But she asked me to come and stay with them at her house for her first dinner with him. "What if he wants to sleep here overnight?" she asked me anxiously.

By that time I was married and living in Chicago. After I heard that Jim would be visiting my mother, I began to worry about her—really, for the first time. What if this man was taking her for a ride? What if he was preying on her? I decided that I needed to stand guard, possibly to save her. I planned to assess this Jim character. So I planned a menu for the two lovebirds and on the afternoon of his flight, I took the train from Chicago to Mother's house in Wheaton, lugging two bags of groceries. I was a rookie cook, but I loved the kitchen and was eager to experiment. When I arrived around four thirty, Mother looked like a million dollars. As she walked down the hall, fastening her fabled rock sharp crystal necklace from Honolulu, a trail of Tweed perfume drifted after her.

I bid her good-bye at the front door, patting her, telling her how beautiful she looked, feeling maternal. She backed her Chevy slowly out of the driveway and headed to the airport to meet Jim. Then in her tiny kitchen, I listened to the Beatles and whipped up recipes I had learned from her: roasted potatoes, carrots, beets, and rutabagas. Salad. And tight, shiny, brown, succulent roast chicken that dripped and popped when I took it out of the oven.

Mother and Jim arrived at the front door just before seven and rang the doorbell. *Bing, bong, bong, bing!* I dashed to open the door, wearing a flowered apron, blushing with the heat of cooking. Mother had somehow lost her key.

I stood holding the door while she introduced me to Jim. He looked like a Brooks Brother's ad standing behind her on the small concrete stoop. He was a nearly bald, portly gentleman with a Georgia accent and a luminous, boyish smile. He shook my hand and ducked his head and growled a few words of greeting. I liked him instantly. Who would not cotton to such a sweet, grown-up Tom Sawyer?

When I held the door open wider and the two of them entered, I saw that Mother was hobbling on one shoe. Weeks ago, she had ordered a pair of satin heels dyed to match her dress. I knew they were expensive, because she had planned every stitch of her wardrobe with me on the phone. I asked her what had happened to her other shoe. She threw up her hands and cried, "I lost it!"

That was all. I lost it. This woman who had worried and planned and worked all her life had slipped into another universe. We all chuckled. How could losing a pricey shoe in the airport seem, not a calamity, but a lucky sign? It did. Mother took off her other shoe and came to dinner, celebrating with bare feet.

After dinner, when Jim excused himself to go to the bathroom, my flushed and erotic-looking Mother whispered to me that I was free to go. She would handle Jim by herself. I laughed all the way back to the city, where my young husband and I pretended to be wiser than my mother. "They'll know a thing or two once they're married," we told one another.

Shortly after that, Mother invited me to lunch in a fancy restaurant, which may have been the first time she had ever done that. We had no more settled into the booth and spread the cloth napkins on our laps than she demanded, "Should I marry him?"

"Good grief, I don't know," I protested. "I've barely met him."

"He's good-looking, don't you think?" she asked.

The man looked nothing like my handsome father, but I didn't mention that. What right did I have? "Is he nice to you?" I asked.

"He's very kind."

"What does he do?"

"He opens doors for me. He walks on the street side of the sidewalk. He knows which silverware to use." Good manners, Mother believed, reveal a kind heart.

"No, I mean work. What does he do?"

She sounded less well versed in this. "Well, it's something about oil wells."

"Does he own them?" I asked hopefully.

"Nooooooo!" The woman who had told me all my life that I could do anything I wanted, studied me as if she were suddenly realizing I was a true imbecile.

"He checks out new sites," she said. "He's an engineer. He graduated with honors from Stanford." She paused to let that sink in.

"Wow!" I exclaimed loyally. "So if you married him, where would you live?"

"We'd have to work all that out."

In the end, I advised her: "Go for it!"

Now as I write this, I suspect that my mother had already decided to marry Jim. Asking me for my opinion was her way of introducing her new husband without forcing him on me. "He has a little money," she said as she paid our lunch bill. "So I hope we can travel." She knew exactly how to commend this new man to my heart.

But the farthest Mother ever traveled with Jim was to Laredo for two weeks for his business. Jim had spent twenty years posted in exotic locations all over Africa and the Middle East and he married Mother hoping to settle down. For most of his life he had supported his own mother and his younger siblings and a very unhappy wife, who had died the year before. Once Jim and Mother were married, he accepted an influential job overseeing the City of Dallas Sanitation Department. So instead of roaming the world, Mother dedicated herself to making a cozy, predictable home for Jim, which she accomplished with affection and high spirits. I remember a morning, for instance, before the two of us left to have lunch at the Museum of Art, when she designed a gourmet sandwich for Jim and stashed it in the refrigerator with a love note. Then she scooped a dish of ice cream, stuck a spoon in it, and left it for him in the freezer. No wonder he worshipped her.

Mother did get to travel, though, after Jim died. It was not just that we took her to the Green Mountains and Kinhaven. When Jack was two, and again when he was four and six, I taught in London and Mother flew over with us for a month each time. The three of us hung out all January in Paddington in a run-down hotel where the heating was so dodgy that some mornings we discovered that the underwear we washed out the night before and hung over the radiator had frozen stiff. I brought a hot plate in my suitcase. Some evenings, to avoid yet another restaurant dinner with a toddler, Mother and I would stir-fry snow peas and Brussels sprouts and onions and we'd all devour it with rice in our room. While I taught class in the morning, Mother played with Jack and served as therapist to our hotel maid, the distraught parent of a toddler who had died several months earlier of a fever. This young woman, who came to love Mother, made Jack's bed with exquisite care, tucking small toys under the covers for him to discover. On our last day she brought him her lost baby's Pooh bear and cried as we all said good-bye.

As for Mother, instead of letting herself sail out into the splendid ether of new experience, she turned every place she traveled into a version of home.

# FIELD NOTE 13

## Is Memory Essential?

*Thinking about memory for years on end has gotten
me nowhere: Mother's memory is getting worse. If a
person's memory is unreliable, is she still a person?
How unreliable does memory have to be before she's not
herself anymore?*

*But before I can answer any of those questions I see that I need
to answer a bigger question. What on earth is a "self"? Is a person
a set of beliefs? Or a set of predictable personality traits? Do we
construct ourselves as social roles? Maybe we're just a patchwork of
relationships like those we form with parents and siblings. Toss in some
learned behaviors, such as knowing that it hurts to touch a hot stove,
like the religious rituals we learned in childhood, and is that a person?
Or is a "self" more than a social construction? Is it more like what we
call a soul? That medieval word.*

*Oh, neuroscience and psychology and sociology and religion!
The disciplines are so cunning and so divergent. They offer schematic
trees with limbs and cruxes and branches. Postulate this, and that
follows. One thing leads to another. And how do you decide? What is
a person?*

## Chapter 43

# THE WHITE ROOM

Early on a November morning in 2007, I pick up the phone. It's Julie. Mother has fallen in her apartment at the Courtyard and fractured her hip. A broken hip often spells the end. I knew something like this was coming, of course. I'd imagined it for years and tried to brace myself against it. But now, when it arrives, I find myself flattened. I am terribly weary, terribly sad. No rehearsal could have prepared me.

I need to be with Mother and Julie.

———

Entering the darkened room, which has been divided by a pull-curtain into a double, I see that Mother's eyes are closed. Under the blinding white sheets and blankets in a hospital bed, she looks tiny. They tell me she's not exactly unconscious, just confused from the anesthesia they gave her when they reset her hip.

I drop into a plastic chair beside her bed.

Her roommate, I'm told by an aide who comes in to feed Mother ice chips, died the night before. Already it looks as if no one ever occupied her empty bed.

I fix my eyes on Mother. She's in a different country, sleeping, under the covers. For an hour she lies in the narrow bed, barely moving. Her head is slightly elevated, her bruised eyelids closed. Her hair, which is finally going gray, spreads around her drawn face like a halo.

I look around the institutional room, the cheap shades pulled down over the windows, the narrow cot, the laminated table they wheel over my mother's bed when they bring her meals of broth and toast and fruit cocktail. There is a big white elementary school clock on the wall. Occasionally its black hands jump.

I don't ask myself why this is happening. I know why it's happening. I am watching the third part of a syllogism I learned in philosophy. *All humans are mortal. My mother is human. My mother is mortal.*

An aide tells me that last night Dr. Wright stopped by for twenty minutes. His report, which I picked up at the desk, says that Mother is dehydrated. She weighs eighty-eight pounds. Her kidney function is declining. Her thyroid is normal. He wants her to resume hospice care. He will treat her pain, but he will not take extraordinary measures to save her. He requested that I sign a DNR order, which Julie signed when we moved Mother to Bentley, but which I have never approved. Now I sign it.

I pace the hall for twenty minutes, then duck back into Mother's room, hoping her eyes will be open. But she's lying in the same position, her eyelids still fluttering over her eyes. I sit for a long time watching her. The room is terribly, terribly white. Except for her breathing, she is so still that she might be a painting of herself. My mind wanders to one of my father's jokes. Ole is sitting in a lawn chair, perfectly still, staring, staring, staring at his fence.

Lars stops by and asks what he's doing.

"Shhhh," Ole hisses. "I'm watching the paint dry!"

It's around noon when Mother abruptly opens her eyes. They dart around. Then she sees me. A slow wave of recognition passes over her face. It's a look that means, finally, the troops have arrived. Help is on its way.

"Let me up," she pleads.

"Dr. Wright says you need to stay in bed, Mom." I get up, move to her, and reach for her hand. She swims restlessly to the other side of the bed.

"Let me go downstairs," she begs. "I don't have good feelings up here."

"You're in nursing care. You fell and broke your hip." I reach for her shoulder, but she squirms away.

"All my life I followed directions, and here I am!"

"I know. You've been wonderful."

"You're at your grandmother's house now! You have to do what she says," Mother warns me fiercely. She is throwing back the covers, trying to get up. She winces and shrinks down again.

I touch her shoulder, trying to calm her. I enter her metaphor. "Grandma wants you to be safe. She said you need to stay in bed."

"You're not talking to us kids. I've known him a long time and I'll tell you he didn't say that."

"Who, Mom?" I ask.

"He didn't say that," she shouts crossly.

"I believe you. I know you're right."

"You do what you want to make yourself happy," Mother declares. "And don't you dare try to push it over into eating!" She struggles up again and casts around for a way out of bed. I get up and stand beside her.

"Please, girls, close this out. It's my request." She's blinking at me. I reach for her hand. I remember she told me that when her father had spinal meningitis at the age of fifty, he got up, dressed, and walked out of the hospital in a delirium of fever. Maybe she wants to leave this room the way he left his.

"Nobody will help me," she murmurs, scanning the room. "That's strange, very strange."

"I'm here, Mom. Look. It's Jeanne, your kid. I'm here."

"I can't do this alone."

"We all want to help you."

"There's enough for all of them. Every single one is taken care of."

I'm holding her restless hand. "What do you want?" I ask her.

"If my husband were here, he would do it for me. I don't have enough history to do it alone." She struggles up again and casts around for a way out of bed. "Will you please let me go?"

I wonder what she means by *go*. "Where do you want to go?" I ask her.

"I want to go to the station and wait."

"Okay," I say, trying to keep my voice low and steady. "You can go." But what does she mean by *go*? By *station*?

"I don't know what to do. I can't do anything. I can't get permission."

Does she want permission to die? Maybe she needs me to release her. "You can go, Mom," I say. "Julie and I are fine."

"My brother's waiting to pick me up. My brother, Lloyd."

I tell her, "Really. No one is keeping you here."

"I don't want to get entangled into anything."

"It's all right, Mom. Julie and I will be fine. You've been such a wonderful mother. You really have. You've done everything for us."

She thrashes around, tussling with the sheets. Then she falls back. She closes her eyes. She sleeps.

I watch her for twenty minutes, an hour, two hours.

Watching is like hearing an alarm wailing, like an arrow slowly going through my heart. It's hard for me to remember that outside her window crape myrtle is flowering. I am trying to recall how hard I had to fight to get away from Mother, how, after years of my struggling to get free she finally released me. When was that? Was it when I went to Peru? When I left for Wheaton? When she married Daddy Jim? I don't know, exactly, but a switch flipped and even though she didn't know what would happen to either of us, she was able to say, *It's okay. Go where you need to go and flourish.*

And now the tables are turned. Now I am giving my mother permission to go. Now I see how terribly difficult it is, that kind of letting go, how a person can say it and still not believe it.

Around nine that night, I sign out and drive to Julie and Rich's house. We hug. I am surprised at how comforted I am to see them. We compare notes. We're all subdued, waiting. What are we waiting for? To see whether Mother's surgery was successful, to see what happens next. We don't have much practice waiting. It's easier for us to act. When we act, it feels like we're in charge.

— ⌒ —

Early the next morning I drive back to the nursing care unit and resume the vigil. Mother sleeps. Julie ducks in at mid-morning. Around noon a young woman wakes Mother for physical therapy. Together with an aide, she lifts Mother into a wheelchair and begins moving her limbs. "Now you try it," she chirps enthusiastically.

Mother turns to me. "Whaaaaa?"

"Try to do what they say, Mom."

The aide moves her left arm. "Mrs. Kelley, can you move your left arm?"

Mother summons all her gumption and tries. She raises it slightly. The aides clap for her. Her hair is wild. Her skin is sagging and one of her brown eyes is out of sync with the other.

The backs of her hands are bruised where needles have been inserted. But she looks pleased with herself.

"Good for you," the young therapist in the pink workout suit says. "Try that again, Mrs. Kelley."

Mother rests a minute, squints, summons her strength, and tries again.

I feel rage, verging into despair. I can't turn away, because this is my own mother. I need to stop her anguish, but I don't have the power to stop it. I have no choice but to sit with it, to wait it out, to try to help in whatever minimal way I can. I wonder how the human heart, which is such a fragile, ramshackle contraption, can stand it.

For four days I sit in Mother's hospital room, waiting. Part of me can't believe this is happening. The hours pass and the days blend into one another. Sometimes she tosses restlessly and talks wildly, but not quite as wildly as before, because, as the nurse at the desk tells me, the anesthesia is leaving her system. Once every two hours the aides come in to turn her. Frequently they come in to change her diaper. Mornings they load her into a wheelchair. I push her up and down the halls. I talk to her. Occasionally she smiles briefly in reply.

One of the aides must guess that I'm lonely, because she talks to me, asking where I live, how long I'll be here, whether I need a glass of water. She's probably in her early thirties, heavyset, with a pretty, tranquil face. She's wearing a uniform. She tells me that she has three little children at home under the age of five. She assures me that people in my mother's condition can relearn to walk. She hopes that our Mother herself will be able to do that. She's seen it happen, she says. She needs to emphasize that this is a possibility. She believes it so powerfully that she almost convinces me it's true.

This young woman deals with the humblest functions of my

mother's body. This is what she gets up every morning to do, this kind of difficult, menial work. It's her life. She's cheerful and resilient. She's been there for two and a half years. She tells me she has faith. I help her turn Mother. I help her change Mother. I feel camaraderie with this aide, however tenuous, however brief.

As I sit here watching Mother, the genius of Christianity occurs to me. The story is, God entered human history and suffered. If God is eternal, then maybe that suffering is always in the "now." I wonder what that means. I think it means God has a good memory. Two thousand years later, he still recalls what it's like to feel confused, abandoned, hurt.

The third day, I begin to feel the tug from the people I love back home, as I always do when I visit Mother. I wonder what my husband, my children are doing. My students' faces bloom before me like water lilies. But this is different from the other times I've needed to go home. Once I leave, I may not see Mother alive again.

At seven on the morning of the day I'm scheduled to fly out, I tell the woman at the nursing care desk what time I need to leave.

Mother is sleeping. I'd like to wake her up. I want her to focus on me and say something I can understand. I want her to summarize our lives together and give me a blessing. I want some last word of wisdom. I know this isn't going to happen, but all morning I watch the big black hands crawl across the face of the clock on the wall, hoping she'll open her eyes.

Three hours before my plane is set to take off, I stand up and kiss Mother good-bye. I tell her I love her. Her eyelids flicker, but that's all. There's no good enough ritual for this kind of leave-taking. So I gather my things and simply walk out the door.

## Chapter 44

# LEARNING TO SEE

A year and a half earlier, long before my mother broke her hip, before we moved her to the Courtyard, before this catastrophe, I signed a contract to fly to London, where I'm scheduled to teach for the month of January. The Study Abroad Program starts in six weeks. I decide I will not do it. I can't. Instead I will fly to Dallas and help Julie take care of Mother. When I get back to Philadelphia, I call Julie and tell her that I will try to cancel the contract for the London program.

No, Julie says. She gives me her point of view: that we both need to go on with our lives. Mother is in hospice care now, and that means Dr. Wright believes that she has less than six months to live. But she was in hospice earlier and then she rallied and Dr. Wright removed her. Maybe Mother will rally again. Who knows how many reversals we'll experience? Julie's not counting on a recovery, though we've seen that several times before, but whatever happens, the two of us can't put our lives on hold indefinitely, she insists.

I thank my sister for her counsel and tell her I'll think about it. And though I do, I look around for someone else to take my twenty students to London. I can't find anyone, and that's not surprising. Six weeks is not enough notice to plan such a complex program abroad, and the program is so idiosyncratic that no one else could manage it, probably. So as Mother stabilizes in the nursing care wing in Dallas, I fly to London with my students.

The students and I work every day of the week for three weeks. Then we take five days off to travel. Daniel and I fly to Paris. It's there early on the morning on the twenty-seventh of January Daniel wakes up with the premonition that Mother has died. He calls Julie and Rich. They tell him he's right.

—

Daniel and I spend all Sunday finding an Internet café and phoning people.

On Tuesday we are scheduled to fly back to London for the final two days of the program.

But meanwhile, we have Monday to get through. We don't know what to do with it; the day is just there, standing in the way of what we must finish. But a Monday is a bit of lifetime, time we'll never get back. It's precious. So we find our way to Musée Marmottan in the suburbs of Paris. There's a subway ride and a lot of walking involved. It's raining so hard our umbrellas can't ward off the deluge. The world is so dark that the lights of the museum shine in the sidewalks.

In the museum, we sit on a bench surrounded by four immense late panels of Monet's water lilies. As the artist aged, he saw his garden through cataracts. He saw how things fall to pieces, and that's what he painted. For a whole afternoon we sit trying to absorb the way things are falling to pieces.

## Chapter 45

# THE GOOD SCAB

That night we surf TV channels for a weather report, because the next morning we need to get to the airport and fly back to London. French news predicts that the next day the city will be in the grip of a taxicab strike. It reports that the Metro staff has canceled trains out of sympathy with cab drivers. And they're slowing whatever underground trains are still running.

We didn't know anything about this. Daniel talks to the woman at the hotel desk, who tells him it's true, so we settle the bill and pack our suitcases and check the map to find Gare du Nord, the rail station where we need to catch a train to the airport.

The next morning we bound out of bed to a five o'clock wake-up call and we're on the street by six thirty, wheeling our suitcases to the nearby underground. For half an hour we wait in the subway for a train, gambling that the underground will be more likely than a cab to get us to Gare du Nord. But half an hour passes and no trains come. With time short now, worried that we'll arrive at the airport too late for our flight, we lug our suitcases up the concrete stairs and through the turnstile to a taxi stand, where we think we spotted a cab earlier.

Joining the taxi line, we eavesdrop, thirsty for news. We have to hope that a few drivers are crossing the picket lines or we'll never make our flight. After about fifteen minutes, a cab circles by to pick up the people ahead of us in line. We scan the streets for another.

In a few minutes, a cab pulls over. We thank the driver, aware that this is no everyday pickup. He is a laconic Frenchman. He turns, grinning, to make sure we're in safely, and then takes off for the station. He chats easily and we like him. With his gray mop of hair and his panache, I think he could teach at the Sorbonne. As the three of us drive across Paris toward Gare du Nord, in spite of the strike and the cold and Mother's death, the January day looks serene.

Then a siren wails, then another, then several more, their decibels crisscrossing one another. We hear thudding, as if of drums, and the rumble of deep voices chanting. Alert now, we stop talking. We listen. Our driver slows down, hanging back till he can see what's going on.

The chanting grows louder. It's ahead of us.

We spot a mob pulsing, surging, and swarming, swelling on the sidewalk to the right of our street, spilling into traffic, thronging into the right lanes of the wide avenue. Some men are shouting slogans in unison, raising clenched fists. Others are beating on cars with baseball bats. Some cock their arms back and hurl eggs at cars.

"They're taxi drivers," Daniel says. "They're mad as hell." They seethe toward us, their faces murderous with rage.

Our driver sees what's happening. He maneuvers wide to the left, to avoid the angled cars and debris in the street. He checks his rearview mirror and expertly floats our cab into the lane to the left. Glancing in the mirror again, he tries to maneuver even farther left, but he's cut off by a car that spurts forward to box us in.

He scans for a way out, but the lane ahead of us is clogged

with cars. The lanes to the right are teeming with angry strikers. They're tearing windshield wipers off several cars like boys tearing the wings from flies. Fistfights have broken out in the street. I see someone going down under a taxi.

Unshaven men press their leering faces against our windows. Some begin pushing at our cab rhythmically, rocking it back and forth. Others pelt our windows with eggs. The eggs make plopping sounds as they rain from every side. Dozens of eggs thump and break, the yolks and whites running like sap down our windows. The eggs are followed by sawdust, which sticks. The last thing I see before our windows go completely dark is a guy raising a baton to smash our windshield. The cab is dark now and rocking violently from side to side, tipping dangerously. I grab for my seat belt. I pull on it so when we go over I'll be buckled in.

Daniel shouts, "Lock the doors!" I reach for the lock, but it's too late, because the door to my left is being pulled open from the outside. I feel a blast of icy air. A hand pitches an egg through the opening. The egg lands on my coat and breaks and runs down my front. I yank at the door, trying to shut it, but I'm not strong enough. I see a hand reaching through the space where the door is opening. I know that soon a dozen hands will be pulling me out of the cab into the mob.

A bolt of raw electric terror twinges through my body. I unfasten my seat belt, turn to face the door, and brace my feet against the floor. Placing both hands on the door handle, I yank hard. Daniel scoots over the seat to help me. Together we slam the door shut and Daniel pounds his fist on the lock.

Meanwhile, our driver, who can't see through his windshield, turns on his wipers, but they stick. He squirts fluid on the windshield. He sprays the windshield over and over, but the wipers are stuck and whirring in a mixture of raw egg and sawdust.

It's dark in the cab. We can't see what's happening, except we know the car is rocking now, dangerously. I fasten my seat belt again. Our driver desperately squirts fluid on his windshield and turns up the speed of the wipers. I'm looking for daylight through his windshield, hoping for daylight.

Finally a tiny ray of sun shines in the left side of the windshield where a small patch of goo has broken loose.

Craning his neck, our driver peers through the hole. He steers the rocking cab forward, maneuvering very slowly toward an opening in traffic. Then he guns the motor, cutting swiftly to the left. Driving blind, or almost blind, he scatters the crowd before him, maneuvering brilliantly out of the cul-de-sac.

Twisting his head to see, inching forward, he feels his way up the boulevard.

When he's gotten beyond the reach of the mob, a mile north of the rioting strikers, he pulls over at the curb. He gets out. From the backseat, we can't see anything thorough the windows. We don't know where we are or what he's doing. We wonder whether he might have spotted another roadblock.

We have twelve minutes to catch our train.

We get out.

He's walking around his cab, checking out damage. He shakes his head, stunned.

When he notices us standing on the sidewalk, he apologizes in French. He tells us it's too dangerous, that he can't see to drive any farther. He needs to get the windshield washed.

He explains that Gare du Nord is six blocks ahead of us. He opens the trunk and helps us lift our suitcases out. He apologizes again and asks whether we're all right. Daniel tells him that we'll be fine and quickly pays him the cab fare and hands him most of our remaining Euros for a tip. We thank him again, though no amount of thanks would be enough.

We grab our suitcases and begin running, pulling them in the direction he's told us to go, toward the station.

—

At the final dinner in London, the undergraduate women wore low-cut dresses, the men, jackets and ties. They took pictures of one another, of the group, of me. They got up from their dinners and danced. Some of them wept at leaving London. They didn't have the faintest idea that my mother had died. They were beautiful and young and for the moment they seemed beyond tragedy.

They asked me to give a speech. A final speech, they pled.

I couldn't find words. I thought I'd found a sentence, fleetingly, but then it swam out of reach. I smiled at my students and just shook my head.

As I watched them celebrate, I was thinking about how strangers had quietly buried my mother's body in Dallas clay several days before. I thought about how simply she had died, how uneventful her death had been, how, with so little Sturm und Drang she had left the earth. And yet to me her death was earth-shattering, an event I hadn't even begun to comprehend, a catastrophe about which I could say nothing, which had taken away my language. It seemed profoundly wrong that her death had gone so unmarked. How could someone so significant leave this world without creating a racket?

The horrific moments in that cab and my mother's death became inextricably linked in my mind. Our dangerous ride, the vicious shouts, the sticks beating on our cab and then the rocking that almost tipped us over, marked my mother's death. Maybe our catastrophic journey in the Paris cab stood in for the wailing and clashing that, by rights, should have occurred when Mother left the world.

Later I meditated on how much that cab driver and I had in common. We had both made a choice. I had decided to stay with my students rather than to fly to Dallas, not quite understanding what that would mean. He had decided to cross the picket line, not knowing what would happen as a consequence. His fellow drivers, those frenzied strikers, were hell-bent on revenge. I worried about him. They probably jotted down his cab and license plate numbers. I feared that he could never drive a cab in Paris again.

For years I have felt mystically tied to the cab driver who saved us from the mob. By some kind of screwy logic, I felt we should help him, partly for the sake of my mother. Daniel and I talked about it for a long time. But we were in Philadelphia and he was in Paris. We didn't know his name.

There was nothing we could do.

As there was nothing we could do to stop my mother's long slide into Alzheimer's. We held both of them in our thoughts, yes. We prayed for them, my mother and that cab driver. But then unless we wanted to be driven crazy, we had to let them go. We were learning how to let go.

## Chapter 46

# TO CELEBRATE HER HOMEGOING

A week or so after we got home from London, we flew to Dallas. My sister and I and our husbands and our children gathered together with Mother's friends at Lake Ridge Bible Church to celebrate what they called her homegoing. We commemorated Mother's intrepid spirit with eulogies and flowers and food and hymns and readings from the Bible. Afterward Julie and Rich and Daniel and I and the children cruised slowly through the cemetery and found Mother's grave. The earth mover that must have dug that hole had left barbaric scars in the lawn. We laid flowers over the scars. Then we grown-ups stood talking in muted voices while four-year-old Sophia, arms out, blond curls flying, sprinted joyfully through the sunshine above Mother's body.

Now, three years later, as I write this, I know that the illness and death of my father and then my brother, and our family's financial peril, and the ongoing crisis of altar calls, the way everything was at stake at every instant, all of it conspired to make our Mother desperate to keep us safe. She needed to preserve her remaining children. To do that she bound us to her by whatever ties she could find. Her love was so seductive that in order to locate myself as a separate person, I had to fight for dear life. Finally, in my twenties, I began to see how different I was from Mother, and we declared a truce, and figured out how to coexist.

When I took care of her at the end of her life, in order to understand her, I began to reflect on her history. As she "lost" her memory, I regained my own memories. This happened, I'm convinced, only because of the thousands of hours I spent with her. It was one of the gifts of Alzheimer's, one of the gifts of the pilgrimage my mother and my sister and I shared. The decade of needing to remember earlier times gave me an opportunity to retrace the stages of my teenage battle against my smart, valiant mother, to discover how oddly like her I am, too, how much of what she told me I was trying to pass on to my own children. That realization is one of the unexpected gifts that Alzheimer's brought. It is, I now think, a universal truth. As T. S. Eliot wrote in "Little Gidding," *We shall not cease from exploration and the end of all our exploring will be to arrive where we started and to know the place for the first time.*

⁓

Now I can say that as my mother journeyed more deeply into the land of Alzheimer's, she was always still a person. I didn't learn that from a book; I discovered it by paying attention to Mother herself. She changed, of course. She entered new stages the way we do all our lives. But fundamentally she was the same person. She continued to be governed much of the time by optimism and faith. Her language, which had always been strewn with images, reeled further into metaphor. I'm not even sure that she lost her memory. She lost control of it, acting out conflicts from other stages of her life as if they existed in the present. Eventually she lost much of her language. But she was still a person, still herself, still my mother.

Habit is the memory of the body. For sixty years I was accustomed to seeing my mother and hearing her voice. I got used to flying to Dallas to take care of her. It's no wonder that for these years since her death, under dreaming and waking, I have been listening for her the way I listened for my children.

The body cries out with the need to escort a loved one back to the earth. To believe in my mother's death, I probably needed to see her dead, distorted face, to throw clods on her coffin and hear the echoing thud. The fact is, I did not understand this when I was deciding whether or not to fly to Dallas to bury her. I see my mother standing at the lip of heaven, shyly, wearing a bright new dress of spirit, wondering exactly when to step over the threshold and go in. But I have trouble sustaining any image of my mother in heaven. Maybe that's not because I lack faith, but because I don't yet entirely believe she's dead. Perhaps it's a failure not of belief, but of my own imagination. I hope someday to correct it.

The fact that most of the time I can't imagine my mother in heaven doesn't mean there is no heaven. My mother never lost her faith. Faith is the conviction this world is not tragic, but comic. Maybe faith gives a person the ability to see whatever joy and beauty and wit flickers in the disorienting darkness. Or maybe it is the result of paying attention more to those flickers than to the darkness itself. I don't know.

How can we know for sure that the flickers are clues to how the story will end? We can't, not for sure. Nevertheless, most mornings I wake up believing that we are perennials, not annuals. That feeling, itself, is a gift. Surely what dies will spring back to life. I suspect it was my mother who taught me that faith—good and true flower show judge that she was.

# FIELD NOTE 14

## ASHES AS A MEMORY DEVICE

*It's Ash Wednesday. Mother died two months before, when Daniel and I were in Paris. Now we're back in Philadelphia. I rehearse these facts as drizzle falls from a gray sky. I hurry into the sanctuary at St. Peter's, slip into a pew, and kneel. Then I join a line of fellow parishioners inching slowly toward the front. It's chilly here and dead silent, except for the low murmur of our priest, who stands center front in his black robe. He cups a silver bowl in one hand and bends, murmuring over an old woman in a red flowered head scarf. Then over a young man clad in a motorcycle jacket. Then over a middle-aged man in a business suit. As I move closer, the drone sorts itself into words:* Remember that you are dust and to dust you shall return. Remember that you are dust and to dust you shall return.

*This is the human pilgrimage we all make.*

~

*I go to St. Peter's partly because I'm so prone to forget. Over and over I need to take the touch and taste and smell of spiritual truths into my body. Sacramental action for me is a memory device.*

~

*Now I'm standing in front of our curly-headed priest, who dips his thumb in the bowl of ashes. He draws a gritty cross on my forehead with his thumb and says,* Remember that you are dust and to dust you shall return.

*I walk the long way back to my pew, lonely now, and kneel to pray.*

## Chapter 47

# REUNION

Half an hour after Mother died, Julie and I promised one another that we would get our families together. At the time I thought, what are the chances? We're busy. We're scattered all over the country. All our connections had been routed through Mother. With Mother gone, how will this happen?

—

Daniel and I celebrated Mother on the first anniversary of her death in January by walking among flamboyant spring flowers in the warm greenhouses of Longwood Gardens. When we got home, I called Julie and again proposed a reunion. I favored renting a house in England. Julie favored getting us together in Dallas. We worked it out.

—

Here's the whole family, sitting on the deck of the big house that belongs to Molly and her husband, Matt, in Webster Groves, Missouri. It's almost too dark to take the picture. Andrew has just lit the lamps and the wind is tugging their flames sideways. Molly is bending over to light the candles on a birthday cake. Daniel is getting up to search for the smallest child's indispensable blanket, which she calls her lovey. Julie steps through the sliding door from the kitchen, carrying peach ice cream, which is already melting in the evening heat. Eve holds a vase of peonies down for Julie's grandson, Grayson, so he can sniff them. Sitting on Rich's lap, Julie's other grandchild, Hayden, clutches a picture book and begs for a story. Molly's child, Sophia, is helping to arrange the plates. Addy, her sister, is toddling behind her. Balloons bob and duck in the wind behind Bobbie and Jack, who are tending a stack of birthday presents. I am the one snapping the picture.

~

When we have our next reunion at Christmas, we will be joined by two more children.

~

We will keep gathering. This is what we have now: the wind, the waning sunlight, the stars and flowers, our mother, the journey we took together during her last decade, the disciplines we learned, the gifts our long pilgrimage together brought us. And here on earth, for a while, we have one another.